Football in the Nordic Countries

This book explores football culture, organisation and development in the five Nordic countries: Denmark, Finland, Iceland, Sweden and Norway. These countries represent an important case study in sport culture, policy and management, being shaped by unique traditions in their civil society and in social welfare and public policy.

The first part of the book explores the development path of football in each country, looking at how football arrived in Scandinavia and how it has been transformed from a voluntary civic activity into a professional sport while becoming closely attached to the global football system. The second part highlights key issues – including historical, contemporary and critical aspects – across three themes: professionalisation and changing practices; equality and gender; and supporters, audiences and culture. Written by a team of authors with a blend of experience as academics and practitioners in football, the book traces the contours of the distinctive Nordic model that occupies a prominent position in the global football system.

Shining fascinating new light on the relationship between football and wider society, this is invaluable reading for students and researchers interested in football, sport management, sport policy, or the history, culture or sociology of sport and for anyone involved in the game.

Mihaly Szerovay holds a joint Professor of Practice position at the University of Jyväskylä, Finland, and the Football Association of Finland. Before taking up his current role that focuses on research and development in football, he worked as Senior Lecturer in Football Studies at Solent University, UK. Szerovay's main research interest lies in the various aspects of sport and globalisation, the professionalisation in the different segments of football, and the changing field of youth sport clubs. Szerovay played football professionally as a goalkeeper in Jyväskylä, Finland.

Arto Nevala is Senior University Lecturer at the University of Eastern Finland. His main topics of research are concerned with the social history of education and sports history. He has published and edited books and articles related to the changes in sports clubs, the development of football and refereeing. Nevala is a former referee in the Finnish Premier League and has also worked as a referee observer and match delegate.

Hannu Itkonen is Professor Emeritus in the Sociology of Sport at the University of Jyväskylä, Finland. His research interests lie in the historical sociology of sport, social control of sport, sports in the civic, public and private sector as well as sport in local and global contexts. He has published books and articles in sport sociology and general sociology as well in social history. Itkonen acted as the president and vice president (2010–2016) of the European Association for the Sociology of Sport.

Critical Research in Football

Series Editors:
Pete Millward, *Liverpool John Moores University, UK*
Jamie Cleland, *University of Southern Australia*
Dan Parnell, *University of Liverpool, UK*
Stacey Pope, *Durham University, UK*
Paul Widdop, *Manchester Metropolitan University, UK*

The *Critical Research in Football* book series was launched in 2017 to showcase the inter- and multi-disciplinary breadth of debate relating to 'football'. The series defines 'football' as broader than association football, with research on rugby, Gaelic and gridiron codes also featured. Including monographs, edited collections, short books and textbooks, books in the series are written and/or edited by leading experts in the field whilst consciously also affording space to emerging voices in the area, and are designed to appeal to students, postgraduate students and scholars who are interested in the range of disciplines in which critical research in football connects. The series is published in association with the *Football Collective*, @FB_Collective.

Available in this series:

Diego Maradona
A Social-Cultural Study
Edited by Pablo Brescia and Mariano Paz

Critical Issues in Football
A Sociological Analysis of the Beautiful Game
Edited by Will Roberts, Stuart Whigham, Alex Culvin and Daniel Parnell

The UEFA European Football Championships
Politics, Media Spectacle and Social Change
Jan Andre Lee Ludvigsen and Renan Petersen-Wagner

Football Fandom, Sexualities and Activism
A Cultural Relational Sociology
Peter Millward

Football in the Nordic Countries
Practices, Equality and Influence
Edited by Mihaly Szerovay, Arto Nevala and Hannu Itkonen

https://www.routledge.com/Critical-Research-in-Football/book-series/CFSFC

Football in the Nordic Countries

Practices, Equality and Influence

Edited by Mihaly Szerovay, Arto Nevala, and Hannu Itkonen

LONDON AND NEW YORK

First published 2023
by Routledge
4 Park Square, Milton Park, Abingdon, Oxon OX14 4RN

and by Routledge
605 Third Avenue, New York, NY 10158

Routledge is an imprint of the Taylor & Francis Group, an informa business

© 2023 selection and editorial matter, Mihaly Szerovay, Arto Nevala and Hannu Itkonen; individual chapters, the contributors

The right of Mihaly Szerovay, Arto Nevala and Hannu Itkonen to be identified as the authors of the editorial material, and of the authors for their individual chapters, has been asserted in accordance with sections 77 and 78 of the Copyright, Designs and Patents Act 1988.

All rights reserved. No part of this book may be reprinted or reproduced or utilised in any form or by any electronic, mechanical, or other means, now known or hereafter invented, including photocopying and recording, or in any information storage or retrieval system, without permission in writing from the publishers.

Trademark notice: Product or corporate names may be trademarks or registered trademarks, and are used only for identification and explanation without intent to infringe.

British Library Cataloguing-in-Publication Data
A catalogue record for this book is available from the British Library

Library of Congress Cataloguing-in-Publication Data
Names: Szerovay, Mihaly, editor. | Nevala, Arto, editor. | Itkonen, Hannu, editor.
Title: Football in the Nordic countries : practices, equality and influence / edited by Mihaly Szerovay, Arto Nevala and Hannu Itkonen.
Description: Abingdon, Oxon ; New York, NY : Routledge, 2023. |
Series: Critical research in football | Includes bibliographical references and index. | Summary: "This book explores football culture, organisation and development in the five Nordic countries - Denmark, Finland, Iceland, Sweden and Norway. These countries represent an important case study in sport culture, policy and management, being shaped by unique traditions in their civil society and in social welfare and public policy. The first part of the book explores the development path of football in each country, looking at how football arrived in Scandinavia and how it has been transformed from a voluntary civic activity into a professional sport while becoming closely attached to the global football system. The second part highlights key issues - including historical, contemporary and critical aspects - across three themes: professionalisation and changing practices; equality and gender; and supporters, audiences and culture. Written by a team of authors with a blend of experience as academics and practitioners in football, the book traces the contours of the distinctive Nordic model that occupies a prominent position in the global football system. Shining fascinating new light on the relationship between football and wider society, this is invaluable reading for students and researchers interested in football, sport management, sport policy, or the history, culture or sociology of sport and for anyone involved in the game"-- Provided by publisher.
Identifiers: LCCN 2022061452 | ISBN 9781032249131 (hardback) | ISBN 9781032249148 (paperback) | ISBN 9781003280729 (ebook)
Subjects: LCSH: Soccer--Scandinavia--History. | Soccer--Social aspects--Scandinavia.
Classification: LCC GV944.S33 F66 2023 | DDC 796.3340948--dc23/eng/20230216
LC record available at https://lccn.loc.gov/2022061452

ISBN: 978-1-032-24913-1 (hbk)
ISBN: 978-1-032-24914-8 (pbk)
ISBN: 978-1-003-28072-9 (ebk)

DOI: 10.4324/9781003280729

Typeset in Goudy
by MPS Limited, Dehradun

Contents

List of Contributors viii
Preface xi

Introduction: Mapping Nordic Countries and Football 1
MIHALY SZEROVAY, ARTO NEVALA, AND HANNU ITKONEN

PART I
Changing Football in the Nordic Countries 9

1 Tradition and Transformation in Denmark 11
SØREN BENNIKE, RASMUS K. STORM,
KARSTEN ELMOSE-ØSTERLUND, NIKOLAJ SCHELDE,
AND LAILA OTTESEN

2 Growing Participation and Slow Professionalisation in Finland 25
ARTO NEVALA, HANNU ITKONEN, AND MIHALY SZEROVAY

3 Preserving the Balance between Amateurism and Professionalism in Iceland 38
VIDAR HALLDORSSON AND OMAR JOHANNSSON

4 Inclusion, Exclusion and Modernisation in Norway 51
ARVE HJELSETH, BENTE OVEDIE SKOGVANG,
FRODE TELSETH, AND PÅL AUGESTAD

5 Between Grassroots Democracy and Professional Commercialism in Sweden 64
ROBERT S. PRIMUS, DANIEL ALSARVE, AND DANIEL SVENSSON

PART II
Specific Issues and Themes 77

Professionalisation and Changing Practices 79

6 Football Companies in Sweden and Their Democratic
  Framework 81
  BJÖRN HORGBY AND CHRISTER ERICSSON

7 The Professionalisation of Finnish Football from the
  1970s to 2000s: From Amateurs to Professionals 94
  JOUNI LAVIKAINEN

8 The Professionalisation of Youth Football in Norway:
  Implications for the "Sport for All" Ideal? 106
  ANDERS BELLING, FRODE TELSETH, AND PÅL AUGESTAD

9 Football Fitness: More of the Same, or a
  Path-Breaking Concept? 119
  SØREN BENNIKE, MORTEN B. RANDERS,
  PETER KRUSTRUP, AND LAILA OTTESEN

Equality and Gender 133

10 Five Decades of Women's Football in Finland 135
   HANNA VEHVILÄINEN, HANNU ITKONEN,
   MIHALY SZEROVAY, AND ARTO NEVALA

11 Breaking Barriers in Norwegian Women's Football 150
   BENTE OVEDIE SKOGVANG

12 Women's Football in Iceland: Don't Wait for Change,
   Just Do It 163
   DAÐI RAFNSSON AND HAFRÚN KRISTJÁNSDÓTTIR

Supporters, Audiences and Culture 177

13 Historical Rivalries in Swedish Club Football 179
   TORBJÖRN ANDERSSON

14 The Development of Supporter Cultures in
   Norwegian Football Since 1990 192
   ARVE HJELSETH AND HANS K. HOGNESTAD

15 Nordic Spectator Studies: The Literature on Attendance
   and Satisfaction at Professional Football Matches   205
   MORTEN KRINGSTAD, TOR GEORG JAKOBSEN, AND
   RASMUS K. STORM

16 Ethnicity and Aesthetics in Swedish Football:
   Playing Like a Swede, Fighting Like a Kurd   219
   TIAGO DUARTE DIAS

   Conclusion: Similarities, Differences and Future
   Research in Football in the Nordic Countries   231
   HANNU ITKONEN, MIHALY SZEROVAY, AND ARTO NEVALA

   Index   243

Contributors

Daniel Alsarve is Researcher in Sport Science at the School of Health Sciences at Örebro University, Sweden and Post Doc Researcher at the School of Business and Economics, University of Jyväskylä, Finland.

Torbjörn Andersson is Associate Professor at the Department of Sports Sciences at Malmö University, Sweden.

Pål Augestad is Professor of Sport Sociology in the Department of Sports, Physical Education and Outdoor Studies, at the University of South-Eastern Norway.

Anders Belling is Research Fellow in Talent Development (football) in the Department of Sports, Physical Education and Outdoor Studies at the University of South-Eastern Norway. Previously Sports Scientist at an elite football academy in the Netherlands.

Søren Bennike is Head of Research at the Danish Football Association.

Tiago Duarte Dias is Doctor in Anthropology at Fluminense Federal University, Brazil, and an independent researcher.

Karsten Elmose-Østerlund is Associate Professor at the Centre for Sports, Health and Civil Society within the Department of Sports Science and Clinical Biomechanics at the University of Southern Denmark.

Christer Ericsson is Professor Emeritus at Örebro University, Sweden.

Vidar Halldorsson is Professor of Sociology at the University of Iceland, a sport consultant and international speaker.

Arve Hjelseth is Professor in the Sociology of Sport at the Norwegian University of Science and Technology, Norway.

Hans K. Hognestad is a social anthropologist and Professor of Sport Sciences at the University of South-Eastern Norway.

Björn Horgby is Professor Emeritus at Örebro University, Sweden.

Tor Georg Jakobsen is Professor in Political Science at NTNU Business School, Norwegian University of Science and Technology, Norway.

Omar Johannsson is a Doctoral Student in Sociology at the University of Iceland.

Morten Kringstad is Associate Professor at NTNU Business School, Norwegian University of Science and Technology, Norway.

Hafrún Kristjánsdóttir is Psychologist, Professor and Department Chair at Reykjavík University's Department of Sports Science, Iceland.

Peter Krustrup is Professor of Sport and Health Sciences in the Department of Sports Science and Clinical Biomechanics at the University of Southern Denmark. He is also the leader of the Football is Medicine platform.

Jouni Lavikainen is a Doctoral Researcher at the University of Helsinki, Finland.

Laila Ottesen is Associate Professor and Head of Section for Social Science in the Department of Nutrition, Exercise and Sports at the University of Copenhagen, Denmark. She is also president of the EASS (European Association for Sociology of Sport).

Robert S. Primus (former Svensson) is Senior Lecturer in Sport Science and Head of the Sport Management Program at Örebro University, Sweden.

Daði Rafnsson holds an UEFA A degree and is a Doctoral Researcher in the Department of Psychology at Reykjavik University, Iceland, and Lecturer in the Department of Sports Science.

Morten B. Randers is Associate Professor in tracking, training and testing in ball games in the Department of Sports Science and Clinical Biomechanics at the University of Southern Denmark.

Nikolaj Schelde is Head of Analytics at the Danish Football Association.

Bente Ovedie Skogvang is Associate Professor at Inland Norway University of Applied Sciences in Norway, and she was the referee of the inaugural Olympic football final in Atlanta 1996.

Rasmus K. Storm is Head of Research at the Danish Institute for Sports Studies. Further, he holds an Adjunct Associate Professor position at NTNU Business School, Norway.

Daniel Svensson is Associate Senior Lecturer in the Department of Sport Sciences at Malmö University, Sweden.

Frode Telseth is Senior Lecturer in Football in the Department of Sports, Physical Education and Outdoor Studies at University of South-Eastern Norway. He is currently working with elite academy football in Norway and is UEFA A licenced football coach.

Hanna Vehviläinen is Communication Specialist at Jamk University of Applied Sciences, School of Health and Social Studies, Finland.

Preface

There is an abundance of research dealing with football in different Nordic countries, but to date there has been no book or study that takes a holistic approach to Nordic football. This edited collection is an attempt to address this gap and to inspire further research avenues in the area.

We have come a long way since we initiated the project in October 2020. As we reached out to colleagues in five Nordic countries to invite them to contribute, we experienced a great amount of support and interest. The project has become an exceptional collaborative effort of 31 authors. Even after the deadline closed, we have been contacted about potential submissions.

We were privileged to gather face-to-face with many of the contributors at the 1st Nordic Football Conference in Jyväskylä, in May 2022. During the special session dedicated to this book and while listening to the other presentations, we fully comprehended how necessary this collection was. There are plenty of nuances in the similarities as well as differences across the Nordic countries that we seek to bring to the fore. As we will show, the Nordic countries share a distinctive Nordic model while fulfilling an active role in the global football system.

We would like to thank the series editors and Routledge for their support throughout this project. Thanks goes out to the Football Association of Finland as well, who strongly supported this initiative. Most of all, we would like to kindly thank all of the contributing authors for their excellent work and seamless collaboration. The editorial process has also turned out to be a great partnership among the three editors.

Finally, we hope this book will inspire many people from various perspectives and positions across the football world and beyond. Although this is a scientific publication, we believe that in addition to helping scholars and students, it can be used by practitioners in sport organisations to stimulate discussion and deepen the understanding of Nordic football.

Mihaly Szerovay, Hannu Itkonen,
Arto Nevala - Jyväskylä and Joensuu
December 2022

Introduction
Mapping Nordic Countries and Football

Mihaly Szerovay, Arto Nevala, and Hannu Itkonen

A shared history and the emergence of the Nordic model

When mapping Denmark, Finland, Iceland, Norway and Sweden – known collectively as the Nordic countries or Scandinavia – as a part of the world as well as of the global football system, we must start by looking at their history. The five Nordic countries have hundreds of years of shared history, while the relations between them and with other countries have obviously changed over time. The 1900s were particularly important for the Nordic countries, when they transformed from being relatively poor and agrarian countries into developed (post)industrial and service societies. At the same time, the so-called Nordic welfare state model became a well-known role model for many countries. The Nordic countries were held up as examples of successful modernisation and social equality (Gustafsson, 2017).

In the 1900s and 2000s, the world's territorial structure was shaped first by the formation of nation-states after World War I and then in the 1990s, after the Cold War between East and West, by the ongoing period of neoliberalism, globalisation and networking. The latter two processes have contributed to the alliance of nation-states into larger and more powerful communities that aim for success in international competition. The most well-known alliance is the European Union, which today comprises 27 states. Although Iceland and Norway are not members of the European Union, the Nordic countries form a cultural, political and economic entity of small states, of which there are only a few in the world. The Nordic Council, the most important cooperation forum of the Nordic countries, was established in 1952. A little later, movement between countries without a passport was allowed, and since 1954 the Nordic countries have formed a common labour market. During the Cold War, Norway, Denmark and Iceland joined the North Atlantic Treaty Organisation (NATO), while Finland and Sweden remained neutral. Despite the different orientations, Nordic cooperation was intensive, and since the 1990s, the countries have become even closer to each other (Gustafsson, 2017).

DOI: 10.4324/9781003280729-1

The development of the Nordic societies has not been identical in the 1900s and 2000s, but common features have dominated and differences between the countries have decreased. It has been suggested that a Nordic model with distinctive economic and social features exists that blends social democracy and liberalism. The model is marked by a strong public sector and civil society with a comprehensive welfare system, high spending on childcare and education, a high degree of taxation, and a significant political role for trade unions (T. M. Andersen et al., 2007; Tin et al., 2020). Nordic countries also experienced a relatively early democratisation that has enabled high levels of gender equality. The Nordic contribution to science and research has been significant, and it seems to have strengthened in the 2000s. In recent years, several studies exploring the similarities and differences of the Nordic societies have been published (e.g., S. S. Andersen & Ronglan, 2012; de la Porte et al., 2022; Eckhardt Larsen et al., 2021; Giulianotti et al., 2019; Green et al., 2020; Tin et al., 2020).

Regarding sport and physical activity, the Nordic sport model was historically based on the voluntary activity of sport associations and an ideological commitment to amateurism (Andersson & Carlsson, 2011). For example, instead of establishing openly professional leagues, Nordic football associations protected amateurism. In voluntary sport clubs, the role of civic activities with a "sport for all" ideal based on egalitarian values as well as a high level of participation remain fundamental (Giulianotti et al., 2019). The wealth of Nordic countries has enabled the establishment of a strong public sector for sport, which has advanced physical activity and sport together with the voluntary and private sectors. The role of the private sport sector and commercial interests have increased both on the grassroots and elite levels. In Sweden, for example, legislation requires 51% ownership by a non-profit club at the elite level. In recent years, however, this has been challenged in football and ice hockey by commercial forces but defended by fan groups (Junghagen, 2018).

Locating Nordic countries in the global football system

The history of football in the Nordic countries also shows both similarities and differences between the countries. With the evolution of modern sport in the second half of the 1800s, association football soon started to emerge as a significant sport. Driven by modernisation, industrialisation and urbanisation, football took root in and then spread from its birthplace, England, to other parts of the world. As a result of its geographical expansion and a shift in social status from the upper classes to become the sport of the working classes, football grew into a competitive sport. That is, teams from different regions and later countries began to compete against each other to prove their superiority. Simultaneously, the emergence of post-industrial societies has shaped football; this local social and cultural practice has increasingly become national, and then international. Consequently, there developed a need for associations to organise competitions. As a result, in 1863 the first national federation was founded in England and the international federation FIFA (International Federation of Association Football) was established in 1904. The gradual widening of football's participant base and its internationalisation created the prerequisites for players, coaches and later for other actors in football to become professional (e.g., Giulianotti & Robertson, 2009; Lanfranchi et al., 2005).

It took a long time, however, for football to become truly global. Until as late as the 1980s, the FIFA World Cup was dominated by European and Latin American sides. The changes of the 1980s and 1990s, such as neoliberalism, marketisation and the breakdown of old structures, had a pervasive impact on many levels of society, and these also fundamentally changed football as both a game and a social phenomenon. In most countries today, football is seen as the primary sport in both participation and as a spectator sport, followed by vast media coverage and the increasing involvement of commercial partners. As football has become more international, a global football system has evolved, with global processes marked by flows of people, technology, capital, mediated images, and ideologies (Maguire, 2001). Some of the features of these flows are the increasing mobility of players and coaches, foreign ownership in elite football, and deterritorialised fan cultures.

Nevertheless, local practices in football have remained fundamental. It is reasonable to talk about *glocal* practices, referring to the global and local interactions and the simultaneous production of both cultural homogenisation and heterogenisation (Giulianotti & Robertson, 2009). Changes brought about by the globalisation of football have varied from locality to locality and contributed to inequalities and unevenness in the global division of labour, power and capital. It is indeed reasonable to examine football through a geopolitical perspective, as it has emerged in various social realities at different points in time with a varying status across countries and continents. It is common to differentiate between English, South American, European and Eastern European football, with each having distinctive characteristics of playing styles, fan cultures, professionalisation, migration routes, and even competition formats and club management. Partly driven by globalisation processes, the involvement of Asian, African and North American football in the global football system has grown considerably in recent decades.

In comparisons to the so-called core football countries, the Nordic countries have not been considered among the major nations when measured by success in international competitions. Scandinavia as a region has often been positioned on the semi-periphery of the global football map (Andersson & Carlsson, 2011; Szerovay et al., 2017), which is, among other factors, based on the history, success, position in migration networks and economic strength of football in international comparison. Yet, football has had a significant status in the sport culture of the Nordic countries and there have been notable achievements on both the women's and men's sides in major international tournaments as well as in club competitions. Just to name a few, the Swedish men's team was among the world's elite in the 1950s, even reaching the World Cup final in 1958, and Umeå FC won the Women's Champions League twice in the 2000s. Iceland's success in the past decade can be seen in the qualification for the 2018 World Cup by the men's team and participation in the most recent European Championships (henceforth Euro) for both men and women. Norway won gold at the second women's World Cup in 1995 and Ada Hegerberg was awarded the first Ballon d'Or Féminin in 2018. In the 1990s, the Rosenborg BK men's team from Trondheim found success in the men's Champions League. As for Finland, the women's team reached the semi-final in Euro 2005 and recently the men's team made their first appearance in a major tournament in Euro 2020 (played in 2021). In total, more than a hundred Nordic players are currently playing in the Big Five leagues in Europe in the 2022–2023 season, which is twice as many as ten years ago. The international importance and visibility of Nordic football continues to rise (player data was obtained from www.transfermarkt.com).

The focus of this book is football examined from a social science perspective in the five Nordic countries, which include the three Scandinavian countries Denmark, Norway and Sweden along with Finland and Iceland. The chapter authors have a strong track record in football research, and many also possess experience as practitioners in various segments of football. Although there is an abundance of research published on football in different Nordic countries, there is no book or study that encompasses five Nordic countries. Previous works have either been written from a national perspective or focused on one Nordic country as part of the international development of football. As one of the reviewers of the book proposal pointed out, "there are no or very few books that take a holistic approach to the Nordic countries. This is perhaps somewhat surprising, given the extremely important role of football in the Nordic countries, which calls for academic exploration".

Despite many similarities, differences across the Nordic countries may be identified. To start with, the historical trajectories and societal developments of the five Nordic countries vary significantly (Berntzen, 2017; Giulianotti et al., 2019). In sport and physical activity, tensions regarding civic activities and professionalisation have been present but differed in their nature and timing. The status of football in society, the number of participants and the pathway of women's football have shown variations as well. When looking at elite sport, differences can be highlighted, for instance, in international competitiveness, migration routes, and the level of commercialisation (Andersen & Ronglan, 2012).

Football research has expanded significantly in all the Nordic countries in the 2000s. In 2009, for example, the journal *Soccer & Society* published a Nordic-themed issue. Despite these advances, football research conducted in the Nordic countries remains poorly known, especially outside Europe. To date, studies have looked at the Nordic countries and societies from many different perspectives, as we wrote earlier. However, the football perspective with a holistic approach is still lacking. In an attempt to fill the gap, this book unwraps and sheds light on the changing football cultures of the Nordic countries while highlighting similarities and differences between them.

Structure of the book

This edited collection is divided into two parts. **Part I** offers a historical-sociological overview of football and society with one chapter dedicated to each of the five Nordic countries. The chapters are presented in alphabetical order of the countries and follow a similar structure while addressing the following dimensions: key societal development paths, football culture and its status within the sport culture, football as a participatory and spectator sport, football based on civil activities as well as professional practices, achievements on the international stage of football, and the development paths and status of women's football.

After providing breadth in Part I, we dig deeper by exploring 11 specific issues in football in the Nordic countries, organised under three themes in **Part II**. The first theme is *professionalisation and changing practices*. The section kicks off with a discussion by Björn Horgby and Christer Ericsson on governance in Swedish football clubs and how clubs have been shaped by three logics: democratic, competition and commercial. Chapter 7, written by Jouni Lavikainen, deals with the professionalisation – and levels of professionalism – of Finnish male players from the 1970s, drawing on empirical data while employing an oral history approach. Chapter 8 explores initiatives to improve elite football in Norway. Anders Belling and colleagues argue that these initiatives create tensions and might challenge the fundamental sport-for-all values and the Norwegian sports model in general. The last chapter of this section (Chapter 9), with a focus on changing practices, looks at football as a health-enhancing activity in Denmark. More specifically, Søren Bennike and his co-authors argue that *Football Fitness* breaks with the traditional organisation of football, drawing on the idea of path-breaking concepts.

The second theme is *gender and equality*, which is addressed by three topical texts on women's football. First, Hanna Vehviläinen and colleagues give an overview of the development of women's football in Finland in the past five decades, starting from the first official women's series in 1971 and walking the reader through how football has become the country's most popular team sport for girls and women. In the second chapter (Chapter 11), Bente Skogvang pinpoints how women have been breaking barriers in the past as well as today and how this has been the case in Norwegian football. In the third chapter (Chapter 12), Daði Rafnsson and Hafrún Kristjánsdóttir – using social and societal transformation theories – examine the evolution of women's football in Iceland through the experiences of five pivotal players during their careers.

The last theme of Part II focuses on *supporters, audiences and culture*. The section starts with Torbjörn Andersson's introduction to the history of Swedish football's classic club rivalries from Gothenburg, Stockholm, and the county of Scania. Then, Arve Hjelseth and Hans K. Hognestad explain how modern supporter culture in Norway developed in parallel to, and was part of, the modernisation and commercialisation of the game from the early 1990s. In the next chapter (Chapter 15), Rasmus Storm and his co-authors review the literature on factors influencing attendance and spectator satisfaction at professional football matches in Nordic countries. In Chapter 16, Tiago Duarte Dias – using an ethnographic approach – shows how aspects related to Kurdishness and Swedishness are expressed through an interpretation of how Dalkurd FF plays on the pitch.

The conclusions chapter brings together the main arguments of the book by highlighting key similarities and differences in the football culture and systems in the Nordic countries. We once again position these countries within the broader Nordic social and political domain as well as within global football, but this time our focus is on recent changes and future pathways. Our book does deal with rather "traditional" approaches to football within the social sciences, so some relevant contemporary perspectives may be lacking, including issues related to sustainable development, disability football, and social impact, just to name a few. However, we close by considering the possibilities, challenges and potential avenues this book presents for future scholarship.

References

Andersen, T. M., Holmström, B., Honkapohja, S., Korkman, S., Söderström, H. T., & Vartiainen, J. (2007). *The Nordic model: Embracing globalization and sharing risks*. Taloustieto Oy.

Andersen, S. S., & Ronglan, L. T. (Eds.). (2012). *Nordic elite sports: Same ambitions – different tracks*. Copenhagen Business School Press.

Andersson, T., & Carlsson, B. (2011). Introduction: Football studies in a broad perspective of centres and peripheries. *Soccer & Society, 12*(6), 719–721.

Berntzen, E. (2017). State- and nation-building in the Nordic region: Particular characteristics. In O. Knutsen (Ed.), *The Nordic models in political science* (pp. 19–44). Fagbokforlaget.

de la Porte, C., Eydal, G. B., Kauko, J., Nohrstedt, D., Hart, P. T., & Tranøy, B. S. (Eds.). (2022). *Successful public policy in the Nordic countries: Cases, lessons, challenges*. Oxford University Press.

Eckhardt Larsen, J., Schulte, B., & Thue, F. W. (2021). *Schoolteachers and the Nordic model: Comparative and historical perspective*. Routledge.

Giulianotti, R., Itkonen, H., Nevala, A., & Salmikangas, A.-K. (2019). Sport and civil society in the Nordic region. *Sport in Society, 22*(4), 540–554.

Giulianotti, R., & Robertson, R. (2009). *Globalization & football*. SAGE Publications.

Green, K., Sigurjónsson, T., & Skille, E. Å. (2020). *Sport in Scandinavia and the Nordic countries*. Routledge.

Gustafsson, H. (2017). *Nordens historia. En europeisk region under 1200 år* [Nordic history: A European region for 1200 years]. Studentlitteratur.
Junghagen, S. (2018). Tensions in stakeholder relations for a Swedish football club: A case study. *Soccer & Society, 19*(4), 612–629.
Lanfranchi, P., Eisenberg, C., Mason, T., & Wahl, A. (2005). *100 years of football: The FIFA centennial book*. Weidenfeld & Nicolson.
Maguire, J. (2001). *Global sport: Identities, societies, civilizations* (Reprinted edition). Polity Press.
Szerovay, M., Itkonen, H., & Vehmas, H. (2017). 'Glocal' processes in peripheral football countries: A figurational sociological comparison of Finland and Hungary. *Soccer & Society, 18*(4), 497–515.
Tin, M., Telseth, F., Tangen, J. O., & Giulianotti, R. (Eds.). (2020). *The Nordic model and physical culture*. Routledge.

Part I

Changing Football in the Nordic Countries

Chapter 1

Tradition and Transformation in Denmark

Søren Bennike, Rasmus K. Storm, Karsten Elmose-Østerlund, Nikolaj Schelde, and Laila Ottesen

Introduction

This chapter provides an understanding of football in Denmark. As in numerous other countries, football is a popular game that engages with men and women of all ages both on and off the pitch, where people are involved as players, volunteers, employees, fans and so forth. According to national sports participation surveys, football is one of the most popular activities (Ibsen et al., 2021; Rask et al., 2021), and at the same time the sport with the highest demand in terms of spectators and live attendees (Nielsen et al., 2019). The empirical backdrop is the existing body of literature and the latest data on issues such as participation and commercialisation. For theoretical underpinning, we will build on an understanding of society formed by four basic social orders viewed as ideal types: *civil society, market, state* and *associations*. Each ideal type has its own characteristics designated the "public sector", the "informal sector", the "commercial sector" and the "voluntary sector" (Pestoff, 1992).

We kick off by describing the early years of football, starting in the 1870s. From there, we highlight decisive landmarks that are essential for understanding Danish football. We continue by exploring the present landscape of football, including grassroots football (self-organised and club-organised) and elite-level football.[1] Finally, we conclude by focusing on selected current issues concerning, respectively, grassroots football and elite-level football. Regarding the Danish history of football, it is important to note that several issues only briefly touched on or not addressed here are described in detail by others. It is worth highlighting two books (in Danish) titled *Football, fair play & business – the history of Danish club football* (Grønkjær & Olsen, 2007) and *Women who win – Football history 1887–2013* (Weber, 2014). Moreover, Bonde (2008) did extensive work on Danish football during World War II.

The early years of football in Denmark

We begin at the "Constitution" of 1849, which is of crucial importance to the development of sports clubs in Denmark. The Constitution established

DOI: 10.4324/9781003280729-3

"freedom of association" and "freedom of assembly", and in the following period many sports clubs were formed. The first sport clubs were established in relation to the Danish-German conflict in the mid/late 19th century, and the activities organised included shooting and gymnastics (Kaspersen & Ottesen, 2001). Subsequently, more clubs were formed around English sports such as cricket, tennis and football (Ibsen & Ottesen, 2003). In the early years of the formalised organisation of sport, shooting and gymnastics activities received state support because a physically strong and "ready-to-shoot" population (men) would contribute to a stronger defence and simultaneously create a more productive, healthy and efficient workforce (Kaspersen & Ottesen, 2001). In contrast, the organisation of other sports, including football, was not (significantly) financially supported by the state until well into the 1900s (Ibsen & Ottesen, 2003). At that time, funding was established because sports associations were highlighted as institutions that contributed to the formation of democratic structures and practices (Gundelach & Torpe, 1999).

The introduction of football in Denmark in the 1870s is described by Toft (1993) and touched on in a recent paper by Grønkjær (forthcoming). Even though it is difficult to conclude how it all began and several myths of the early days exist, the link to the United Kingdom seems clear (McDowell, 2017). Grønkjær (2022) states that the introduction came with the help of British engineers working in Denmark. Firstly, football gained a foothold in the boarding school environment in Zealand at Sorø Academy and Birkerød Boarding School. In 1878, the first club to organise football in Denmark, and in mainland Europe, was Copenhagen Ball Club (KB), primarily organised around cricket. In the early years, the game was strongly dominated by (predominantly) men from the upper-middle class, both as players and leaders (Toft, 1993). There is documentation that women did also play football, though in very limited numbers. The first women's football club was founded in 1887 (Weber, 2014).

In the following years, more football clubs came into existence, enabling the first official club-based men's match in 1887 (Toft, 1993). One year later, in 1888, KB arranged the first tournament, in which 15 teams participated (Toft, 1993). As more clubs were formed, for football to spread and further consolidate it was necessary to secure better organisation, unified rules and organised tournaments. This led to the foundation of the Danish Ball Games Association (DBU) in 1889, which represented football, cricket and tennis.[2] Women's football was not included in DBU until 1972 (Brus & Trangbæk, 2003). In the first league tournament organised by DBU, held in 1889, seven "near Copenhagen" based clubs participated. The first official national men's team match was played at the 1908 Olympics against France, and the first national league tournament was held in 1912–1913 (Grønkjær & Olsen, 2007). The first mention of a women's football match was in 1902 (Weber, 2014), and the first women's (unofficial) national team match was played at the (unofficial) women's world cup in Italy in 1970. Denmark was represented by the club BK Femina and was crowned champions.

The following year, more than 200 clubs participated in the national women's tournament, making the recruitment basis large enough to pick a "real" national team (Brus & Trangbæk, 2003), and the Danish team won the world title for the second successive year in 1971.

The DBU, the first national football association in mainland Europe, had a difficult start and almost dissolved in 1895 with only two clubs as members (Olsen & Grønkjær, 2009). The struggles came to an end at the beginning of the 1900s as the popularity of the game grew. An important point raised by Toft (1993) is that in 1896 the Danish Ministry of Culture recommended that football should be incorporated in physical education lessons in schools, thus pushing forward the popularity of the game. It was emphasised that football contributed to character building and health for both boys and girls (Brus & Trangbæk, 2003). This was an early example of state involvement in the game, which had massive importance for its popularity and uptake.

Rather quickly after it was founded, the DBU transformed into something resembling its present structure as an umbrella organisation comprising six regional Football County Unions (FCUs).[3] Moreover, the National Olympic Committee and Sports Confederation of Denmark (DIF) was established in 1896 with the DBU as a member. In this structure, the clubs were no longer members of the DBU; they were members of the regional FCUs, which were members of the DBU operating at national level and functioning as members of DIF. This structure is illustrated in Figure 1.2, which depicts the present organisation of Danish football. It is important to note that all clubs and organisations functioned as associations, being non-profit and relatively autonomous. With reference to Pestoff (1992), these are positioned in the "voluntary sector".

The consolidation of football in Denmark

The consolidation of football and sports club activity was hugely influenced by state laws in the period from 1937 to 1968. In 1937, a new school law required the local authorities (municipalities) to provide public schools of a certain size with a playing field and to make the facilities available to local sports clubs after school hours (Ibsen & Ottesen, 2003). This included football clubs and solved a major issue regarding playing fields. Furthermore, in 1948 the Danish Parliament adopted an Act on Receipts from the State Football Pools,[4] which secured DIF a relatively large part of the national monopolistic betting profits (including the national lottery profits in 1989), bringing funding to the DBU. This led to a professionalisation of sports organisations in the years that followed. Women's football also requested stronger organisation as part of the DBU but was turned down. Instead, three clubs formed their own union – the Danish Women's Football Union (Brus & Trangbæk, 2003). In 1968, the Danish Leisure Act[5] was adopted. It provided favourable conditions for sports clubs, as it obligated the local authorities to support all leisure-time activities, including football, organised in associations (Ibsen & Ottesen, 2003). Leisure time was considered a welfare benefit, and the culture and leisure-time policy became significant for building municipal welfare. The Leisure Act obligated each municipality to provide facilities and financial support for clubs. In its present form, it is important to highlight that financial support is primarily provided for the organisation of activities for children and young people below the age of 25. In relation to the following, this is an important point for understanding the purpose and interest of grassroots clubs. By this time, a subsidised structure was created that remains within association-based club sport and football today; the state supports the work of the DBU (through DIF) and the local authorities (municipalities) support non-profit football clubs, to whom the citizens pay membership fees. Kaspersen and Ottesen (2001) define this as the "double democratic principle", in which the financial support and state recognition of sports clubs creates an "associative democracy" as a parallel form of government to "representative democracy", forming a dual strategy. The passing of these laws was a key factor in the continually growing numbers of people playing football up until 1980. Another aspect regarding the increasing number of players in the DBU is the inclusion of women's football in 1972 (Brus & Trangbæk, 2003). See Figure 1.1 for an overview of participation numbers and clubs from 1930 to 2020 (DIF, 2022).[6]

At the same time, the above-mentioned state laws were a key factor in maintaining the amateur code and associative structure of the clubs, as funding and facilities could not be assigned to for-profit organisations. Meanwhile, while the countries around Denmark introduced professional football, Denmark retained its amateur code up to 1978, based among other things on state funding and the argument of its importance. As related by

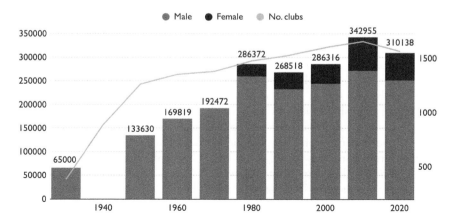

Figure 1.1 Participation numbers and clubs.

Figure 1.2 The organisational system of football in Denmark.

Grønkjær (2022), there were strong amateur ideals in DIF and the DBU, for example that professional players playing abroad were not allowed to represent the national team. These ideals were heavily challenged over time, and from 1978 onwards the mixture of football and money finally resulted in some clubs establishing a stock-based foundation, which was private and for-profit and thus positioned in the "commercial sector". An important step towards the introduction of professional football was the founding of the Danish League Association (LA) in 1969 as an organisation representing men's top league clubs and addressing issues in favour of professional football. The female equivalent is the Women's League Association (WLA), established in 1981. Note that the WLA is not an official member of the DBU. Instead, it has cooperative agreements with the LA and the DBU, respectively, and is represented in both the DBU's board of directors and boards of representatives. For detailed insights, see Bennike et al. (2020). With the introduction of professional football and for-profit activity, the football landscape found its present form, which is presented in Figure 1.2 and further explored in the following.

The current landscape of football in Denmark

Overall, the present organisation can be divided into different ideal types, also reflecting the organisational structure of Danish football. Grassroots football is positioned either in the voluntary sector as club-organised football or in the informal sector as self-organised football. The latter can be exemplified by a group of friends meeting in the park to play football. Elite-level football is positioned in both the voluntary and commercial sectors, depending on the economic foundation of the club. In the following, we focus first on grassroots football, including both club- and self-organised settings, before providing insights into elite-level football, with a strong commercial perspective.

Insights into grassroots football

Football is a popular grassroots sporting activity in Denmark, particularly among children. In 2020, the number of children aged 7–15 years that had played football regularly within the last year was estimated at 31%. Among boys, 45% were reported to have played football, while the figure among girls was 17% (Rask et al., 2021). Among the children who play football, nearly all are involved in a sports club setting. For adults aged 15+ years, the percentage that had played football within the last year was estimated at 11%. More men (17%) than women (6%) are playing (Ibsen et al., 2021). Thus, participation in football is highest among children, with a significant drop-out in adult life. In respect of adults, 5% play football at least once a week, 3.5% play in a sports club setting and 1.4% play self-organised football (Ibsen et al., 2021). Approximately 0.4% are reported to play both self-organised football and in a club setting. This leaves 1% of adult Danes who play self-organised football on a weekly basis without any connection to a sports club (Elmose-Østerlund, 2022). While for children club-organised and self-organised football are mainly complementary activities (Pilgaard & Rask, 2016), these organisational forms seem to be more exclusionary among adults. And the fact that one in five regularly active adult football players is active outside football clubs indicates that grassroots football should be looked at in a broader perspective than solely as a club-based activity. Recent data concludes that most adult Danes who are not club-active but play self-organised football at least once a week are young adult men aged between 15 and 29 who play with friends (Elmose-Østerlund, 2022).

As mentioned, the dominant organisational form of football is as a club-organised sport. In Denmark, there are 1,577 grassroots football clubs of different sizes organised under the umbrella of the DBU (DIF, 2022). The distribution of club size is portrayed in Figure 1.3. It is important to note that Denmark has other national sporting umbrella organisations besides the DBU (and DIF) that have different structures and ideologies, but all work to improve conditions for grassroots sport, including football. As the DBU is the supreme authority for organised football and officially represents Danish football in national and international matters, our focus will rest with them.

Typically, the purpose of grassroots clubs is social interaction, training and tournament participation (Bennike et al., 2020). Even though almost all clubs are involved in competitive activities, most club chairpersons perceive their club to be largely social and agree that it is important to organise football with a focus on social benefits (Bennike et al., 2020). This perspective, in which

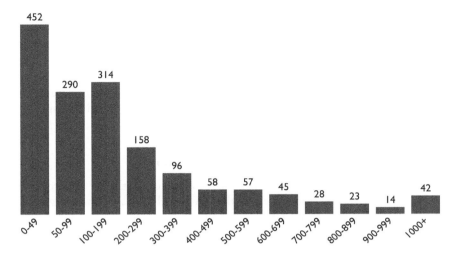

Figure 1.3 Distribution of club size based on number of members (DIF, 2022).

competitiveness and social interaction exist side by side, is also expressed by Ibsen and Seippel (2010) and Breuer et al. (2016) independently of sports club activity. Furthermore, Bennike et al. (2019) show that the clubs see their main purpose as being to create sound leisure-time activity for young people, a social community for members and a cultural centre of attention for the local community. This is exactly what the state wants in order to create a strong civil society in which people's leisure time is believed to be important. This did not just grow out of nothing; rather, the state created a policy system beneficial to associationism, cf. the previously mentioned passing of state laws. In relation to the creation of a social community, providing a place where members feel comfortable and enjoy spending their leisure time should be considered important because their membership fees and voluntary work are important for the running of the club. The importance of membership fees and voluntary work is also indicated by the fact that most clubs agree that it is important to recruit more members and more volunteers (Bennike et al., 2019).

Overall, 344,678 members are active in grassroots clubs (DIF, 2022) and an estimated 126,000 are taking on volunteer tasks, such as board membership, coaching, etc. (DBU, 2018). In 2019, Bennike and Schelde (2020) led an extensive analysis of grassroots players focusing among other things on age, gender, ethnicity and sexuality. It is worth highlighting that more than 50% of club members are children and young people, and internal DBU data shows that participants are active for the whole lifespan; there are more than 3,000 club members over the age of 70 (DBU, 2022). The analysis also concluded that there was an underrepresentation of members with immigrant or descendant-of-immigrant status compared to Danish society as a whole. It can also be observed that sexuality varies according to gender (i.e. relatively more bisexual and gay women than men participate in football). For further perspectives on diversity in Danish football, see Bennike et al. (2020). The analysis was conducted because a political commission (DBU, 2017) employed by the DBU recognised the need for a higher degree of diversity, and this present analysis represents a change from sweeping yet passive statements relating to football being "for all" towards the explicit recognition that specific groups are underrepresented.

Insights into elite-level (commercial) football clubs

Disregarding the national teams, which are organised under the DBU, elite-level football in Denmark is represented by the LA and the WLA. These organisations work to create the best possible conditions for elite-level football and to develop Danish professional football. As already mentioned, the DBU lifted the ban on professional football in 1978. At this point, the transitioning of the (men's) clubs from amateur status to commercial entities began, and it slowly developed up to the 1990s, when revenues in the Danish men's clubs grew significantly (Storm, 2009). In short, the top-tier men's clubs broke from the voluntary sector into the commercial sector, incorporating formal hierarchical organisational structures and a private, for-profit foundation (Bennike et al., 2019). Even if the top-tier men's clubs are for profit, it does not mean that the clubs are genuinely profit-maximising entities in the traditional sense of private firms. Following contemporary studies, they are merely win-optimising entities using money as a means to sporting success (though with some exceptions; Storm, 2009). In respect of top-level women's football, the players are still mainly amateurs, with only a few Danish top-tier clubs fielding professional and semi-professional players, though resting on a non-profit foundation in grassroots clubs and thus positioned in the voluntary sector (Brandt-Hansen & Ottesen, 2019). Furthermore, the difference between men's and women's club revenues is significant, as it is for men's and women's salaries. While there is no data available for Danish women's professional football, anecdotal evidence reveals that even the highest female wages are minimal, in significant contrast to the best male players.

When money enters football due to commercialisation, financial resources become a powerful competitive tool, as the increased revenue enables clubs to buy up players to improve their chances of success (Szymanski & Kuypers, 2000). However, the financial dimension of the professional game also constitutes a problem. As pointed out by Whitney (1993) and Dietl et al. (2008), European professional clubs are faced with a competitive structure that is creating a rat race for players. This goes for Danish clubs as well. Financial difficulties and indebtedness are the direct result (Nielsen & Storm, 2017). In the Danish league, all clubs have faced financial problems due to this ruinous competitive structure, and most clubs operate with deficits year by year (Storm, 2013). Fortunately, because the clubs face soft budget constraints (Storm & Nielsen, 2015), they are usually bailed out or rescued by creditors, sponsors or shareholders, thus keeping them afloat.

In addition to receiving capital injections, clubs have developed various solutions to the central problem of remaining competitive. Storm (2013) argues that during commercialisation clubs have developed certain "programmes" to optimise their chances of becoming successful – both financially and in sporting terms. These programmes, including *talent development, engaging sponsors, floating shares, facilities and stadium development,* and *diversification,* constitute the Danish business model of professional football and will be briefly examined in the following. On the commercialisation timeline, *talent development* was the first programme developed by the clubs. In fact, it already started being institutionalised before the commercialisation process in which the clubs transferred from the voluntary to the commercial sector. However, talent development now helps the clubs commercially and in relation to sporting performance by developing players who can be utilised by the clubs themselves or sold on the international transfer market. The second programme developed was *engaging sponsors,* which naturally follows from the commercialisation process. By selling sponsorships and using football players as advertising stands for various products, the Danish clubs have aimed to earn income that can be used for improving sporting performance and, in turn, revenue. The third programme is turning clubs into stockholding companies and *floating shares.* This is essential to understanding professional clubs as part of the commercial sector. In 1987, Brøndby IF became the second football club in Europe (after Tottenham Hotspur a year earlier) to float shares and become a stockholding company. This development should be seen as part of the process of attracting investors and financial investment to the club to remain competitive, making the idea of floating shares a significant trend in the commercialisation process of Danish professional football. *Facilities and stadium development* programmes have also been part of the commercialisation process. Most facilities are owned by the municipalities, though some clubs, such as FC Copenhagen, FC Midtjylland and Brøndby IF, have bought or built their own stadiums. Over the years, league clubs have pushed for improvement of existing facilities to attract more spectators or sponsors, and during the 2000s many had their home grounds renovated, mainly paid for by municipalities. This means that the public sector (the municipality) is investing in facilities built to support actors in the commercial sector (Storm & Brandt, 2008). It is clear that Danish professional football clubs have played an active role in promoting these investments. Upgraded facilities are necessary to improve demand among sponsors and spectators and are thus an essential tool for success. Finally, *diversification* into other leisure and entertainment activities was a strategy of the Danish clubs from the 2000s up to the international financial crisis in 2008/09. Many clubs saw it as a means to gain additional income from, for example, property investments and leisure-activities such as concerts and events. Even investment in fitness centres and hotels – or other property – was part of the diversification process. FC Copenhagen, in particular, was successful in building a highly diversified business by buying the Danish national stadium, a chain of fitness centres and a large holiday resort. Other Danish football clubs were inspired by this and started to diversify into other businesses as well. From 2000, nearly all Danish top-tier clubs diversified to some extent. However, after the crisis of 2008/09, many clubs started to de-diversify and focus on the core football business due to financial difficulties and problems capitalising on the new investments. During the last ten years, the clubs have been finding new business models, but many are still struggling to make financial ends meet sporting ambitions.

Final remarks and current issues

To sum up, all organisations except the professional elite-level clubs represent a specific institutionalisation of associative democracy built on state laws from 1849 to 1968. In a Scandinavian context, Andersson and Carlsson (2009) refer to this as football having historical roots in the development of the welfare state. If we look into grassroots football, this is extremely clear, whereas elite-level football, when organised in a professional football context, extends into the market and the commercial sector, with clubs organised as for-profit (stock-holding) companies and not therefore resting on a democratic platform. These historical roots have resulted in a relatively high number of non-profit democratically organised grassroots clubs of different sizes spread around the country involving volunteers and creating local cultural and social communities, especially for children and young people. These aspects can be traced as direct outcomes of the state-initiated political system, which at the same time contributed to late professionalism.

This final section will focus on three emerging issues that we pinpoint as "points of attention". Two are related to grassroots football – one with a focus on self-organised football and the other on club-organised football – while the third is related to elite-level football. Each point of attention is related to different societal sectors and will arguably influence the future organisation of football. The first point of attention relates to self-organised football, which is positioned in the informal sector, and the point that grassroots football should not be addressed as solely a club-sport activity. So far, self-organised football players have not received much attention from research or practice, and we know very little about these football players beyond what is presented in this text. Nevertheless, self-organised football is part of a general trend in sports participation towards a growth in self-organised sports, especially those practised outside (Rask et al., 2021). In order to better understand the motives and barriers of these players for practising self-organised football, a strengthened focus from both research and practice seems highly relevant. Questions regarding whether self-organised players are drop-outs from club-organised football, why and how they were recruited and how they organise their activities seem particularly relevant. This knowledge could inspire the Danish national sports organisations, DIF (representing the DBU) and DGI,[7] with regard to initiatives to increase the number of self-organised football players as part of their "vision 25-50-75" in which they aim to promote both club-organised and self-organised sport.

The second point of attention relates to grassroots football clubs, which are positioned in the voluntary sector, and the observation that cooperation and co-production with public authorities are apparently becoming increasingly more common among football clubs. Specifically, the DBU is now entering into "welfare alliances" with municipalities, with the mission for grassroots football to contribute explicitly to the resolution of societal challenges such as health, integration and unemployment. It is hardly revolutionary for sports clubs and sports organisations to be used for non-sporting objectives (Bennike et al., 2018; Thing & Ottesen, 2010). However, the role of sport, and in this case football, within the "welfare alliance" initiatives seem to have progressed from a passive and symbolic focus on resolving societal challenges to something more explicit and ambitious. This development brings organised grassroots football closer to the public sector in a form that will arguably challenge the autonomy of clubs. Moreover, and as discussed by Bennike and Ottesen (2020), implementational challenges must be expected as the DBU and organised grassroots clubs explicitly enter policy arenas other than sport.

The third point of attention relates to elite-level football, and more specifically professional football positioned in the commercial sector. One central issue remains a recurring challenge for the Danish clubs: finances and dependence on the market. The question of economic power is top of the agenda because clubs are trying to balance financial stability with sporting success nationally and internationally. During the last couple of years, a growing number of new foreign investors have looked to Denmark and even acquired Danish clubs (for example, FC Nordsjælland, FC Midtjylland, FC Vejle and FC Amager), while others have provided capital to financially distressed clubs. It is reasonable to believe that Denmark's work with talent development in an international context plays an important role (FIFA, 2021). Denmark is highlighted by FIFA as "a unique example of how to maximise talent" (FIFA, 2022). Providing access to Danish clubs for such investors could be a future development aspect of the business model of Danish football mentioned earlier. Whether Danish fans and stakeholders will welcome foreign ownership to a larger extent than before remains to be seen.

Notes

1 A contemporary profile of the organisation of club football in Denmark is thoroughly analysed by Bennike et al. (2020), which is recognised as a key paper for this chapter. Several perspectives from this peer-reviewed article are incorporated in this chapter.
2 Tennis was included in the DBU until 1920 and cricket until 1953.

3 FCU Jutland (1895), FCU Zealand (1902), FCU Copenhagen (1903), FCU Funen (1904), FCU Lolland-Falster (1906) and FCU Bornholm (1907).
4 Today's version is the Allocation Act (*Udlodningsloven*).
5 Today's version is the Enlightenment Act (*Folkeoplysningsloven*).
6 The figures for participation in 2021 were 344,678 members and 1,577 clubs (DIF, 2022).
7 Denmark has three significant national sports umbrella organisations (DIF, DGI and DFIF), which have different aims, structure and ideology but all work to improve conditions for associatively based recreational sport.

References

Andersson, T., & Carlsson, B. (2009). Football in Scandinavia: A fusion of welfare policy and the market. *Soccer & Society*, *10*(3–4), 299–304.

Bennike, S., & Ottesen, L. S. (2020). 'Welfare Alliances' – a new social role for football in Denmark: Reflections on changes and challenges. *Idrottsforum.org*. Retrieved November 2, 2022, from https://idrottsforum.org/bennike-ottesen201123/

Bennike, S., & Schelde, N. (2020). *Diversiteten i dansk fodbold* [The Diversity in Danish Football]. DBU. Brøndby.

Bennike, S., Schelde, N., & Evans, A. B. (2020). The diversity of organised grassroots football in Denmark. *Idrottsforum.org*. Retrieved November 27, 2022, from https://idrottsforum.org/bennikeetal200908/

Bennike, S., Storm, R., Wikman, J., & Ottesen, L. (2020). The organisation of club football in Denmark: A contemporary profile. *Soccer & Society*, *21*(5), 551–571.

Bennike, S., Thing, L. F., & Ottesen, L. (2018). Health through state supported voluntary sport clubs. In D. Parnel & P. Krustrup (Eds.), *Sport and health: Exploring the current state of play* (pp. 111–131). Routledge.

Bonde, H. (2008). *Football with the foe – Danish sport under the swastika*. University Press of Southern Denmark.

Brandt-Hansen, M., & Ottesen, L. (2019). Caught between passion for the game and the need for education: A study of female football players in Denmark. *Soccer & Society*, *20*(3), 494–511.

Breuer, C., Feiler, S., Llopis-Goig, R., & Elmose-Østerlund, K. (2016). *Characteristics of European sports clubs*. Centre for sports, health and civil Society, University of Southern Denmark.

Brus, A., & Trangbæk, E. (2003). Asserting the right to play – women's football in Denmark. *Soccer & Society*, *4*(2–3), 95–111.

DBU. (2017). *Kommission anbefaler politiske reformer* [The commission recommends political reforms]. Retrieved April 15, 2022, from https://www.dbu.dk/nyheder/2017/marts/kommission-anbefaler-politiske-reformer/

DBU. (2018). *Fodboldens værdi for Danmark* [The value of football for Denmark]. DBU. Retrieved April 10, 2022, from https://www.dbu.dk/media/12378/dbu-samfundsbog online.pdf

DBU. (2022). *Internal database*. DBU.

Dietl, H. M., Franck, E., & Lang, M. (2008). Overinvestment in team sports leagues: A contest theory model. *Scottish Journal of Political Economy*, *55*(3), 353–368.

DIF. (2022). *Medlemstal 2021* [Number of members 2021]. Retrieved September 4, 2022, from https://www.dif.dk/idraetten-i-tal

Elmose-Østerlund, K. (2022). *Analysis of self-organised football players*. Unpublished raw material.
FIFA. (2021). *Increasing global competitiveness – an analysis of the talent development ecosystem in Denmark*. FIFA. Retrieved September 16, 2022, from https://gamechanger.nu/pdf/DEN_Final_2021.pdf
FIFA. (2022). *Denmark – a unique example of how to maximise talent*. FIFA Training Center.
Grønkjær, A. (forthcoming). Struggling with the amateur identity: The self-perception of the Danish football movement, 1880s to 1970s. *Soccer & Society*.
Grønkjær, A., & Olsen, D. H. (2007). *Fodbold, fairplay og forretning* [Football, fairplay and business]. Turbineforlaget.
Gundelach, P., & Torpe, L. (1999). Befolkningens fornemmelse for demokrati: Foreninger, politisk engagement og demokratisk kultur [People's feeling for democracy: Associations, political commitment and democratic culture]. In J. Andersen (Ed.), *Den demokratiske udfordring* [The democratic challenge] (pp. 70–91). Hans Reitzels Forlag.
Ibsen, B., Høyer-Kruse, J., & Elmose-Østerlund, K. (2021). *Danskernes bevægelsesvaner og motiver for bevægelse* [Movement habits and motives for movement in Denmark]. Centre for sports, health and civil Society, University of Southern Denmark.
Ibsen, B., & Ottesen, L. (2003). Sport and welfare policy in Denmark: The development of sport between state, market and community. In K. Heinemann (Ed.), *Sport and welfare policies: Six European case studies* (pp. 31–86). Hofmann.
Ibsen, B., & Seippel, Ø. (2010). Voluntary organized sport in Denmark and Norway. *Sport in Society: Cultures, Commerce, Media, Politics, 13*(4), 593–608.
Kaspersen, L. B., & Ottesen, L. (2001). Associationalism for 150 years and still alive and kicking: Some reflections on Danish civil society. *Critical Review of International Social and Political Philosophy, 4*(1), 105–130.
McDowell, M. L. (2017). 'To cross the Skager Rack'. Discourses, images, and tourism in early 'European' football: Scotland, the United Kingdom, Denmark, and Scandinavia, 1898–1914. *Soccer & Society, 18*(2–3), 245–269.
Nielsen, C. G., Storm, R. K., & Jakobsen, T. G. (2019). The impact of English Premier League broadcasts on Danish spectator demand: A small league perspective. *Journal of Business Economics, 89*(6), 633–653.
Nielsen, K., & Storm, R. K. (2017). Profits, championships and budget constraints in European professional sport. In U. Wagner, R. K. Storm, & K. Nielsen (Eds.), *When sport meets business: Capabilities, challenges, critiques* (pp. 153–166). SAGE Publications Inc.
Olsen, D. H., & Grønkjær, A. B. (2009). Dansk fodboldhistorie: Var der fodbold før 1980? *Forum for Idræt* [Danish football history: Was there football before 1980?].
Pestoff, V. A. (1992). Third sector and co-operative services: An alternative to privatization. *Journal of Consumer Policy, 15*, 21–45.
Pilgaard, M., & Rask, S. (2016). *Danskernes motions- og sportsvaner 2016* [Sports participation in Denmark 2016]. Idrættens Analyseinstitut.
Rask, S., Eske, M., Petersen, F., & Hansen, K. (2021). *Danskernes aktivitetsvalg og organisering i 2020* [Activity choice and organisation of sport among Danes 2020]. Idrættens Analyseinstitut.
Storm, R. K. (2009). The rational emotions of FC København: A lesson on generating profit in professional soccer. *Soccer & Society, 10*(3–4), 459–476.

Storm, R. K. (2013). *Kommercielle sportsklubber: Følelser eller forretning?* [Professional team sports clubs in Europe: Emotional attachments or a profitable business?] [PhD Thesis]. University of Southern Denmark.

Storm, R. K., & Brandt, H. (2008). *Idræt og sport i den danske oplevelsesøkonomi [Sport in the Danish experience economy]*. Forlaget Samfundslitteratur.

Storm, R. K., & Nielsen, K. (2015). Soft budget constraints in European and US leagues – similarities and differences. In W. Andreff (Ed.), *Disequilibrium sport economics: Competitive imbalance and budget constraints* (pp. 151–171). Edward Elgar.

Szymanski, S., & Kuypers, T. (2000). *Winners and losers: The business strategy of football*. Penguin Books.

Thing, L. F., & Ottesen, L. (2010). The autonomy of sports: Negotiating boundaries between sports governance and government policy in the Danish welfare state. *International Journal of Sport Policy, 2*(2), 223–235.

Toft, J. (1993). Fodbold mellem myter og kilder [Football between myths and realities]. *Forum for Idræt*.

Weber, L. (2014). *Kvinder der vinder – Fodboldhistorie 1887–2013* [Women who win – The story of football 1887–2013]. Hillerød, Forlaget Lennart Weber.

Whitney, J. D. (1993). Bidding till bankrupt: Destructive competition in professional team sports. *Economic Inquiry, 31*(1), 100–115.

Chapter 2

Growing Participation and Slow Professionalisation in Finland

Arto Nevala, Hannu Itkonen, and Mihaly Szerovay

The early years

Football came to Finland in the late 19th century, above all with English seamen. Since 1809, Finland had been an autonomous part of the Russian Empire. Due this, Finland gradually became a nation with geographical borders, its own system of government, economic life and national identity. On the other hand, industrialisation and modernisation started in Finland later than in other Nordic countries. At the beginning of the 20th century, Finland was a largely non-industrialised and only slightly urbanised country with only 12% of the population living in the cities, much less than in many countries in Western Europe (Koponen & Saaritsa, 2019).

The modernisation process in Finland had three key elements at the turn of the 20th century. Industrialisation meant above all growth of the forest industry, which created wealth in both the cities and the countryside. In the parliament reform of 1906, Finland suddenly became one of the most democratic states in the world in terms of the right to vote and stand for election. The enlargement of civic society meant a strong expansion of organisations, including the sport sector. Since then, one of the characteristics of Finnish physical culture has been the multiplicity of civic society. The importance of the public sector grew in the 20th century after independence in 1917 (Itkonen, 2000; Koski et al., 2015).

The spread of football in Finland was part of a wider revolution in sports. The traditional competitions held at national festivals turned into modern competitions organised according to international examples, common rules and measuring (Koski et al., 2015). The breakthrough of modern sports was closely related to the nation-building process, the expansion of civil society and the formation of an international sport movement. In the early years, football was most popular in coastal and school towns, whereas for example track and field sports, cross country skiing and wrestling were more sports of the countryside. Teachers' colleges took an important role, starting to teach football as early as the 1890s. The school system played an important role in the early phases of football in Finland in exactly same way as in England (Itkonen & Nevala, 2012; Winner, 2005).

DOI: 10.4324/9781003280729-4

In the beginning on the 20th century, football was a small sport: Only four clubs attended the founding meeting of the Football Association of Finland (FAF) in 1907. The first years of the FAF were characterised by uncertainty, and the competition system did not stabilise until the late 1920s, when over 20 teams were competing for the Finnish Championship. Another indication of stabilisation was the founding of regional associations, as was the case in other areas of civic society too. The first regional football association was founded in Helsinki in 1922, and just a decade later there were 11 associations around the country (Itkonen & Nevala, 2012).

Finland integrated into the international football community as early as 1908, with a permanent membership of FIFA. Four years later (1912), Finland took part in the Olympic football tournament in Stockholm, surprisingly reaching fourth place. However, only seven international games were played before World War I (WWI). The Stockholm Olympics was a turning point in the relationship between sport and nationalism. Olympic success became a key goal of the Finnish sports movement. Olympic medals were thought to measure the superiority and vitality of nations. That is why football, even though it was an Olympic sport, was overshadowed by track and field sports and wrestling. In addition, Finland's long, dark and snowy winter, as well as the lack of decent football fields, prevented football from developing into a sport of importance in nation-building, as occurred in many other Western European countries (Goldblatt, 2006; Itkonen & Nevala, 2012; Kokkonen, 2015).

The spread of football

The outbreak of the First World War, the gaining of independence from Russia in 1917 and the bloody civil war of the following year fundamentally changed the political and social situation in Finland. Three important elements can be highlighted. State independence provided momentum to several different kinds of social reform. The constitution law of 1919 consolidated democracy and the citizens' rights, as did the democratisation of municipal decision-making. Secondly, Finland was a politically divided nation between the World Wars and even later. The losing party in the Civil War, the political left, was partly restricted. However, Finland did not degenerate into an undemocratic state, as did many other states which gained independence after WWI. This was a result of the strong civil society and of the fact that many important politicians on the bourgeois winning side were in favour of moderation and social reforms. After the Civil War, the establishment of small, independent farms was important in stabilising the political situation and forging the unity of the nation. The number of small farmers grew rapidly until the 1930s. This meant that urbanisation and modernisation in Finland were much slower than in other Nordic countries. Unity and stability were also promoted by many social policy reforms and the implementation of compulsory education in the early 1920s (Meinander, 2014).

Thirdly, Finland's position as a neighbour of the Russia/Soviet Union had a significant effect on national identity. The political right saw the Soviet Union as a threat to Finland's independence. Resistance to this threat had to be prepared by military means, but also by raising decent citizens: a free, Christian and hard-working small farmer was the ideal citizen. Alongside the Defence Forces, the paramilitary organisation Civil Guard played an important role in national defence. The Civil Guard was an important organisation in the sport sector too, as its organisation was more comprehensive than that of the public sector. The goal of the Civil Guard's sports activities was to strengthen national defence, but the organisation also built many sports venues. The role of the state and municipalities as builders of sport venues increased in the 1920s, but still the Civil Guard was an important actor in physical activity and sports, especially in rural areas, where almost 80% of Finns lived (Itkonen & Salmikangas, 2015; Kokkonen, 2015).

At the core of Finnish sports life in the 1920s and 1930s was Olympic success in individual sports. Considering its population size, Finland succeeded excellently in the Summer and Winter Olympics. Olympic success was important to the young nation. Many Olympic athletes became well-known public figures due the news coverage by newspapers and radio. On the other hand, team sports were overshadowed by individual sports in popularity. The only exception was Finnish baseball (*pesäpallo*). The Civil Guard included Finnish baseball as part of its sports programme and spread the sport to the countryside. However, football did not play an important role in the Civil Guard. On the contrary, the unwelcoming attitude of the Civil Guard marginalised football in the 1920s and 1930s when the position of football strengthened elsewhere (Kokkonen, 2015; Vasara, 2007).

Nonetheless, the popularity of football grew between the World Wars and the number of clubs in the FAF increased sevenfold. Unfortunately, no data is available on the number of registered players. However, football was played on three serial levels in the mid-1930s, which indicates the expansion of the game. Furthermore, the internationalisation of Finnish football continued. About six to eight international matches were played annually. In addition, Finland participated in the Nordic Cup since 1929 and even in the Olympic tournament in Berlin (1936), although only by losing one match. Finland participated in the World Cup qualification for the first time in 1937–1938, but the result was again nothing but losses. As part of internationalisation, the FAF had to resolve its attitude towards professionalism, which became more and more important in football. The decision in favour of amateurism was made in 1920 and was influenced by the principles of the International Olympic Committee (IOC). Internationally, top football developed towards professionalism, but Finland chose differently (Itkonen & Nevala, 2012).

In terms of football, Finland lagged behind the other Nordic countries and the rest of Europe during the interwar period. In building national identity, both Summer and Winter Olympics medals, but not football, were crucial. Until the

1960s, football, as well as ice hockey, were overshadowed by Olympic sports. Team sports were the sports of cities, and industrial centres were still populated by only a minority of the population. Top athletes in track and fields, wrestling and cross-country skiing came mostly from the countryside, although some of them were born in the cities. The structure of Finnish society thus strongly affected the development of sports. It was not until the rapid modernisation of Finnish society since the 1960s that the structure and power relationships of sports culture slowly began to change.

Consolidation

The Second World War (WWII) changed European societies fundamentally. Finland's position changed when the war against the Soviet Union ended in defeat. Finland had to hand over one tenth of its territory to the Soviet Union and pay war reparations. In addition, the country had to resettle people coming from the ceded areas and those displaced from the army. Furthermore, the political situation changed when all left-wing parties were once again allowed to operate freely (Meinander, 2014).

The post-war reconstruction required financial resources and national unity. Reforms to prevent social conflicts from escalating were also needed. One of the most important solutions was once again the establishment of small farms. In this way, a large part of the population was bound to the countryside for decades, which slowed down the urbanisation and modernisation of society. The small farms policy was faced with crisis at the turn of the 1950s and 1960s, leading to a drastic social restructuring: transition from agriculture to industry and services and migration to cities and also to Sweden. In order to control this change, Finnish society was modernised in accordance with the Nordic welfare state model. The transition from a warfare state to a welfare state took place in Finland almost two decades later than in many other countries. However, the transition was rapid, and Finland soon caught up with the other Nordic countries in terms of well-being and living standards (Allardt, 1976; Koponen & Saaritsa, 2019).

The reconstruction and war reparations strengthened the role of the state in Finland and in the other Nordic countries too. The state became a strong actor in the economy. The public sector – the state and the municipalities – took a key role in building the welfare state, which meant major social reforms for example in the education system, health care and social services. In short, the public sector became an important actor in many areas of social life (Allardt, 1976; Arnason & Wittrock, 2012; Giulianotti et al., 2017).

The welfare state changed the relationship between civil society organisations, including sport organisation and public authorities. In the 1970s and 1980s, the state had a strong guiding role in municipal sport through funding the building of facilities and counselling. The Sport Act of 1980 established sport boards in municipalities and strengthened local sport services by increasing the number of sport officials, supporting voluntary sport clubs and building sports facilities. The Act confirmed the still-existing work distribution between public and civil actors in sport. According to this model, also known elsewhere in the Nordic countries, the public sports administration system creates equal conditions for all citizens, while sports organisations are responsible for the arrangement of sport activities (Giuliantti et al., 2017; Kokkonen, 2015).

Sport activities grew rapidly on the 1960s, 1970s and 1980s, due partly to the availability of better sport facilities built by public funding. Swimming pools, indoor ice skating rinks, fitness and gymnastics halls were built especially in the cities, while in rural areas athletic fields were more common. These sport facilities provided the long-term infrastructure and environment essential for sport organisations, including football (Giuliantti et al., 2017; Kokkonen, 2015).

After WWII, Finnish sporting life was still divided into two parts, bourgeois and working-class. Football was the first major sport to establish a joint series between the two federations, in 1954. This was important in building the national organisation for Finnish football. Another important factor was the growth in the number of players. In 1949, the FAF had approximately 16,000 registered players. Two decades later, the number had doubled to 33,000 players and in 1989 to nearly 62,000 (Itkonen & Nevala, 2012).

The growth of football also brought new cities to the scene. Helsinki was the most successful football city, but gradually football spread inland and north to the Tampere, Kuopio, Oulu and Rovaniemi regions. As the activity increased, so did the requirements for the organisation of the FAF. One answer was the creation of regional associations. In the late 1940s, the FAF comprised 17 regional associations, which remained approximately the same until the 1990s. Although most activities were taken care of by voluntary work, the need for more and more hired professionals was also felt in the FAF (Itkonen & Nevala, 2012).

In Finland as well as in many other countries, women's football started in the early 1970s. The first women's football championship was organised in 1971. The number of registered female players reached almost 2,000 in the first few years, and the first international match was played against Sweden in 1973. Later, the growth in the number of registered female players was slow until the late 1980s. The situation was different in Sweden, where the number of registered female football players in 1972 jumped to over 9,000. Ten years later the number was more than 30,000 in Sweden but only 3,000 in Finland. Women's football started in Finland and Sweden at around the same time, but the differences grew during the 1970s and 1980s. This demonstrates that the position of football in the Finnish sports system was weaker than in Sweden or in the other Nordic countries (Ericsson & Horgby, 2021; Väisänen, 2019).

In the early 1970s, the FAF made other important reforms in addition to starting women's football. First, the winter game bandy, which had belonged to the FAF, became separated, founding an association of its own in 1972.

Second, the football series was reorganised in 1973 by establishing a new level, Division 1, below the Premier League level. The aim was to reduce the problematic difference in playing skills between the top level and the next one down (Itkonen & Nevala, 2012).

In the decades after WWII, internationalisation gradually became a more important part of Finnish football. Two important dimensions were the increase in the number of matches played by the National teams and clubs and the movement of players across borders. The competitions for National teams and clubs, organised by the European Football Association (UEFA, established in 1954), made a significant contribution to internationalisation. At the end of the 1950s, the men's and youth's national teams played a total of 12 matches a year. Ten years later, the number was 20. On the other hand, there were only a few international matches for clubs in a year. In addition, Finland's success in international matches was quite poor. The unofficial men's Nordic Football Championship in 1966 was one exception, and second place in the boys' under-18 UEFA final tournament in 1975 was another. However, Finland did not make it to either the European Championships or the World Cup finals (Itkonen & Nevala, 2012; Suomen Palloliitto, 1958, 1969).

Until WWII, the mobility of players across national borders was limited: football was a sport of nation states. The situation changed in the 1950s and in the first stage, South American players moved to Europe, especially Spain. Later, the mobility of European players increased: first the mobility focused on top players, later on a larger group of professional footballers. Still, mobility was low compared to later decades. For example, only 6% of the players in the 1966 World Cup final represented a club other than their homeland (see Lanfranchi & Taylor, 2001).

The first Finnish player to move abroad was Aulis Rytkönen (Toulouse FC France) in 1952. During the following years, four other Finns played as professionals in France, Germany and Belgium. Having players abroad opened a new link to international football. However, compared internationally, the number of Finnish players going abroad in the 1950s and 1960s was modest. For example, between the years 1948 and 1965 more than 50 Swedish players played abroad as professionals (Eliasson, 2009; Itkonen & Nevala, 2012).

The number of Finnish players abroad did not increase until the 1980s, when the number rose from 20 to 40. Finnish players moved mainly to Sweden due to neighbourhood and cultural reasons, but also to Central European countries, such as the Netherlands and Belgium, as well as to England. Finns did not play in the top clubs of premier series; usually they represented mid-level clubs or played in secondary level clubs. However, the increased movement of players was important in the internationalisation of Finnish football. Equally important was the entry of foreign players into the Finnish series from the 1970s onwards. These first "brave men" came mainly from England. The situation changed significantly in the 1980s, when there were about 15–20 foreign players in the Premier League every year. Most foreign players still came from England (about 60%), but Eastern Europeans, Poles and Hungarians also played in Finland. In addition, foreign players also appeared in lower levels than the Premier League in the 1980s. The mobility of players to and from Finland was part of two wider phenomena: The globalisation of football and the increased migration of labour force (Hognestad, 2009; Itkonen & Nevala, 2012; Lanfranchi & Taylor, 2001; Naakka, 2013; Szerovay & Itkonen, 2015).

Football slowly established its position in Finnish sports from the late 1940s to the 1980s. The number of football players increased, conditions improved, and internationality became an important part of football culture. However, football still did not become a national sport and internationally Finland was a "football dwarf". The modernisation and urbanisation of Finnish society, the building of the welfare state and becoming a consumer society improved the position of team sports. From the 1960s, team sports challenged the dominance of individual sports. However, ice hockey was the most successful in the struggle between the sports. Ice hockey improved its facilities, and by the 1980s the network of indoor ice rinks covered almost the whole country. Ice hockey shifted to the category of indoor sports. In football, conditions were clearly more modest, although training facilities improved (Isotalo et al., 2020).

Ice hockey also stood out from other sports in terms of professionalisation. From the 1970s onwards, the players became first semi-professionals and then professionals, the top clubs professionalised, and in 1975 the main series became the Hockey League in accordance with the North American model (Backman, 2018; Lämsä et al., 2020). Finland also consolidated its position in ice hockey among the top six countries. This increased its popularity and visibility in the national media. Finland's rapid social development created a new space for a modern urban sport. Ice hockey took advantage of this opportunity better and faster than other sports, including football, even though the number of registered players in football was higher than in ice hockey. Therefore, ice hockey took a leading position in Finnish sports, and for long time there was no room for another professionalised sport (Isotalo et al., 2020).

Popular, global and fragmented football

The years of strong economic growth after WWII ended in the oil crisis and recession of the 1970s in many Western countries. This led to a political and social turnaround, often called the breakthrough of neoliberalism, followed by globalisation, technologisation and marketisation. Western liberal democracy had clearly superseded socialism in Finland by the turn of 1990s but was soon faced with new challenges both globally and nationally. Liberal democracy was challenged by totalitarian states, increasing right-wing opposition and the supremacy of global economy (see Harari, 2018).

In Finland, the late structural and social change, the migration to Sweden and favourable trade with socialist countries supported the economy until the end of the 1980s. However, the economic recession of the 1990s in Finland was exceptionally deep and long-lasting. It changed the structure of the economy, weakened the welfare state, and changed the balance of political power. Unemployment remained permanently at a high level, and many social payments remained at a lower level than before the recession. As a result, social polarisation accelerated, despite a strong economic boom from the mid-1990s until the crisis in 2008 (Meinander, 2014).

The crisis of the 1990s fundamentally changed Finnish sports culture. Old structures, based partly on political divisions, crumbled but were not replaced by as strong actors as the former sport organisations. At the same time, the private "sport industry" expanded. As a result, strong sports, especially ice hockey, rose to prominence. The position of ice hockey was also strengthened by Finland's international success, including the first Finnish world championship in 1995. Professionalised and well-organised ice hockey also conformed well to the fragmentation of civil society and the strengthening of the sport markets (Giulianotti et al., 2017).

The international changes of the 1990s improved the position of Finnish ice hockey. In football, the situation was almost the opposite. Major changes in the football world, such as the birth of new states in the ruins of the Soviet Union and Yugoslavia, marketisation, explosion in television visibility, increase in player migration and the differentiation of top and grassroots football had a strong impact on Finland. Closer integration into the global football community had many significant and long-term effects on the national level as well (Isotalo et al., 2020).

The formation of a new top league in 1990 started a new era in Finnish football. The Premier League was named *Veikkausliiga* (Pools League), after its main sponsor. Thus, football switched to a league system that had been proved viable in ice hockey, drawing a clear distinction between market-driven top sports and "ordinary" competitive sports. In women's football, the same reform was not implemented until 2007, which shows that women's football played a smaller role in Finnish football for a long time (Isotalo et al., 2020; Itkonen & Nevala, 2012; Vares, 2022; Väisänen, 2019).

On the other hand, an important element increasing the number of football players was in fact female players. In the early 1990s, female players accounted for about 10% of the total number of players. By the turn of the millennium, their share was already around 15% and at the beginning of the 2020s almost 27%. In three decades, the number of registered players all in all doubled, but the number of female players increased more than fivefold during the same period. In addition, the women's national team qualified for the first time in UEFA Women's Euro 2006. The men's national team did not achieve the same goal until 2020 (organised in 2021) (Väisänen, 2019; Vares, 2022).

Globalisation in Finnish football can be seen in the doubling of the number of international matches during the first decade of the 2000s. In particular, the international matches played by female and junior teams increased. Another clear indication of globalisation since the 1990s was the increase in players moving abroad, and foreign players coming to Finland. In the background was the so-called Bosman case. This led to increase in the migration of football players across borders, especially in Europe. In the Finnish Premier League, there were already about 100 foreign players per year during the 2010s. In addition, the home country of the players was often other than England, Sweden or Eastern Europe. The number of African players in the Finnish league grew rapidly in the beginning the 21st century, as in many other European countries. For example, in 2014, almost 40 African players played in the Finnish Premier League, compared to about ten in the early years of the 2000s (Acheampong et al., 2020; Giulianotti & Robertson, 2012; Itkonen & Nevala, 2012). Not only players migrate, but also coaches and other football practitioners. Finland has experienced an influx of foreign coaches – most of them professionals – in youth football over the past decade. This serves as an example of a "trickle-down" of professional practices and to a certain extent, globalisation on the youth level, with organisational structures, training and managerial methods known from the top-level game (Szerovay et al., 2016).

The ice hockey league has been the only fully professional series in Finland from the 1980s onwards. In football, the professionalisation of clubs and players was slow. To illustrate, in 1990 there were only ten players in the premier league and five from the first division whose profession was indicated as "football player" in the Football Yearbook. Most of the full professionals were foreign players at the time. The audience of the football league remained small; the average number of spectators was only about 2,000 in the 1990s (see Kringstad et al., 2023, this volume). Finnish football also appeared only rather rarely on television. The resources needed for professionalisation were scarce. Many league clubs operated in a traditional way and players' fees rarely permitted full-time playing. In addition, the growing visibility of top international football was also a kind of rival for Finnish football.

In the 21st century, professionalism is a more important part of football than before, but Finland still lags behind the other Nordic countries in terms of salaries in the top leagues. The flip side of modest professionalisation is that football in Finland is not as strongly differentiated as in larger football countries. One example of this is the modest technologisation of Finnish football. For example, the so-called VAR technology is not in use in the Finnish Premier League in the season 2023. On the other hand, better training and playing conditions as well as better coaching have raised the level of Finnish football. Both the men's and women's football national teams have qualified for the European Championships. Futsal as an alternative playing format has also seen an increase in popularity and success, with the men's team making it to the European Championships. In addition, more Finnish players than before have moved to good-quality foreign clubs, although there are still fewer Finnish players in the European top five leagues than players from other Nordic countries. Today, Finland is a more "footballisationed" country and is closer to the Nordic level than ever before. Finland is still not a big football country, but no longer a "football dwarf" either, and the country is more than ever an integral part of the global football community.

Conclusion

The change in Finnish society and football over a period of more than 100 years can be summarised in three time periods. From the late 19th century until the 1960s, Finland was an agricultural country, dominated by small farms and only a slightly urbanised and industrialised society. Football was played above all in towns and industrial centres, but in rural areas the most important team sport was the Finnish baseball that football competed with. However, success in individual sports, especially in the Olympic Games, was the most important thing in sport culture. Finnish identity in sport was based primarily on success in the Olympics, and as a rather small sport, football played no role in building national identity – unlike in many other Western European countries.

The second period stretches from the 1960s to the 1990s. During that time, Finland underwent a rapid social restructuring and modernisation process. At the same time, migration moved the population from the countryside into the cities. In sports culture, as in society more generally, the importance of the public sector increased. This was reflected in the increase in building of sporting facilities. On the other hand, sport became more competitive and professional than before. Urbanisation, rising living standards and the transition to a consumer society strengthened the position of team sports, although individual and Olympic sports remained dominant. The strongest of the team sports was ice hockey, which determinedly developed facilities and a culture that suited the modern environment, for example by establishing an independent league system for top hockey in accordance with a North American model.

The number of football players increased and the game spread across the country. Women's football also began in Finland in the early 1970s. However, football, as a conservative sport, was still overshadowed by ice hockey. This was partly because Finland did not achieve international success in football – unlike in hockey since the late 1980s. During this period, Finland began to be identified as an ice hockey country, as success in traditional Olympic sports weakened, and Finland remained internationally a "football dwarf".

At the beginning of the third period, Finland went through an exceptionally deep and long-lasting economic recession. This changed Finnish society at the same time as the international environment also changed. Globalisation, technologisation, mobility and polarisation were the keywords of change, both in Finland and around the world. In the Finnish sports culture, old structures were demolished in the 1990s as part of a broader social change. The culture of physical activity became more segregated and dominated by strong sports. Finnish ice hockey benefited from international and national changes from the 1990s onwards. Even in the worst recession years, new indoor ice rinks were built in Finland at a record pace. In the beginning of the 21st century, Finland was undoubtedly an ice hockey country: in a small but appropriately sized sport, Finland had a strong international position and was very successful in major tournaments.

Despite the international success of ice hockey, football has for a long time been the most popular sport in Finland in terms of the number of players. In particular, the increase in the number of female players has been an important factor in the popularity of football. Another important element has been the professionalisation of football, both in terms of organisation, clubs and, ultimately, players. The professionalisation of the Finnish Premier League has been fundamentally influenced by the rapid increase in the number of foreign players since the 1990s. On the other hand, more Finnish players have also moved abroad as part of the growth in mobility and football work. In this way, Finland has become closer to the international football community than before. This is one of the most significant changes in the third period. The other most important change has been international success, i.e., qualifying into the men's and women's major tournaments. In this sense, too, Finland has become closer to other Nordic countries. Finland, a football lightweight for 130 years, is no longer far behind.

References

Acheampong, E., Bouhaouala, M., & Raspaud, M. (2020). *African footballers in Europe. Migration, community, and give back behaviours.* Routledge.

Allardt, E. (1976). Dimensions of welfare in a comparative Scandinavian study. *Acta Sosiologica, 19*(3), 227–240. 10.1177/000169937601900302

Arnason, J. P., & Wittrock, B. (Eds.). (2012). *Nordic path to modernity.* Berghahn Books.

Backman, J. (2018). *Ishockeyns amerikanisering: En studie av svensk och finsk elitishockey.* Malmö University. Studies in Sport Science, no. 27.

Eliasson, A. (2009). The European football market, globalization and movement among players. *Soccer & Society, 10*(3–4), 386–397. https://doi-org.ezproxy.uef.fi:2443/10.1080/14660970902771449

Ericsson, C., & Horgby, G. (2021). Kvinnorna inom den kommersiella fotbollen [The women in commercial football]. *Idrottforum.org.* Retrieved March 8, 2022, from https://idrottsforum.org/wp-content/uploads/2020/09/ericsson-horgby200921.pdf

Giulianotti, R., Itkonen, H., Nevala, A., & Salmikangas, A.-K. (2017). Sport and civil society in the Nordic region. *Sport in Society, 22*(4), 540–554. 10.1080/17430437.2017.1390906

Giulianotti, R., & Robertson, R. (2012). Mapping the global football field: A sociological model of transnational forces within the world game. *British Journal of Sociology, 63*(2), 216–240, 10.1111/j.1468-4446.2012.01407.x

Goldblatt, D. (2006). *The ball is round: A global history of football.* Penguin Books.

Harari, Y. N. (2018). *21 Lessons for 21th the century.* Penguin Random House.

Hognestad, H. (2009). Transglobal Scandinavia? Globalization and contestation of identities in football. *Soccer & Society, 10*(3–4), 358–373. https://doi-org.ezproxy.uef.fi:2443/10.1080/14660970902771423

Isotalo, K., Itkonen, H., & Nevala A. (2020). Miksi Suomesta tuli vuosikymmeniksi jääkiekko- mutta ei jalkapallomaa? [Why did Finland become a hockey country but not a football country for decades?] *Ennen ja Nyt: Historian Tietosanomat*, 20(3), 2–23. 10.37449/ennenjanyt.94378

Itkonen, H. (2000). *Sport and civil society. Sociological perspectives.* University of Joensuu. Publications of Karelian Institute No. 134. Joensuu.

Itkonen, H., & Nevala, A. (2012). A popular game in Father Christmas' Land? Football in Finland. *Soccer & Society*, 13(4), 570–584. 10.1080/14660970.2012.677229

Itkonen, H., & Salmikangas, A.-K. (2015). The changing roles of public, civic and private sector in Finnish sport culture. *Public Policy and Administration*, 14(4), 545—556.

Kokkonen, J. (2015). *Suomalainen liikuntakulttuuri – Juuret, nykyisyys ja muutossuunnat* [Finnish sports culture – Roots, present and directions of change]. Suomen urheilumuseosäätiön tutkimuksia n:o 3. Otavan kirjapaino Oy.

Koponen, J., & Saaritsa S. (Eds.). (2019). *Nälkämaasta hyvinvointivaltioksi. Suomi kehityksen kiinniottajana* [From a starving country to a welfare state. Finland as a catcher of development]. Gaudeamus Oy.

Koski, P., Itkonen, H., Lehtonen, K., & Vehmas, H. (2015). Sport clubs in Finland. In C. Bauer, R. Hoekman, S. Nagel, & H. van der Werff (Eds.), *Sport clubs in Europe. A cross-national comparative perspective* (pp. 147–160). Springer.

Kringstad, M., Jakobsen, T. G., & Storm, R. K. (2023). Nordic spectator studies: The literature on attendance and satisfaction at professional football matches. *This volume*.

Lämsä, J., Nevala, A., Aarresola, O., & Itkonen, H. (2020). Ammattilaisuus amatörismin kriisiyttäjänä suomalaisessa joukkueurheilussa 1975–2018 [Professionalism and the crisis of amateurism in Finnish team sports 1975–2018]. In H. Roiko-Jokela & A. Holmila (Eds.), *Urheilun kriisejä. Suomen urheiluhistoriallisen seuran vuosikirja 2019–2020* (pp. 57–85). Suomen urheiluhistoriallinen seura.

Lanfranchi, P., & Taylor, M. (2001). *Moving with the ball. The migration of professional footballers*. Berg.

Meinander, H. (2014). *A history of Finland*. Oxford University Press.

Naakka, A.-M. (2013). *Foreign players in the Finnish Football League 1970–2010* [Master's thesis, University of Jyväskylä]. https://jyx.jyu.fi/handle/123456789/43409

Suomen Palloliitto. (1958, 1969). *Annual report of the FA of Finland*.

Szerovay, M., & Itkonen, H. (2015). Suomalaisten ja unkarilaisten huippujalkapalloilijoiden aseman muutokset 1980-luvulta nykypäiviin [The professionalisation of Finnish and Hungarian top-level football players since the 1980s]. In H. Roiko-Jokela & E. Sironen (Eds.), *Urheilun toinen puoli. Suomen urheiluhistoriallisen seuran vuosikirja* (pp. 109–127). Suomen urheiluhistoriallinen seura.

Szerovay, M., Perényi S., & Itkonen, H. (2016). Glocal processes in peripheral football countries: Elite youth football clubs in Finland and Hungary. *Hungarian Review of Sport Science*, 17(65), 26–33.

Vares, V. (2022). *Enemmän kuin peliä. Naisten jalkapallo tasa-arvon tiellä maailmalla ja Suomessa* [More than a game: Women's football on the way to equality worldwide and in Finland]. Suomen urheiluhistoriallisen seuran julkaisusarja n:o 3. Jyväskylän yliopistopaino.

Väisänen, A. (2019). *Vertaileva tutkimus naisten jalkapallon kehityksestä ja nykytilasta Suomessa ja Ruotsissa* [Comparative research of the development of women's football and its current state in Finland and Sweden] [Master's thesis, University of Jyväskylä]. http://urn.fi/URN:NBN:fi:jyu-201906243380

Vasara, E. (2007). Jalkapallo – Suojelukuntajärjestön vieroksuma urheilumuoto. [Football – A game rejected by the Civil Guard]. H. Itkonen & A. Nevala (Eds.), *Kuningaspelin kentät. Jalkapalloilu paikallisena ja globaalina ilmiönä* (pp. 84–99). Gaudeamus, Helsinki University Press.

Winner, D. (2005). *Those feet. A Sensual history of English football*. Bloomsbury Publishing.

Chapter 3

Preserving the Balance between Amateurism and Professionalism in Iceland

Vidar Halldorsson and Omar Johannsson

The early years: 1899–1911

Sports in Iceland can be traced back to the Saga Age (which lasted from around the second half of the ninth century to around 1100) (Thorlindsson & Halldorsson, 2020; Wieting, 2015). Pre-modern sports were, however, very different from sports as we know them today (Guttmann, 1978). Even though such games were often governed by rules there was no formal referee, so it was up to the participants to uphold rules of conduct. Sports in the Saga Age became characterised and bound by individual honour and prestige to fair and skilful play (Thorlindsson & Halldorsson, 2020). The sporting spirit of the Icelanders is evident in the Icelandic Sagas (Bjarnason, [1908]/1950; Wieting, 2015) and this spirit has characterised Icelandic sports and athletes to date (Thorlindsson & Halldorsson, 2020).

Modern sports began to emerge in Iceland in the late nineteenth century (Lúðvíksson, 2012). This was a time of great transition in Iceland as people were moving from rural areas to the capital, Reykjavík, which was developing and expanding. All kinds of social associations were established around the turn of the twentieth century, such as workers unions, abstinence societies, and sport and youth associations (Thorlindsson & Halldorsson, 2020). Sports in Iceland were rooted in the volunteer movements in the early twentieth century and were intended to foster democracy and civic society. Furthermore, Icelandic sports were important for Iceland's fight for independence from the rule of Denmark although being influenced by their Nordic neighbours and built on what has been termed as *the Nordic sports model* (Thorlindsson & Halldorsson, 2019).

It was in this social context and period that football arrived in Iceland. Football, as most other sports the Icelanders started to play at the time, was introduced and established due to foreign influences that have remained strong all through its history. A Scottish printer, by the name of James B. Ferguson, is acknowledged to have brought football to Iceland and to have taught the Icelanders the sport (Sigurðsson & Friðjónsson, 1997, pp. 19–20). Ferguson only spent a year in Iceland, in 1895–1896, but during his time there he established

DOI: 10.4324/9781003280729-5

the Reykjavík Gymnastic Club which, as the name suggests, emphasised and exhibited gymnastics. Ferguson, however, encouraged some young boys to take up the sport of football, which they did. The first football club, KR Reykjavík (formerly Fótboltafélag Reykjavíkur – the Football Club of Reykjavík), was established in 1899, but since KR was the only Icelandic club at the time it only played against foreign teams, which were mostly based on seafarers who had a layover in Iceland.

In 1908, an Icelandic scholar, Björn Bjarnason, recognised how the Icelanders were finally following the initiative of others, such as their fellow Nordic nations, in taking up sports. Bjarnason argued:

> Physical sports have for a long time not been prevalent here in Iceland; as people have believed the practice of sports to be a waste of time and not worthy of attention. But now we are seeing brighter times as the domestic leaders of civic education have finally understood, what the leading educationalists in the world have long fought for and the most courageous nations, such as the English, have made happen, the equality of the physical culture with the spiritual education. Youth associations have been established, partly to give rebirth to national and healthy physical sports ... Is this not the dawning of a new age in sports, the upcoming of a courageous generation? ([1908]/1950, VII)

It was at this time that other teams began to be established, and the sport began to grow, although at a slow pace. Reykjavik clubs Fram and Víkingur were formed in 1908. The previously mentioned influence on sports and football in Iceland originating from the nation's ongoing independence battle was very visible when these new clubs were formed. Apart from the obvious reference to the Saga Age era in the name of Víkingur (Viking), Fram sought its name from a home rule organisation where many of the players were active members. Furthermore, their team logo consisted of a blue flag with a white cross, in line with the Icelandic flag at the time. The sport clubs were established locally and represented different neighbourhoods in the capital area or the various towns around Iceland. With time, local sport clubs became multi-sport clubs which served their local communities.

In 1910, the work on Melavöllur stadium started, a multi-function stadium located centrally in the capital Reykjavík (Friðþjófsson, 1994). The new stadium was a giant leap for Icelandic football when it came to facilities as previously football had been played in open public spaces with various interruptions, even having to stop a match or training because a road went through the "pitch". The stadium, and especially after the relocation and renovation of the stadium in 1926, made Melavöllur the growth centre of football in Iceland, as for decades it hosted the bulk of domestic and international football matches in Iceland (Friðþjófsson, 1994). It was on 20th of June 1911 that the first formal football game was played in Iceland when KR and Fram played in front of 1,500 spectators in the newly built Melavöllur. A year later, or in 1912, the first Icelandic football championship took place (Steinarsson, 2011a, pp. 10–12).

The spread of football: 1912–1947

The first Icelandic championship in 1912 consisted of three teams, KR and Fram, as well as KV from Vestmannaeyjar, or the Westman Islands, off the south coast of Iceland. On KV's request, the tournament was moved forward one day till the 28th of June and the entire tournament was played on Melavöllur during that weekend at end of June. The reason for KV's request was that they needed to return to their island through a connection with an ocean-going vessel departing from Reykjavík on the 1st and calling at the Westman Islands on its journey. KR ended up as the first Icelandic champion in football, but KV had to withdraw their team from the competition after their first match against KR due to injuries. KV did not participate again in the Icelandic championship again until 1926 but until then only four Reykjavík teams participated, KR and Fram, as well as Víkingur and Valur periodically (Steinarsson, 2011a, pp. 14–16).

The Icelandic championship consisted of these four teams in the following decades with the periodic participation of KV and KA from Akureyri, located on the north coast of Iceland, that first took part in 1929 – interestingly, the Reykjavík area population comprised just under 20% of the total population of Iceland in 1912, compared to about 64% in 2022 (Statistics Iceland, 2021). It was not until 1946 that a new team emerged, IA from Akranes, located on the west coast of Iceland. Only rarely did all the above-mentioned teams participate and usually the Icelandic championship consisted of three to five teams. The first and only all-women's football club, Fótboltafélagið Hvöt, from Ísafjörður in the west fjords of Iceland, was established in 1914, and the girls played some unofficial matches against boys in 1914–1916. It was, however, not until 1970 that women's football was recognised by the Icelandic Football Association (Steinarsson, 2017, pp. 6–9).

Foreign influence on Icelandic football and football culture, not least from the United Kingdom, has been prominent ever since James Ferguson introduced the sport to Icelanders. In the years of football development, several UK coaches led Icelandic teams in the Icelandic championship, although at that time coaches also came from Norway, Denmark, Sweden and Germany. The first international football matches in Iceland were in 1919 when the Danish club Akademisk Boldclub (AB Copenhagen) played five matches against an unofficial Icelandic national team. The visitors won the first four matches, whereas the Icelandic team won the fifth and last match (Steinarsson, 2014). In the years to come, Iceland played several unofficial matches, but an Icelandic "national" team played its first away match in the Faroe Islands in 1930 and won 1-0 (Steinarsson, 2014, pp. 12–14).

Football soon became the sport most written about in the media after the Icelandic championship competition started. In the newspaper Vísir on 19th June 1913, there was a report of the first half of the match played between Fram and KR that took place on 15th June. The report of the second half then appeared in the paper on the 22nd of June so readers had to wait a few days before knowing the result of the match (Steinarsson, 2011b, bls. 489). In 1935, the first live radio broadcast of a football game in Iceland took place. It was the final of the Icelandic championship between Valur and KR, but it was estimated that around 25,000 people listened to the broadcast or about 22% of the Icelandic population at the time. Furthermore, there were just over 3,000 spectators at the game, underlining the widespread popularity of football amongst Icelanders at the time (Steinarsson, 2011a, p. 89).

Facilities and weather have set their mark on Icelandic football; in 1943 the first football match was played on grass in Iceland. The pitch was in the Laugardalur area in Reykjavík, where the national football stadium and headquarters are currently located. Even though there were mixed opinions as to the quality of the pitch at the time, this marked the biggest improvement in football facilities since the creation of Melavöllur. Other circumstances, such as the remote location of Iceland in the middle of the Atlantic Ocean became obvious in the World War II which affected football in Iceland in many ways, as elsewhere. A grave shortage of footballs in Iceland at the time prevented people from playing the sport as much as they would have liked (Steinarsson, 2011a, pp. 135–137). Also, due to an economic upsurge in the war years, many young men chose work over playing football at the time. Improving socioeconomic conditions would continue to set their mark on Icelandic football and move it in a direction of more professionalism.

On 17 June 1944, Iceland formally became an independent republic and suitably soon thereafter, or in 1946, Iceland played its first official national game against their former rulers, Denmark. The game, which attracted great interest among the Icelandic public, was played in Melavöllur in front of about 8,000 spectators (Steinarsson, 2014, p. 36). Matches against the other Nordic countries have been met with similar interest up to the present, as Iceland often compares itself to the Nordic countries when it comes to football, frequently combined with the narrative of the small, oppressed, yet independent nation. The Icelandic Football Association (KSÍ) was established in 1947 and the Icelandic football landscape continued to walk hand in hand with the overall Icelandic social context. It was also in 1947 that Iceland acquired its first professional player, when Albert Guðmundsson paved the way for coming generations of Icelandic football players.

Consolidation: 1948–1973

The economic growth following the Second World War transformed Iceland from one of the poorest nations in Europe to one of the richest (Ólafsson &

Kristjánsson, 2017). However, football in Iceland remained an amateur sport. Again, highlighting the amateur status of football in Iceland, the players of ÍA Akranes, for instance, dropped out of the Icelandic championship due to high demand for workers in the herring season in 1948 (Steinarsson, 2011a, p. 169). In 1951, ÍA and became the first club outside of Reykjavík to become Icelandic champion and alongside population growth in Iceland and increasing socioeconomic prosperity, new football teams emerged quite rapidly in the following decades; in 1955 division 2 was founded and later in 1966, Icelandic football counted three leagues. In 1960, the Icelandic Cup competition began and up until 1973, the final was played at Iceland's first football pitch, Melavöllur. Since 1973, the cup final has been played in the National Arena, Laugardalsvöllur, that still serves this function today and is located in the same place as Iceland's first grass pitch (Steinarsson, 2011a).

The Icelandic national team played for the first time in the World Cup group stages in 1957 and despite big losses against Belgium and France, the journey towards a major tournament had started. Then, in 1959, the Icelandic national team played both Denmark and Norway in the Olympic preliminaries and although a draw against Denmark and a win against Norway met with huge celebrations in Iceland, this was not enough to qualify for the Olympics (Steinarsson, 2014, pp. 112–115). Despite some good results Icelandic track and field athletes and the men's national handball team enjoyed greater attention and recognition than did football, due to their international success at this time (Lúðvíksson, 2012; Thorlindsson & Halldorsson, 2019).

Icelandic clubs also entered the international stage in 1964 when KR became the first Icelandic team to compete in the European Cup and Icelandic teams have since then competed in the different European competitions. The opponents in the European Cup, who by coincidence were also playing their first European match, were FC Liverpool. This was the start for many lifelong fans in Iceland of Liverpool who have since then built one of the biggest fanbases in Iceland of any English club; their popularity has even been compared to the worship of a religious cult (Ormarsson, 2020).

The first official women's football match was in 1970 between Reykjavík and Keflavík and the first Icelandic championship for women was in 1972. It was Albert Guðmundsson, then chairman of KSÍ, who was said to have played a key role in the first steps of Icelandic women's football. He felt it was of much importance to start a women's league as soon as possible so as not to lag behind other countries that had started a women's league before Iceland. In the first championship in 1972 eight teams competed in two groups and finally it was FH from Hafnarfjörður that took home the first Icelandic championship trophy for women (Sigurðsson & Friðjónsson, 1997, p. 239).

Ásgeir Sigurvinsson started the second wave of Icelandic professional football players emigrating. Sigurvinsson is by many considered one of the most successful Icelandic player of all times and following his venture into professional football in 1973 the number of Icelandic professional football players started to grow steadily. Football remained the most popular sport in Iceland and matches drew relatively high attendances per capita but it was not only Icelandic football that attracted interest in Iceland. English football radio broadcasts could be reached through the BBC and Icelanders listened with enthusiasm. Thus, it certainly helped boost interest in English football when the national television (RÚV) started showing one game a weekend, from the previous week, in 1968. English football has ever since played a dominant role in the Icelandic football community with devoted fans of English teams exceeding those of their Icelandic counterparts (Ormarsson, 2020).

Popular football: 1974–2000

Following the move into professional football by Ásgeir Sigurvinsson, the number of Icelandic players going abroad seeking adventure as well as payment for playing football grew steadily. This, in turn, prompted the Icelandic clubs to act and find ways to compensate players in Iceland for playing despite rules stating that football should be an amateur sport in Iceland. Also, increasing professionalism amongst Icelandic clubs, in terms of training and matches, meant that more time was devoted to football amongst players, trainers and other staff, further escalating the argument of a compensation for playing football (Halldorsson, 2017). Transfers of players between Icelandic clubs also became more common during this development, but previously it had been exceptional for players to transfer between Icelandic clubs. It became more common that coaches began to get paid, even for coaching children and thus the foundation for the highly structured youth football system that Iceland has today was laid. These steps towards some sort of professionalism were confined to men's football; women's football in Iceland was still very much at its developing stage (Halldorsson, 2022).

Football, however, remained only a summer sport, played for three months in the middle of the summer. It was common that Icelandic football players at the time played other sports than football as well, mostly during the wintertime when conditions for playing football were poor. Football was mostly played indoors during winter, in the sport halls around the country that were primarily intended to host sports such as handball, basketball, volleyball and other traditional indoor sports. Iceland has, therefore, seen several athletes who were national team players in more than one sport, such as in football, handball, basketball and volleyball, both amongst men and women. It may therefore not be a coincident that the Icelandic handball was doing well in international comparison, competing regularly in the World Cup, European Cup and Olympics. Iceland even hosted the World Cup in handball in 1995 but at the same time the Icelandic football national team had never qualified for a final tournament. Even today the official football season in Iceland begins in May and ends in October, which makes is the shortest football season in the world (Kuper & Szymanski, 2014, pp. 235–259).

Women's football in Iceland grew steadily during this period, especially after 1980. This also happened to be the election year of Vigdís Finnbogadóttir as the first female president of Iceland and previous years had seen politics and public discourse highly influenced by movements fighting for the social rights of women (Halldorsson, 2022). Following an increasing number of participants and teams, the Icelandic women's league system was extended into two leagues in 1982. Icelandic women played their first international game in 1981 when they lost against Scotland away 3-2. Competition in the Icelandic Cup also started in 1981 on the women's side so it is easy to identify those years as a turning point for Icelandic women's football in the developing stages (Steinarsson, 2017, pp. 67–79).

By the mid-1980s, more than 20 Icelandic men were playing professional football outside Iceland, but no foreign player was at the same time playing in Iceland. This started to change around 1990 and the number of foreign players in Icelandic football began to rise (Magnússon, 2001). Most prominently, these players were from war-ridden Yugoslavia and between 1990 and 2000 about 100 players came to Iceland from the different countries of former Yugoslavia. This influx of foreign professional players, although many of them had work alongside playing football, introduced new ways of thinking and a more professional approach to football than had previously been the case in Iceland (see discussion in Halldorsson, 2017). Furthermore, as the labour market became more open to individuals within the European Union (EU) and European Economic Area (EEA) and because of the effect of the Bosman case in 1996, transfers between countries and clubs continued to rise in the late 1990s in Iceland as in other countries within the EU and EEA (Magnússon, 2001).

Present and future: 2001–2022

The current organisation of sports in Iceland builds on similar foundations as in the other Nordic nations, as it emphasises sports-for-all with the intention of improving the lives of participants and contributing to better and healthier societies (Green et al., 2019; Tin et al., 2020). Thus, youth sports take place in formally organised grassroots sport clubs nested in the local communities all over the country and intended to serve everyone. The structure and ideology of Icelandic sports, however, contrasts with that of many other nations, and even its Nordic neighbours (see Andersen & Ronglan, 2012). While the Icelandic Sports Model emphasises both the positive personal development of participants through sports and sport performance at the same time, within a sports-for-all system, a clear distinction is made between participation sports and performance sports in most other countries, the latter being available only for the selected few. The "non-elite" system of Icelandic sports has, however, been extremely successful in guiding players and teams to the elite level, as well as having a positive impact on the psycho-sociological development of its participants (Halldorsson, 2020a).

The organisation of the Icelandic sport clubs has attracted attention from abroad as it differs from the organisation of formal football in most countries (Halldorsson, 2020a). Thus, when Iceland's male national team qualified for Euro 2016 and the 2018 World Cup, reporters, documentary film makers, coaches and scholars from all over the world came to Iceland to try to gain insight into how such a small nation could be so successful in the world's most popular sport. What appealed to the visitors was the organisation of the Icelandic sport clubs. A reporter from the English newspaper *The Telegraph* for instance stated:

> And really at this point I have to stop to take a breath. Facilities for all; professional coaching for kids; a state provision that unburdens parents of the after-school childcare juggle: what I see at Breidablik [sport club] is the positive side of social democracy writ large on a sports field. I think I want to be a child again, only this time, I want to be Icelandic. (Cooper, 2018)

Today, up to 90% of children and adolescents in Iceland practise sport in the formal sport clubs, sometime in their youth, where boys practise on average 1.9 sports and girls 1.6 sports (Halldorsson, 2018). Football is by far the most popular sport in Iceland with around 28,000 participants, followed by golf with 21,000 and gymnastics with 14,000. Other popular team sports such as basketball and handball have around 8,000 participants. Around two-thirds of all football participants are male and one-third female. Likewise, just over two-thirds of football participants are under the age of 18 and up to one-third are older. At the senior levels there are five football leagues for men (with a total of 76 teams) and three for women (with 30 teams) (ÍSÍ, 2019). Placing these figures in a larger context shows the limited resources the adult national football teams can select players from. The men's team can select players from a pool of 6,600 and the women's team from a pool of 1,800.

This high involvement may be explained by the sport-for-all policy of the Icelandic system, but more recently thanks to the considerable investments in football facilities accomplished after several years of planning when the first full-size, indoor football pitch was completed in 2000. This, along with football turf pitches and mini-football pitches all around Iceland, transformed Icelandic football from a summer sport, played only a few months a year, to a full-year sport where individuals of all ages could devote their time to playing football in the best possible conditions despite harsh winter weather. Currently there are 179 full size football pitches in Iceland (natural grass, football turf, outdoor/indoor); that is, one full-size pitch per every 1,800 inhabitants, and one per every 128 registered players. Furthermore, Iceland has more coaches with UEFA coaching certificates per capita than its neighbouring countries or one qualified UEFA B coach per close to every 400 Icelanders, compared to one per every 1,500 elsewhere in Europe. About two-thirds hold a UEFA B or more and just over one-third a UEFA A or more (KSI, 2022). These investments were implemented at the same time as Icelandic society saw an unprecedented economic rise from the middle of the 1990s, but this came to a halt along with the bank crash in 2008 (Durrenberger & Palsson, 2015). As the Icelandic economic system bounced back quickly after the bank crash (Ólafsson & Kristjánsson, 2017), so did investments in football facilities around the country.

Although football is highly visible in Iceland which has even measured as the country that loves football the most according to several per capita appraisals (Kuper & Szymanski, 2014, pp. 235–259), attendance at football matches is low, however. In the men's top football league, attendance is around 1,000 spectators per game, and in the women's top league, attendance is around 100–200 spectators per game (KSÍ, 2021). But the national teams raise bigger crowds, for example the men's teams often sell out the national stadium, which has a capacity of 9,800. The women's team has once sold out the national stadium, but spectators at women's national team matches are usually a few thousand. Attendance at national team games depends on team performance; when the teams are doing well more people show up to watch them play. There are ongoing initiatives to build a new and bigger national stadium which could host up to 20,000 spectators.

At the same time, Icelanders have never taken more interest in the English teams and their matches (Ormarsson, 2020). There are several active fan clubs relating to various teams in England and English football is shown on big screens in every second home and pub. In addition, Icelanders flock to England to witness their favourite team perform. It has even been suggested that Icelanders take more interest in the English Premier League than the Icelandic top division (Karlsson, 2015). In recent years, Icelandic investors even bought the English clubs Stoke City and soon afterwards West Ham United (Bullock, 2021). These investments in English football clubs both highlight Icelandic interest in English football and also reveal the overconfident characteristics of Icelanders who tend to characterise themselves as brave and heroic ambassadors of the tiny nation, in their quest to conquer new territories abroad – and during the banking boom were frequently referred to as "outvasion Vikings" (Durrenberger & Palsson, 2015; Halldorsson, 2017, p. 14). However, Icelandic ownership of these clubs did not last long.

As football in Iceland has developed at an ever-faster pace in recent years, it is the success of the national teams that highlights this development. After first witnessing the Icelandic women's team reach the European final competition 2009 the Icelandic nation was overcome by a football frenzy, not least when the men's national team attained a corresponding level in 2016. Reaching the quarter finals with a win over England, the nation most Icelanders view as the focal point of football, marked perhaps the greatest achievement in Icelandic football history. Revisiting the Saga Age again, Icelandic fans also made their mark with the trademark "Viking clap" since the Viking affiliation is never far away from various contexts relating to football performance (Halldorsson, 2017). By qualifying for the European competition, the men's team represented the smallest country per capita to enter the competition. Two years later, Iceland became the smallest country per capita to enter the World Cup as the national men's team continued their march of success thereby attracting international attention (Gregory, 2018) and kindling the national pride of their countrymen (Halldorsson, 2020b). Since qualifying in 2009, the women's teams have maintained a high international status, playing in the European final competition again in 2013, 2017 and 2022 (Halldorsson, 2022). Following the international success of the national teams it can be said that football in Iceland took the final step in becoming the number one sport in Iceland ahead of handball and other popular sports in Iceland. While the men's national football team has reached 18th place in the official FIFA ranking, the women's national team has climbed to 15th place (FIFA, 2022).

In recent years there has been an immense expansion in players playing professionally abroad, both amongst men and women, as well as players moving abroad at an increasingly younger age (see e.g., Sverrisson, 2019). Statistics from CIES show that Iceland has by far the highest number of expatriates in World football (CIES, 2018). The Icelandic leagues have also seen a successive rise in the number of foreign players in the teams since the 1990s as infrastructure and facilities keep improving. Despite the giant steps Icelandic football has taken in recent years, the Icelandic league system is semi-professional with most players receiving little or no compensation for playing football. The majority of youth players stay with their neighbourhood clubs until and even after they reach adult football. It is in this mix of amateurism and professionalism that the success of Icelandic football is rooted (Halldorsson, 2017).

Conclusion

The foresight of Bjarnason, who over a century ago hypothesised about the "dawning of a new age in sports" and "the upcoming of a courageous generation" in Icelandic sports ([1908]/1950) has undeniably become reality. The twentieth century and the beginning of the twenty-first century have marked Iceland as a sporting nation. Due to the international sporting success of its national athletes and teams, sports have played an important part in the identity-making of the Icelanders (Halldorsson, 2020b). Football, as other sports in Iceland, however, remains nested in the voluntary movements which emerged in the beginning of the twentieth century and were intended to help to build up communities and later to provide children and adolescents with an opportunity to have fun and develop their skills through sports. This sports system has been highly valuable to the Icelanders (Halldorsson, 2020a).

The recent international success of Iceland's national football teams has strengthened football's position on the Icelandic sports scene as football is expanding in terms of participation, infrastructure and interest, to a greater extent than other sports in Iceland. Currently football can be considered to be in a league of its own as the giant of Icelandic sports as other sports, such as team handball, do not hold the same international prestige or financial and cultural global power as does football. However, given football's enhanced status is Iceland, due to its recent successes and the intensified globalisation of the game, Icelandic football stands at a crossroads. While some want to professionalise football in Iceland to a greater or full extent – and follow the path of professional football clubs elsewhere – others want to protect and sustain the grassroots sport-for-all system, which Iceland has been recognised for in the past. Probably the professionalisation of sports in Iceland will continue, as everywhere else, but whether the Icelanders will be able to protect their valuable sport-for-all system for years to come is yet to be seen. Constrained by the smallness of the population, it is hard for Icelandic football to take the final steps towards professionalism, but perhaps this mix of amateurism and professionalism is the optimum place for football in Iceland for years to come (see Halldorsson, 2017; 2020a; McGinn, 2020).

References

Andersen, S. S., & Ronglan, L. T. (Eds.). (2012). *Nordic elite sport: Same ambitions – different tracks*. Universitetsforleget.

Bjarnason, B. ([1908]/1950). *Íþróttir fornmanna á norðurlöndum* [Pre-modern sports in the Nordic countries]. Bókfellsútgáfan.

Bullock, L. (2021). *Twinned with Reykjavik. Stoke City: The Icelandic years*. Pitch Publishing.

CIES. (2018). World football expatriates: Global study 2018. *CIES Football Observatory Monthly Report, 35*. Retrieved November 15, 2022, from https://www.football-observatory.com/IMG/pdf/mr35en.pdf

Cooper, J. (2018, May 11). The story behind Iceland's assault on world football. *The Telegraph*. Retrieved August 22, 2022, from https://www.telegraph.co.uk/sport/2018/05/11/story-behind-icelands-assault-world-football/

Durrenberger, E. P., & Palsson, G. (Eds.) (2015). *Gambling debt: Iceland's rise and fall in the global economy*. University Press of Colorado.

FIFA. (2022). *Iceland ranking*. Retrieved August 25, 2022, from https://www.fifa.com/fifa-world-ranking/ISL

Friðþjófsson, S. (1994). *Íþróttir í Reykjavík* [Sports in Reykjavík]. ÍBR.

Green, K., Sigurjónsson, T., & Skille, E. Á. (Eds.). (2019). *Sport in Scandinavia and the Nordic countries*. Routledge.

Gregory, S. (2018, June 18). The little country that could: How tiny Iceland crashed the party. *Time*, 34–39.

Guttmann, A. (1978). *From ritual to record: The nature of modern sports*. Columbia University Press.

Halldorsson, V. (2017). *Sport in Iceland: How small nations achieve international success*. Routledge.

Halldorsson, V. (2018). Sport participation in Iceland. In K. Green, T. Sigurjónsson, & E. A. Skille (Eds.), *Sport in Scandinavia and the Nordic countries* (pp. 87–108). Routledge.

Halldorsson, V. (2020a). The black swan of elite football: The case of Iceland. *Soccer & Society, 21*(7), 711–724.

Halldorsson, V. (2020b). National sport success and the emergent social atmosphere: The case of Iceland at the 2018 FIFA World Cup. *International Review for the Sociology of Sport, 56*(4), 492.

Halldorsson, V. (2022). The rise of women's football: A case study of Iceland. *Soccer & Society, special issue on Nordic football, 23*(8) [in press].

ÍSÍ. (2019). Tölfræði Íþróttahreyfingarinnar [Statistics of the Icelandic Sport and Olympic Association]. Retrieved June 11, 2021, from https://www.isi.is/library/Skrar/Efnisveita/Tolfraedi/Samantekt/Stutt%20samantekt%202020

Karlsson, G. (2015). *What are the motivating factors behind Icelanders' interest in the English Premier League and the men's Pepsi League?* [Master's thesis]. Skemman. https://skemman.is/handle/1946/20317

KSÍ. (2021). *Áhorfendatölur* [Attendance Figures]. Retrieved April 27, 2021 from https://www.ksi.is/heim/ahorfendur/?tournamentID=39256

KSÍ. (2022). *Þjálfarar* [Coaches]. Retrieved September 7, 2022, from https://www.ksi.is/fraedsla/ymsar-upplysingar/thjalfarar/

Kuper, S., & Szymanski, S. (2014). *Soccernomics: Why Spain, Germany and Brazil win, and why the USA, Japan, Australia – and even Iraq – are destined to become the kings of the world's most popular sport*. HarperSport.

Lúðvíksson, S. J. (2012). *Íþróttabókin* [The book of sports: The history of Icelandic sports and community]. ÍSÍ.

Magnússon, G. K. (2001). The internalization of sports: The case of Iceland. *International Review for the Sociology of Sport, 36*(1), 59–69.

McGinn, M. (2020). *Against the elements: The eruption of Icelandic football*. Pitch Publishing.

Ormarsson, O. P. (2020). *Í faðmi ljónsins: Ástarsaga* [In the lion´s embrace: A love story]. Sögur.

Ólafsson, S., & Kristjánsson, A. S. (2017). *Inequality in Iceland: Distribution of income and wealth in a multinational context*. Iceland University Press.

Sigurðsson, V., & Friðjónsson, S. Á. (1997). *Knattspyrna í heila öld: 1895–1996* [A century of Icelandic football: 1895–1996]. Knattspyrnusamband Íslands.

Statistics Iceland. (2021). *Mannfjöldi í einstökum byggðakjörnum og strjálbýli 1880–2020. Árslokatölur* [The population of Iceland 1880–2020]. Retrieved August 10, 2022, from http://px.hagstofa.is/pxis/pxweb/is/Sogulegar/Sogulegar__sogul_mannfjoldi/SOG01010.px

Steinarsson, S. Ó. (2011a). *100 ára saga Íslandsmótsins í knattspyrnu, fyrra bindi* [100 year history of the Icelandic championship in football, volume 1]. Knattspyrnusamband Íslands, Sporthamar ehf.

Steinarsson, S. Ó. (2011b). *100 ára saga Íslandsmótsins í knattspyrnu, síðara bindi* [100 year history of the Icelandic championship in football, volume 2]. Knattspyrnusamband Íslands, Sporthamar ehf.

Steinarsson, S. Ó. (2014). *Saga landsliðs karla* [The history of the Icelandic men's national football team]. Knattspyrnusamband Íslands.

Steinarsson, S. Ó. (2017). *Stelpurnar okkar. Saga knattspyrnu kvenna á Íslandi frá 1914* [Our girls: The history of women's football in Iceland from 1914]. Knattspyrnusamband Íslands.

Sverrisson, S. (2019). Metfjöldi í atvinnumennskunni [Record number of players playing professional football]. Retrieved September 10, 2022, from https://www.mbl.is/sport/efstadeild/2019/02/07/metfjoldi_i_atvinnumennskunni/

Thorlindsson, T., & Halldorsson, V. (2019). The cultural production of a successful sport tradition: A case study of Icelandic handball. *Studies in Symbolic Interaction*, 50(1), 237–266.

Thorlindsson, T., & Halldorsson, V. (2020). The roots of Icelandic physical culture and sport in the Saga Age. In M. B. Tin, F. Telseth, J. O. Tangen, & R. Giulianotti (Eds.), *The Nordic model and physical culture* (pp. 101–116). Routledge.

Tin, M. B., Telseth, F., Tangen, J. O., & Giulianotti, R. (2020). *The Nordic model and physical culture*. Routledge.

Wieting, S. G. (2015). *The sociology of hypocrisy: An analysis of sport and religion*. Routledge.

Chapter 4

Inclusion, Exclusion and Modernisation in Norway

Arve Hjelseth, Bente Ovedie Skogvang, Frode Telseth, and Pål Augestad

Introduction

This chapter presents and analyses the introduction of football in Norway, how it spread and consolidated, and how it gradually turned into a more professional and commercial enterprise. The analysis is based on two main narratives: one of modernisation (international influences, the gradual development of professional football, the establishment of, and changes in, the league systems, and the influence of commercial interests and the media), and one of inclusion and exclusion (football and social class, the growth of children's and youth football, and the gradual recognition of women's football). Both narratives are contextualised in terms of the broader social, political and cultural trends in Norway. They reflect tensions and conflicts that characterise modern society, including the relation between democracy and the market, "play" and work/school, organised and unorganised activities, voluntary and professional work, men and women, etc.

Methodically, we make some incisions into the historical body, and then use the surfaces of these incisions to detect changes in the field. There are no clear-cut distinctions between the phases. Thus, the periodisation is based on substantial changes and processes rather than exact years. Yet in chronological terms, the analysis is divided into three main sections. The first part roughly covers the period from the late 19th century to 1920, the second part analyses the years between about 1920 and 1970, and the third phase covers approximately the last 50 years. Events and provisions that occurred at a certain historical time may be converted into effective processes several years later. In a final concluding section, we discuss possible futures of Norwegian football.

The early years

The rise of modern sport in Norway was closely connected to industrialisation and urbanisation. The first reports on "futbål" stem from the 1880s when it was introduced by engineers and sailors from the British Isles. Claims have been made by both Oslo and Bergen to have hosted the first men's football match

DOI: 10.4324/9781003280729-6

(Goksøyr & Olstad, 2002; Larsen, 1977) but, from what we know, Christiania Fotballclub was the first club of its kind, established in May 1885 (*Norsk Idrettsblad*, 5 November 1887, cited in Larsen, 1977). Christiania was, at that time, the name of the Norwegian capital (now Oslo).

In the emerging English tradition, modern sports were exclusively leisure activities, which were often initially reserved only for the male upper classes. The sports that had traditionally been promoted in Norway were said to reflect and develop skills that were important in everyday routines, like cross country skiing. In fact, skiing was not a widespread activity before modern sport emerged in Norway other than for transport purposes (Lidström, 2021). Nevertheless, cross country skiing soon became a symbol of Norwegian identity. Whilst football was a game that certainly could serve socialisation purposes, such as the development of discipline and teamwork (Walvin, 1994), these skills were not required to master everyday routines. Thus, some regarded football as a less useful form of physical activity compared to other emerging sports in Norway at the time (Goksøyr, 1991).

In the decades following the introduction of football, some thought of it as an ideal summer sport for men in an otherwise winterly nation, while others remained critical. To the latter, football reminded people more of children's play in urban streets than of the sports traditionally valued in Norway (Goksøyr, 1991). From a hegemonic perspective, a combination of the use of the English language and the requirement for extensive bodily contact led football to be perceived as being unproper for "real sportspersons". Male players were subject to ridicule, much like the experiences of their female counterparts 80 years later (Goksøyr & Olstad, 2002).

At the turn of the century, football was thus a counterculture to traditional sports (Andersen, 2007), in two ways. First, competition for the sake of competition ran counter to the established values of the aesthetical style and the societal demands that sport should somehow be *useful*. Sports were supposed to build character, bring the body under control of will and strengthen individual capacity for restraint and discipline (Augestad, 2003). Second, the nature of football has its own specific values. It is a team sport, played with friends and against opponents, and entails bodily contact and the chance to improvise. Hence, football's inherent nature is an extension of children's ways of playing games.

Due to a widespread reluctance to football, the number of clubs and organisations was limited prior to World War I (WWI). As it was mainly played by young boys, adults were often not involved and the boys served as their own leaders (Andersen, 2007, p. 94). Arvid Skappel (cited in Goksøyr & Olstad, 2002) described football as a form of youth rebellion against tradition and values. Youths made their own footballs, used the game as a free space and often played against the will of their parents. Larsen (1977) pinpoints that "football was used as a tool to keep up zest of life and in fact a kind of surviving safeguard for unemployed youth" (p. 17).

The contested status of football meant that many of the leading clubs in the late 19th century disappeared within a few years, while the game survived in schools (Goksøyr & Olstad, 2002). Especially in cities, it was mainly played by children and youth from the upper and middle classes. Still, a national federation (The Norwegian Football Association, hereafter NFA) was formed in 1902, and the first champion was crowned through a cup tournament consisting of five clubs. Norway joined the international football association, FIFA, in 1908 and played its first international game in the same year against Sweden, losing 3–11. Norwegian football was far behind Sweden and Denmark prior to WWI, both in terms of tactics and skill. In 1911, it was reported that forwards only recently had recognised that they could play together rather than just running with the ball by themselves (Goksøyr & Olstad, 2002). The need of a "Norwegian" mode of play was called for, as the English style was regarded too brutal (Andersen, 2007). Later, a distinction emerged between the styles of Odd Skien and Brann Bergen, two of the biggest clubs at the time. Odd Skien became known for their "direct" play with long passes, while Brann Bergen conversely adopted a style more reminiscent of the Scottish way of playing short passes (Goksøyr & Olstad, 2002).

Besides playing most international games in the first years against Sweden and Denmark, England and partly Scotland were the main international influences on Norwegian football. Even before WWI, several English coaches were invited to Norway to improve skills and training methods. England has continued to act as a major inspiration for the development of the Norwegian game (Goksøyr & Olstad, 2002).

The spread and consolidation of football

As mentioned, football first drew attention in urban areas linked to industrialisation. The strongest teams came from industrial cities, notably in the Oslofjord area. Bergen, the largest city of Western Norway, also became an early stronghold of football. Football gradually developed into a source of regional and national pride in the 1920s and, in line with tactical distinctions between different styles of play, the style of the team in a city could serve as markers of local football identities (Goksøyr & Olstad, 2002).

Regional associations became important in the spread of football. They were allowed a certain autonomy towards the NFA and were influential in making football popular in most parts of the country. It is also likely that these "decentralised" features of the organisation have contributed to keeping Norwegian football within one major organisation. Goksøyr and Olstad (2002) concluded that a major strength of football as an organised sport is that it has remained de-centralised in this sense. Small clubs can enjoy considerable influence. That the regional associations – of which there are currently 18 in Norway – were important in organising and spreading grassroots football, also meant that the interests of these groups could be raised against the central association. Small clubs make up a majority at the general assembly (Fotballtinget).

In most parts of Norway, the climate did not favour football for much of the year. It was hard to establish and maintain grass fields, and football was thus often played on sub-optimal surfaces, mostly gravel. The first grass arena was opened in Stavanger in 1917, a city with a relatively mild, but also wet, climate. Still, football soon became the most popular summer sport and the best male football players gradually became national heroes, although not to the same extent as speed skaters and skiers.

During the 1930s, football became the largest organised sport for men. The men's national team also started to perform relatively well, winning the bronze medal in the 1936 Olympic Games and qualifying for the World Cup in 1938, losing marginally in the first round to eventual winners Italy. The spread of newspapers and particularly the radio contributed to making football a national game (Goksøyr & Olstad, 2002).

Football also spread through more sections of the population. Around 1915, it slowly emerged as a sport also for the working classes and industrial cities became vital for further growth. From 1924 onwards, Norwegian sport was split between the established association (NFA) and a competing association from the organised working class, Workers' Sport Association (AIF). AIF organised their own national tournament from 1924 to 1939 (known as the Worker's championship). However, the working classes also played in the established clubs from the "old" association and increasingly football became an important spectator sport for the working classes.

After World War II (WWII), Norway entered a period characterised by economic growth and the political dominance of the social democratic Labour party. Class conflicts from the interwar years lessened and AIF and The Norwegian Sports Federation (NIF) merged (Goksøyr, 1991). The number of young people entering higher education rose sharply from the late 1960s and the industrial cities around the Oslofjord area gradually lost ground in sporting terms to emerging cities that offered education through universities or colleges (e.g. Sogndal, Molde and Tromsø in the 1970s and 1980s), as football – at least formally – was still amateurish. Larger cities also profited from the structural changes from the 1960s onwards. Rosenborg of Trondheim became a stronghold of football during the 1960s, Brann were another major force, and Oslo clubs Vålerenga, Skeid and Lyn all won the league during the 1960s.

For several decades, the NFA cup, a traditional cup tournament, was the major national competition. It took many years before a proper and transparent league system came into place. Clubs were not too keen to join regional or nationwide leagues as spectators would often prefer unofficial games between clubs from rival cities rather than league games against clubs from different regions (Goksøyr & Olstad, 2002). The transport infrastructure also posed challenges.

Still, a league system appeared as a more just way to crown the strongest team. The forerunner of the current league system can be traced back to the late 1930s, and from 1948 a top division consisting of two sections or groups was formed. The league champion was crowned through a final between the group winners. This model was maintained throughout the 1950s. In these years, the league was dominated by clubs from the Oslofjord area. At the start of the league in 1948, 13 of the 16 clubs were based here. From 1961 to 1963, a transition took place where the number of clubs was restricted to ten and the system of two groups was abolished. From then on, the season ran from April to October rather than from August to May (the latter including a winter break lasting for several months). In 1972, the league was extended to 12 clubs, then to 14 in 1995 and 16 in 2009.

Even before WWII, Norway participated on the international arena, if they qualified, and took part in several Olympic tournaments. International influences were also visible in the hiring of international – predominantly British – coaches. Key Norwegian figures returning from abroad were also important. Among these, the most notable figure was Asbjørn Halvorsen, who had a career in Germany before returning to Norway. He was vital in the emergence of the – by Norwegian standards – famously strong national team of the 1930s (Goksøyr & Olstad, 2002).

A national lottery (Norsk Tipping) was established in 1948. Significant parts of the surplus were allocated to build sport facilities all over Norway, including football grounds. This contributed to the spread of football to new groups and new regions. Sports were used politically to erase cultural differences and political divisions (Slagstad, 1998), and football contributed to cultural integration (Augestad, 2001).

Broadly speaking, the history of sport, including football, is a history where new groups have struggled for the right to play or for their right to participate on equal terms. While class was the most notable category in the interwar years, children and youth became a major target of Norwegian sport policy from the 1960s. Women's football, however, was not recognised before the late 1970s, when Norwegian football gradually started to enter the professional and more commercial phase of development.

Football became *the* major spectator sport in Norway in the post-war decades. Even if the major ski and speed skating events could attract even larger crowds, football entered everyday (or every week) routines to a larger extent, as people were attending matches week in, week out during the football season. Leading clubs came to be symbols of local pride and local identity. Partly, they could also be symbols of class identities.

Popular football: Professionalisation and commercialisation

Professionalisation and further spread

The three northernmost counties were gradually integrated into the football pyramid. Mjølner of Narvik were the first northern club to compete in the top

Division in 1972. Bodø/Glimt won the cup in 1975 and were promoted to the top division from 1977. Not until 1979, though, were the northern districts fully integrated into the pyramid, meaning they could qualify for promotion on exactly the same terms as any other club (Goksøyr & Olstad, 2002). On the women's side, a nationwide top division was formed as late as 1987 (Goksøyr & Olstad, 2002).

Until the 1970s, most of Norwegian sport was strictly amateurish. Even if turnovers in the largest clubs could be considerable due to the number of spectators, Norwegian football stuck to the principles of amateur sport. For example, professional players were not allowed to represent Norway's national team until the late 1960s. It was, however, a badly hidden fact that the best players received payment in the 1970s. In 1984, a regulation called "non-amateur" football was set up. This meant that clubs could pay players who had a contract, but players were not allowed to have football as their major source of living (Goksøyr & Olstad, 2002).

From the early 1970s, another aspect of professionalisation was introduced (Goksøyr & Olstad, 2002). The Norwegian School of Sport Science (NIH), established in 1968, quickly became a key institution in coaching education. Gradually, formal skills were demanded for acting as a coach. Academic studies of football tactics, nutrition, technical skills and physical education more generally were gradually influencing football. These processes were not straightforward. Many opposed the idea of making football a subject of science. In the 1970s and 1980s, these tensions were often labelled as a distinction between "joyous football" (*gladfotball*) and "systems football", and many would support the former. When the Swede Gunder Bengtsson arrived at Vålerenga of Oslo in 1983, he was inspired by the pressing style brought to Scandinavia by the English coaches Bob Houghton and Roy Hodgson (Andersson & Radmann, 1999; Peterson, 2000). Vålerenga won the league two years in a row under Bengtsson, but attendances dropped.

It was not until around 1990 that the scientific approach started to dominate the way football was played. Nils Arne Eggen of Rosenborg Trondheim and Egil "Drillo" Olsen, coach of the national team between 1990–1998 and 2009–2013, achieved results previously unknown in Norwegian football by anchoring tactical principles in academic and scientific knowledge (Hjelseth & Telseth, 2022). In the 1990s, Norwegian football was arguably among the most research-based in the world, before the significance of science in sport and football was increasingly recognised in the stronger football nations. During these years, Rosenborg of Trondheim was the stronghold of club football, winning the league for 13 consecutive years and qualifying for the UEFA Champions league for eight consecutive seasons. The national team qualified for the World Cups in 1994 and 1998, and for the 2000 European Championship (Euro). After the turn of the millennium, Norwegian men's football went into sporting decline. It is reasonable to assume that the science-based approach to tactics, nutrition and physical education in the 1990s served as an advantage, while larger football nations caught up in the years that followed (Hjelseth & Telseth, 2022).

As a result of the scientific approach, a clearly defined systems football emerged, with specific roles and role relationships that limited the number of choices and increased confidence and predictability. This also contributed to the standardisation of training methods. By using all available knowledge, one can detail and control the training process, and its execution, for the individual role holder. All training and all development plans were aimed at maximising output or results.

The inclusion and spread of women's football

Football was predominantly a male sport, but women did play football during the early days. In general, women's football developed earlier in the Oslofjord area than in other regions (Goksøyr & Olstad, 2002). Women's football started as entertainment matches against men, and "... women were seen as something strange and monstrous" (Skogvang, 2022, p. 72). The earliest recorded matches featured Moss Ladies Team and Askim in 1921 in the industrial area of South-Eastern Norway (Johnsen & Lien, 2019), and the actor and ice-dancer Sonja Henie played against a men's team in 1928 (Goksøyr & Olstad, 2002). Other show games included one in Tromsø in 1931 to make money for a club banner (Hansen, 1994), a Hamar Ladies team match against Bolton Wanderers in 1931, and events in several other towns and cities. Many of these events were stopped due to negative attitudes from the NFA. They instructed referees not to take on women's games and clubs to ban ladies from their arenas as football was a male sport. Skogvang (2022) summarises that, although girls' and women's football was not formally banned, it might still be labelled the "ban period" as the NFA put much effort in keeping women's football outside of the organisation.

From the early 1970s, female football was gradually introduced against harsh opposition among key actors in the NFA. Women had continued playing outside the NFA. For example, some handball players started to play football before the women's game was officially recognised (Skogvang, 2007) and they were finally included in the federation in 1976. An increasing number of girls wanted to play football and girls could play in boys' teams, which was crucial in rural areas. From 1984, classes dependent on age were established for girls in the same way as for boys.

Until recently, women's football has been heavily discriminated in terms of financial support, training facilities, professional support and general recognition (Skogvang, 2022). The ignoring of women can be traced back to several factors. In Norwegian schools, girls had been excluded from games and play that involved bodily contact and duels. Football did not fit the traditional stereotype of femininity (Skogvang, 2007) and there was a real and subsequent struggle for recognition before widespread popularity and acceptance was gradually achieved.

In the late 1980s and early 1990s, women's football started to spread internationally and Norway became a leading force. They won the Euro 1987, the unofficial World Cup in China in 1988, Euro 1993, the World Cup in 1995 and the Olympic Games in 2000. Since the turn of the millennium, results have declined over a long period, but the national team still regularly qualifies for major tournaments. They were eliminated at the group stage in Euro 2022 but qualified for the World Cup 2023 by winning the group with nine wins and a draw and a goal difference of 47-2. At the club level, Norwegian female teams have struggled to compete, not least as clubs in the larger football nations have been able to invest heavily due to the increased popularity of women's football. Over the last few years, female club teams have merged with male top clubs in Brann, Lillestrøm, Rosenborg, Stabæk, Tromsø and Vålerenga. Players underline the positive effects in terms of improved playing conditions, medical support, more supporters and more media attention, but at the same time discrimination is still prevalent (Skogvang, 2022).

The development of women's football has been substantial and women accounted for 29% of all Norwegian players in 2020. It started out with 75 registered teams and about 1,500 registered players in 1975, increased to about 52,000 registered players in 1980, and in 2020 there are 108,962 women and girls playing football in Norway (NFA, 2021). Football has been the largest organised sport for women in Norway since 1995.

Norway in the international football community

Norway was eager to compete in international tournaments like the European Cups at an early stage, but generally both clubs and the national teams had performed poorly in the 1970s and 1980s. The men's national team could win surprisingly, like when they beat England in a World Cup qualifier in 1981, but they regularly finished at the bottom of their qualifying group. As we have seen, the women's national team performed much better from the mid-1980s.

Being known as a country of gender equality, Norway has also played an important part in promoting women's football and women's rights of representation on the international scene. The Norwegian Executive Board member Ellen Wille was the first woman ever to speak at the FIFA congress in Mexico City in 1986. She criticised FIFA's annual report because it did not mention women's football. She also suggested a World Championship for women and the inclusion of women's football in the Olympic programme. An official women's World Cup was organised for the first time in 1991 and women's football entered the Olympic programme in 1996. Per Ravn Omdal was another key figure at the international level. After serving as president of the NFA for a total of 13 years between 1987 and 2004, he has, among other positions, sat on the boards of both UEFA and FIFA and led FIFA's TV and Marketing Committee and Women's Committee. Karen Espelund was the first female vice president of the NFA as well as the first female general secretary of the NFA and she has also sat on UEFA's board and led its committee of women's football.

In 2022, Lise Klaveness was elected as the first female president of the NFA. At the FIFA Congress in Qatar on 31 March 2022, she addressed topics of human rights, transparency and equal opportunities for everyone who wants to play football, and stated: "Let us stand together and live up to the promise and dreams we give to everyone who takes the first kick of the ball" (NFA, 2022).

Ada Hegerberg, playing for Lyon, became the first player to receive the Ballon d'Or Féminin in 2018. The award may be seen as a symbol of the tradition in the Scandinavian countries of fighting for women's right to play football. At the same time, however, she rejected playing for the national team between 2017 and 2021, at least partly due to the ignorance of women's football on the part of the NFA. She returned to the national team for the 2022 season. This illustrates the neglect of women's football from the NFA and contributed to Norway losing ground to many other nations that had recognised the potential of women's football, including in commercial terms.

The growth of commercial football

Football was by far the most popular sport after 1970, both in terms of participation and spectatorship. The gradual introduction of artificial surfaces from the late 1970s also meant that football could be practiced throughout the year, and in the 1980s, the dominance of football as *the* most popular sport for children and youth was further strengthened.

In the 1980s, football also gradually became an integral part of popular culture. The most popular male players were as attractive on the front pages of magazines as film stars or rock musicians (Goksøyr & Olstad, 2002). Football also became a topic within high culture, such as when the highly respected novelists Dag Solstad and Jon Michelet wrote books from five consecutive World Cups (1982–1998).

Norway became a wealthy nation during the 1980s and the political hegemony of the social democratic party was broken. Norway became a more liberal society, which meant it gradually became less reluctant to commercial sport. Sponsors and the media enjoyed increased influence on football from the late 1980s onwards.

Norwegian top clubs were allowed to wear small sponsor logos on the back of jerseys from the late 1970s, and from the early 1980s they were also introduced on the chest of the shirt. In this period, there was little opposition towards this kind of commercialisation. In the 1990s commercialisation increased significantly, which led groups of supporters to contest the strengthened influence of sponsors and the media and demand influence on such issues. For example, supporter groups have often opposed unpredictable fixture schedules for TV needs and have criticised the introduction of sponsor logos that do not fit the colours of the shirt.

Still, most forms of commercial influences have been accepted by most parties, as it was a necessary means to introduce fully professional football in

Norway. Amateurism was fully abandoned in 1992. From then on, top clubs were *obliged* to have formal contracts with players. Several other functions were also professionalised, including formal qualifications for coaches in children's and youth football.

The same year, in 1992, the first national, commercial broadcaster (TV2) was established. This meant that there was more competition for sport rights. At that time, live coverage of Norwegian league games was quite scarce. Clubs feared that TV coverage would reduce attendances and it took many years before any league game was televised as a rule. A hallmark of commercial TV football was reached in 2004 when TV2 paid NOK 1 billion (EUR 97.1 million) for a three-year deal to cover Norwegian top football. While sporting results were in fact starting to decline, the deal was symbolic of the increasing status of the game and attendances increased significantly in the short run.

Conclusion: The future of Norwegian football

Based on participation rates, especially among children (up to 12 years) and youth (13–19 years), the position of football as the most popular sport remains unchallenged. Current numbers show that, by 2021, there were 1,747 men's teams and 518 women's teams, 4,044 youth boys' teams and 2,036 girl's teams, 12,873 children's boys' teams and 5,786 children's girl's teams (NFA, 2021), although these numbers have declined due to the COVID-19 pandemic. Girls and women still make up about one-third of the memberships in the NFA.

Attendances at top football matches have, however, declined significantly for more than ten years. At the time of writing (May 2022), the Norwegian 2021 cup final (postponed due to COVID restrictions) has just been decided. For the first time in decades, there was no scarcity of tickets at a cup final. While this was probably partly due to the post-COVID situation and the unfamiliar timing of the cup final (traditionally played in late November or early December), it is also a symbol of a game that is increasingly struggling to engage the people. Norwegian football probably appears unfashionable compared to English, Spanish and German football, which is televised throughout the year. It may also signal more fundamental problems in football's relation to its fans. On the other hand, the number of spectators in women's matches in Norway is increasing in line with the development in Europe.

We started this chapter by pointing out two narratives that have been the cornerstones of our sketch of the history of Norwegian football. The first was a narrative of modernisation. Professional football, commercial football and the academic, science-based approach to football, all belong to this category. These developments follow the trajectory of most sports during the same period. However, parts of these processes have been challenged by football supporters, both at the national and the international level. According to politically conscious supporter groups, football has entered a state of moral decline, which has severely damaged its reputation. At the international level, the fact that many clubs are in the hands of political regimes and commercial corporations with highly questionable records of human rights has led to increasing concerns. This criticism has also influenced Norwegian football, and campaigns to boycott the Qatar World Cup have put the NFA in a position where they are seen as allied to the highly questionable regime of FIFA. Contrary to most other sports, football has groups of supporters that can mobilise against aspects of the modern game. Campaigns such as "Against modern football" have limited numerical support, but the intensity of such campaigns means that football must take heed of them. Further, it is reasonable to assume that Norwegian football is more vulnerable to such criticism compared to football in leading countries where the global following of the top clubs means that those protesting can be substituted by new crowds. On the other hand, the engagement in such football-political issues by the fans is in itself an illustration of the value that is put on football as a sporting and cultural practice.

The second narrative was linked to inequality, inclusion and exclusion. The spread of football in this sense came in three waves at different points in time. Class was a major issue in the interwar period, children's and youth football spread rapidly in the 1960s and 1970s, while women's football was introduced in the late 1970s and quickly spread as a popular sport for girls. Women's football was mostly ignored by the media and partly by the NFA for a long period, but as growing international popularity is visible for all to see, this has slowly started to change. Games in the women's top league are now regularly televised and some of the major clubs have become involved in women's football. This is the case in Rosenborg, Brann, Lillestrøm and Vålerenga. There are clear signs that attendances at games are rising as well-known club names attract spectators.

On the grassroots level, professionalisation has led to increasing costs of participation and the question of social inequality in sport due to economic inequality is heavily discussed. The popularity of football also means that private football academies are offering professional coaching, even for young children in some of the larger cities. Social inequality in sport participation is generally increasing in Norway (Strandbu et al., 2017) and issues of exclusion are yet again on the agenda.

The professionalisation and commercialisation of Norwegian football also entails an increasing pressure for elite clubs to develop their own players. This, in turn, has created a pressure towards specialisation and increased training volumes at an early age, which has challenged the Norwegian ideal that a focus on performance and competition must wait until the players turn 12 years old. When the demands on the clubs and young players increase, there is a risk that the Norwegian football family will be split in two when it comes to children's and youth football, creating a distinction between grassroots clubs and elite clubs.

References

Andersen, E. (2007). *Det store gjennombruddet – Norsk fotballs kulturhistorie 1885–1925* (The great breakthrough – The cultural history of Norwegian football 1885–1925). [Doctoral dissertation]. Norwegian School of Sport Sciences.

Andersson, T., & Radmann, A. (1999). Everything in moderation: The Swedish model. In G. Armstrong, & R. Giulianotti (Eds.), *Football cultures and identities* (pp. 67–76). Macmillan.

Augestad, P. (2001). Nasjonen og idretten [The nation and sport]. *Sosiologisk tidsskrift*, 9(3), 233–253.

Augestad, P. (2003). *Skolering av kroppen. Om kunnskap og makt i kroppsøvingsfaget* [Educating the body. On knowledge and power in physical education]. [Doctoral dissertation]. University of Oslo, Telemark University College.

Goksøyr, M. (1991). *Historien om norsk idrett* [The history of Norwegian sport]. Abstrakt.

Goksøyr, M., & Olstad, F. (2002). *Fotball! Norges Fotballforbund 100 år* [Football! The Norwegian Football Federation 100 years]. Norges Fotballforbund.

Hansen, J. (Ed.). (1994). *I "futtbollens" tjeneste. 75 år med Troms Fotballkrets* [In service of "futtboll". 75 years with the Troms regional football association]. Troms Fotballkrets.

Hjelseth, A., & Telseth, F. (2022). Scientification of Norwegian football in the 1990s and the emergence of a new regime of knowledge. *Soccer & Society*. 10.1080/14660970.2023.2179193

Johnsen, L., & Lien, M. (2019). Den lange kampen. 100 år med norsk kvinnefotball [The long battle. 100 years of Norwegian women's football]. *Josimar – tidsskrift om fotball*. Dype skoger.

Larsen, P. (1977). *75 norske fotballår, Norges Fotballforbund 1902–1977* [75 Norwegian years of football. The Norwegian Football Federation 1902–1977]. Norges Fotballforbund.

Lidström, I. (2021). *På skidor i kulturella gränsland: Samiska spår i skidsportens historia.* [Skiing in cultural border areas: Sami traces in the history of ski sport]. Malmö University.

NFA (Norges fotballforbund). (2021). *Annual Report*. Norwegian Football Federation. Norges Fotballforbund.

NFA (Norges fotballforbund). (2022). *Lise Klaveness calls for at change at the FIFA Congress*. Retrieved April 12, 2022, from https://www.fotball.no/tema/nff-nyheter/2022/calls-out-for-change-at-the-fifa-congress/

Peterson, T. (2000). Split visions: The Introduction of the Svenglish model in Swedish football. *Soccer & Society*, 1(2), 1–18.

Skappel, A. (n.d.). *Fotballkamp paa grus og græs i 25 aar* [Football game on gravel and grass]. Christiania.

Skogvang, B. O. (2007). The historical development of women's football in Norway: From "show games" to international successes. In J. Magee, J. Caudwell, K. Liston, & S. E. Scraton (Eds.), *Women, football, and Europe: Histories, equity and experiences* (pp. 41–54). Meyer & Meyer Sport.

Skogvang, B. O. (2022). Hitos en el desarrollo del fútbol femenino en Noruega [Highlights of the development of women's soccer in Norway]. In A. Janson,

J. Branz, B. O. Skogvang, T. Arimoto, & M. Santino (Eds.), *Del jugar por jugar a jugar en serio – La profesionalizacion en el fútbol femenino* (pp. 46–87). Aurelia Rivera Libros.

Slagstad, R. (1998). *De nasjonale strateger* [The national strategists]. Pax.

Strandbu, Å., Gulløy, E., Andersen, P. L., Seippel, Ø. L., & Dalen, H. B. (2017). Ungdom, idrett og klasse. Fortid, samtid og framtid [Youth, sport and class. The past, the current and the future]. *Norsk sosiologisk tidsskrift 1*(2), 132–151.

Walvin, J. (1994). *The people's game: The history of football revisited*. Mainstream.

Chapter 5

Between Grassroots Democracy and Professional Commercialism in Sweden

Robert S. Primus, Daniel Alsarve, and Daniel Svensson

The early years, ca. 1860–1903

How did football become the biggest sport in a country traditionally focused on skiing and Ling gymnastics? The answer to this question is closely linked to the 20th century transformation of Sweden from a rural periphery to a more urbanised, industrialised and internationalised country. Due to the urbanising and industrialising processes that permeated the Nordic region at the time, the 1880s was a decisive decade for the development of a modern and democratic Swedish society. New social and economic challenges led to the formation of a more comprehensive state apparatus. As a result, more effective infrastructures were created involving fire protection, water and sewage treatment and other areas related to public health (Hedenborg & Kvarnström, 2009).

A consequence of these processes was the growth of popular movements. This growth is often explained as an effect of people's lost sense of community in the urban landscape, which motivated individuals to gather to discuss and challenge contemporary political and social issues. Due to a specific interest in issues related to public health, citizens' bodily hygiene and nature became the embryos of the Swedish sports movement (Hedenborg & Kvarnström, 2009).

Between the 1860s and the 1890s, several clubs organising different types of physical activities were founded. While the first clubs focused on promoting health, social camaraderie and demarcations of class status, later clubs focused on competition and the sporting activity *per se* (Janzon, 1978; Ljunggren, 2020; Yttergren, 1996). During this period, hundreds of sports associations were established in Sweden at local, regional and national levels. In Stockholm alone, 160 sport clubs were founded between 1860 and 1898 (Yttergren, 1996). These clubs organised several sports, thus inviting members to be active all year round. Consequently, an increase in the number of working-class men engaging in sport changed its social markers and led to a more explicit, yet controversial, focus on competition and performance enhancement (Andersson, 2002). Specifically embracing male workers, this expansion completely sidelined the participation of females, which during the late 1800s almost disappeared from the sporting scene (Ljunggren, 2020).

DOI: 10.4324/9781003280729-7

The first comprehensive sports organisation in Sweden was the Swedish Central Association for the Promotion of Athletics (Centralföreningen för idrottens främjande, SCIF), founded in 1897. Viktor Balck, who is recognised as the founding father of Swedish sport, was its first chairman. SCIF applied to host the Olympic Games in Stockholm in 1912 (Balck was also a member of the International Olympic Committee) and was a key factor in the popularisation of competitive Swedish sport in the late 1800s and early 1900s. However, founded in 1903, the Swedish Sports Confederation (Riksidrottsförbundet) was to become the hegemonic organisation of Swedish sport.

At the end of the 1800s, and as part of a sportification process, football was introduced through three different yet interrelated procedures. First, British workers and officials within the industry introduced the new sport in western coastal cities such as Gothenburg. Second, Swedish gymnasts who had visited England and learned the game started to mimic and play it. Finally, in southern cities like Halmstad and Malmö Danish teams were invited to show and play exhibition games against Swedish teams (Sund, 1997). On arrival, football was perceived as a controversial attraction with a violent, problematic, yet popular and competitive character suitable for "real" men (Andersson, 2002).

During the 1880s and 1890s, clubs like Örgryte IS (1887), AIK (1891), Djurgårdens IF (1891), GAIS (1894) and IFK Norrköping (1897) were founded. The first organised game with English football rules was played in 1892 between two Swedish clubs in Gothenburg. Subsequently, regional sports associations started to organise tournaments and in 1896 the Swedish Sports Association (Svenska Idrottsförbundet) in Gothenburg organised the first Swedish Championship (Sund 1997). Stockholm Sports Association (Stockholms idrottsförbund) was founded in 1898 and in the following year launched the football cup tournament known as *Rosenska Pokalen.* In the eastern regions of Sweden this was perceived as more prestigious than the Swedish Championship (Sund, 1997).

Initiatives to solve the organisational and geographical divisions and organise Swedish football at joint national level were started but several clubs in Gothenburg protested against such a construction. In 1902, a group of Stockholm-based clubs founded an association focusing on football (and bandy) – The Swedish Ballgame Association (Svenska Bollspelsförbundet). However, the association never managed to gain legitimacy outside the Stockholm region (Sund, 1997; Sund, 2007).

Understandably, the conditions and resources were somewhat limited in these early years. Football training was conducted in parks, games were played on gravel pitches and several of the players lacked adequate footwear (Sund, 1997; Svensson, 2019). Even though some PE teachers allowed their female pupils to practise ball games similar to football, in general the sport was not perceived as appropriate for women. Many of the players came from the working-class, while middle-class men were more involved in organising, refereeing and writing about the game (Andersson, 2002).

The spread of football, 1904–1923

At the beginning of the 20th century democratic tendencies were strengthened in Swedish society. The universal right to vote for all men was established in 1909 and the Swedish Sports Confederation was based on an associative democracy, where each member had one vote at the club's annual meeting. Despite these progressive initiatives, Swedish society in general was characterised by a patriarchal power structure with weak positions for workers in the labour market (Hedenborg & Kvarnström, 2009). Sport – and not least football – became important identity-creating activities in industrial cities (Andersson, 2002, 2011; Ericsson, 2004, 2013; Ericsson et al., 2019; Horgby, 2012).

When the Swedish Sports Confederation was founded in 1903 it organised 2,000 members in 35 clubs. A decade later it had 63,000 members and 600 clubs. The expansion was not only numerical, but also social and geographical, and sport became a popular movement (Ljunggren, 2020). In short, the democratic and patriarchal context conditioned the ways in which sports clubs were governed. On the one hand, patriarchal elements could be emphasised, resulting in a club governed by a strong man as the chairman for several decades. On the other hand, democratic elements could also be prevalent, where members, in addition to the qualities promoted by the sport itself, learned languages and other societal skills (Alsarve, 2014; Andersson, 2002).

Stockholm hosted the Olympic Games in 1912. With this event, the modern sports movement became public and visible and increased its political impact. From 1913 onwards, it gained annual governmental funding, since sport was perceived as beneficial for public health by creating character, promoting sobriety, and strengthening the military defence. There were also critical voices, not least from the previously dominant Ling gymnastics, arguing that sport was too much about winning and beating records, thereby causing a degeneration of younger citizens due its brutal nature (Ljunggren, 2020).

At a local political level, larger cities started to be involved in sport by lending land to sports clubs and granting sports facilities. Arenas and other facilities therefore became common in the urban landscape (Sjöblom, 2006). An increased visibility was also evident in the media. For example, *Idrottsbladet* was established in 1910, with three issues published per week (Ljunggren, 2020). Unexpectedly, this visibility and popularity affected the education system so that instead of mainly consisting of Swedish gymnastics (Linggymnastik), sport was also included in the PE curriculum (Annerstedt, 2000).

As the number of football clubs and competitions increased, the need for a national association arose and in 1904 the Swedish Football Association (Svenska Fotbollförbundet, SvFF) was founded. From 1906, SvFF exclusively organised Swedish football. At its inception SvFF listed 77 football clubs. At the beginning of the 1920s, it organised more than 500 member clubs (Svenska Fotbollförbundet, 2004).

Several competitions were launched in the first decade of the new century. In 1910, the first national league – the Swedish Series (Svenska serien) – was established and several regional competitions were soon cancelled. The series consisted of eight clubs. In 1912, SvFF took over responsibility and a parallel regional series was launched that soon became official and included lower divisions of the Swedish series system (SvFF, 2004). The number of participating clubs grew and in 1922 the Swedish series was divided into two groups. However, a suggestion for a larger all Swedish series was presented (SvFF, 2004). In short, football became one of the cultural expressions of the urban public, i.e., the male working-class youth. The number of spectators also increased, making the crowd an important aspect of an attractive game (Andersson, 2002).

Sweden was one of the seven countries to found FIFA in 1904 (SvFF, 2004). As preparation for the Olympics in London in 1908, the first international match ever to be played was against Norway. During the years leading up to the Paris Olympics in 1924, the national team played almost 100 games (Sund, 1997). In addition, Swedish clubs attracted coaches from countries such as England, Hungary and Austria (Sund, 1997; Svensson, 2019).

The years of consolidation, 1924–1958

From the end of the First World War to the "Happy Fifties", Sweden changed from a poor peripheral country, characterised by constant strikes, into a rich industrial country with strong ties between the political sphere and the trade union branches of the labour movement (Hedenborg & Kvarnström, 2009). Through majority and a hegemonic position, the Social Democratic Workers' Party planned and socially engineered a Swedish welfare society (Horgby, 2012). Women gained the right to vote in 1921 and women's sports grew in scope, although early attempts to create space for women's football did not gain support from the leading sports organisations. In the wake of social reforms, and an increased population with more leisure time, the entire sports movement expanded (Tolvhed, 2015). After almost half a century and more or less intense conflicts with other organisations, the Swedish Sports Confederation became the dominant umbrella organisation that brought together the entire Swedish sports movement.

While sport continued to gain status in Swedish society, it was not always straightforward. During the 1920s government grants for sport decreased, as sport was criticised for focusing too much on the competitive element and less on public health. However, the sports movement managed to get grants in other ways. During the interwar period recession, several sports facilities were built as part of putting people into labour (Norberg, 2014). After the Second World War, the benefits of sport increased in importance and were perceived as not only benefiting the public, but also contributing to citizens' physical and moral standards. Sport balanced the negative effects of industrialisation and urbanisation by offering a recreational and meaningful leisure time.

By the 1950s, the government's sports policy was no longer about *if* the sports movement should receive government funding, but rather *how much*. New grants had a significant impact, which meant the development of coach education and the employment of sport consultants. This funding, together with new youth policies, contributed to a professionalisation of the Swedish sports movement (Norberg, 2014). In the 1950s, the involvement and institutionalisation of sport at municipality level expanded further, which facilitated an extensive societal planning of sport and sports facilities (Sjöblom, 2006).

Sport in general, and football in particular, grew in tandem with the media. During the 1920s, daily newspapers included sport reports, which broadened the media landscape. In 1925, Swedish public radio was launched and included the first outdoor coverage of a sporting event – *Vasaloppet*. Perhaps as a response to the critical voices, clubs started to organise sporting activities for young people. In the 1920s, IFK Norrköping launched summer camps, where children could enjoy "sun, water, fresh air, sport, gymnastics and simple but good food" (Svensson, 2019, p. 177). Additionally, in PE, sport ultimately replaced gymnastics as the core content (Annerstedt, 2000). TV was introduced in the 1950s and the broadcast of the World Cup in 1958 contributed to the development of the radio and TV network in Sweden. This worried the Swedish FA and the clubs because it meant that radio and TV coverage could lead to a decline in spectators on site, which in turn would have negative economic consequences (Dahlén, 2008).

Indeed, sports clubs saw a commercial potential in public interest. Sports arenas were enclosed so that spectators had to pay to enter, and for some time entrance fees were by far the most important income for football clubs (Andersson, 2002; Zethrin, 2015). Activities like lotteries were offered in order to increase the attraction of the games, and sometimes the games were combined with other sport competitions. Zethrin (2015) suggested that these market-orientated sporting events during the 1920s and 1930s formed the backbone of the commercialisation of sport in Sweden.

With the Swedish series as a foundation, *Allsvenskan* was launched in 1924. It consisted of 12 clubs and it is still the highest division in Swedish male football. In terms of spectators, it was a great success, averaging 3,000 spectators in the first year to up to 13,000 at the beginning of the 1950s. However, Allsvenskan also meant greater costs, as the trips were longer and SvFF demanded a guarantee sum for participation. Consequently, smaller and poorer clubs tended to be excluded (Andersson, 2002). Similar problems have proved to be a challenge for women's football clubs even today.

From approximately 500 clubs and 72,000 members in 1924, SvFF organised almost 3,000 clubs and 350,000 members by the end of the 1950s (SvFF, 2004). These clubs started to offer sporting activities for children. In the 1940s, SvFF formed a youth committee (Ungdomskommittén) that started to educate youth coaches with the aim of inspiring clubs to initiate a youth section (Peterson, 1993). The focus, however, was only on boys.

In the 1920s, women's football became more popular in many countries. Despite this, the lack of support from football federations and other organisations, as well as paternalistic ideas of protecting women from the physical dangers of playing football, limited the potential growth of women's football (e.g., Cox, 2012; Jenkel, 2020; Macbeth, 2002; Williams, 2003). Sweden was no exception, although there were a few scattered, loosely organised and short-lived initiatives of women's football (some as early as 1917) and even an attempt at organising a women's league in Umeå in 1950–1951 (Hjelm & Olofsson, 2003).

A common way of disarming the potentially controversial idea of women's football was to downplay its seriousness. Teams often played against so called *gubblag* (i.e., teams of older men) and such games were framed as an amusement rather than as serious sport. Despite these games and the continuous efforts of female footballers to establish their sport, there was little support from the governing organisations (i.e., SvFF or the Swedish Sports Confederation). Football thus remained a predominantly male domain up until the 1960s.

While almost all European countries were suffering from the Second World War, in 1948 Sweden enjoyed a successful football decade. Sweden won gold at the Olympics that year, bronze in the World Cup in 1950 and at the Olympics in 1952, and a silver medal in the 1958 World Cup. The fact that Sweden hosted the World Cup in 1958 emphasised Sweden's strong position in the international football community at the time. The international successes were also mirrored at club level. During the 1940s, IFK Norrköping excelled in international games and was at the time regarded as one of the best European clubs (Sund, 1997; Svensson, 2019).

When the Swedish Sports Confederation was founded, the amateur regulations were a top priority and for many years led to several disputes between the Swedish Sports Confederation and SvFF, between SvFF and the clubs and amongst the clubs themselves (Andersson, 2002; Sund, 1997, Wikberg; 2005). As the financial, symbolic and cultural meaning of competitive sport grew, the players were asked to invest more time and, consequently, wanted more in return. Several clubs pressed for higher financial compensation and professional football. Some clubs also gave players certain benefits, such as allowances, clothing, dinners and supplied them with work opportunities at sponsoring companies (Andersson, 2002; Zethrin, 2015). However, from time-to-time SvFF also punished clubs for violating the regulations (Sund, 1997; Wikberg, 2005).

At the international level professional football was on the rise. In the 1920s, FIFA abandoned the Olympics and established the World Cup (1930) in which amateurs and professionals could participate. At that time many countries had already legalised professional football (Wikberg, 2005), but Sweden had not. As several of the best Swedish players were not amateurs, Sweden did *not* attend the 1928 Olympics (Sund, 1997; SvFF, 2004). Slowly but steadily, the regulations became more permissive and what has been labelled a "rational amateurism" developed (Andersson, 2002). The main reason for this was that at the end of the 1940s Swedish players started to become contracted by European professional clubs. Thus, if Swedish football did not professionalise it ran the risk of being drained of skilled players, losing quality and public interest and, consequently, declining in popularity. At the end of the 1960s, it was decided that the amateur regulations would be overturned (Peterson, 1993; Sund, 1997).

But professionalisation is not only about contracts and salaries. Education is also an important element (Peterson, 1993; Yttergren, 2012). In the initial decades SvFF and Swedish clubs had engaged foreign coaches, but in order to secure a more sustainable quality in Swedish football Sweden needed its own cadre of coaches. Hence, in 1931 SvFF launched a coach education programme (Sund, 1997). During the 1950s the programme was developed and SvFF started to engage scientists from the Swedish School of Sport and Health Sciences, which in turn led to the formation of a more modern coach education programme (Peterson, 1993).

Popular football, 1959–2000s

At the beginning of the 1960s Sweden was deeply involved in the globalisation of commerce and politics. This meant that the Cold War, with its intensified conflicts between a global east and west during the 1960s and 1970s, also affected the Swedish society and economy. Unemployment rates rose, strikes broke out more frequently and the social democratic hegemony was challenged and gradually "replaced" by neoliberalism. The assassination of Prime Minister Olof Palme in 1986 can be described as the symbolic end of the era of the People's Home (Folkhemmet). Palme's death left the entire country in shock, with a vacuum-like situation in terms of political power. When the Iron Curtain collapsed Swedish society was struggling with declining economic conditions and major cuts in public finances affected the sports movement negatively. Reduced public subsidies resulted in inferior facilities and more challenging conditions for the civic society in general. After a referendum in 1994, when the yes-side won with 52.3% of the votes (the no-side received 46.8%), in 1995 Sweden joined the European Union (EU) (Hedenborg & Kvarnström, 2009). This would prove to be important for football.

The changing political climate and new international obligations affected the ideas and structure of Swedish football in several ways. Starting with the overturning of the amateur regulations in 1967 and rapidly accelerating with the Bosman ruling in 1995, most of the players in Allsvenskan became full-time professionals. A gradual change can be discerned from volunteers to employed experts/professionals amongst coaches and other staff (Alsarve, 2014; Svensson, 2019). At the same time, coaches became more dependent on scientific knowledge and formalised education, rather than practical experience (Svensson, 2019; Svensson & Svensson, 2021).

By the 1960s, Swedish society had seen gender equality rise on the political agenda, which paved the way for a more inclusive football movement. Barriers remained, though, and had to be challenged. It was Öxabäck, a team from a small village with the same name, that managed to secure the support of the regional FA for a women's football league in the late 1960s. During the 1970s the number of women's teams increased and several new local and regional football leagues started. In 1972, female football was formally organised into a national league by SvFF.

Youth football also grew substantially during this period. When the second wave of women's football swept across Europe in the early 1970s, the breakthrough was manifested by the establishment of national leagues and international competition. For Sweden, the first international fixture was played in 1973, against Finland. This was an important step in the general sportification of women's football, and one that set Sweden on the path towards becoming one of the leading women's football nations. The expansion was evident, especially in terms of the rapid increase in the number of registered players from some 700 in 1970 to more than 26,000 in 1980 (Hjelm & Olofsson, 2003). Today, the number of registered female players is close to 100,000.

The rise of Swedish women's football has been most visible at the international level with the outstanding performances of specific teams (e.g., Öxabäck, Jitex, Djurgården, Umeå, Rosengård, the Swedish national team) and players. However, there are also structural explanations, such as rational training, regimentation, and equalisation, for the promotion and development of women's football and the securing of organisational and public support (e.g., Brus & Trangbæk 2003; Hjelm & Olofsson, 2003; Svensson & Oppenheim, 2018). All this was largely managed without any far-reaching professionalisation. Although women's clubs in Sweden were among the most successful in Europe during the 1990s and early 2000s, very few players were full-time professionals. Many players from other countries moved to Scandinavia to play football, while Scandinavian players moved in the other direction (Botelho & Skogvang, 2013) – in the 1970s and 1980s primarily to Italy, in the 1990s and early 2000s to Japan and the United States, and in the 2010s to England, Germany, France and Spain. This illustrates how, perhaps counterintuitively, Swedish clubs were amongst the best in the world in terms of sportification and results, but not in terms of salaries and turnovers. This was in line with the Scandinavian sports model, which emphasised non-commerciality, mass participation and voluntary work (e.g., Ljunggren, 2020; Wikberg, 2005). As one of Sweden's most successful players of all time, Pia Sundhage, put it in relation to her move to Italy in 1985: "I played and worked as a professional, so I wanted to be recognised as a professional" (Botelho & Skogvang, 2013, p. 804).

Given Sweden's relatively small population, historically speaking Swedish football has been rather successful. Swedish clubs had a very limited impact on the international football scene in the first half of the 20th century, but from the 1970s and until the Bosman ruling in 1995, several men's football clubs achieved notable results. For example, Malmö FF reached the European Cup final in 1979, in 1982 and 1987 IFK Göteborg won the UEFA Cup and, in the

1990s, featured for several seasons in the UEFA Champions League and reached the quarter finals in 1994/1995. However, since the Bosman ruling and the accelerating economic growth of international football that followed, Swedish clubs have struggled to reach these heights. It has been argued that Swedish football benefited from a form of rational amateurism (Andersson, 2002), where players were amateurs but trained rationally and systematically – acting like professionals without full-time employment. In a football world where transfers and club economies were less decisive, rational amateurism served Swedish clubs well. For men's football, the Bosman ruling changed the landscape completely (see, e.g., Svensson, 2019), although for women's clubs rational amateurism continued to be a competitive edge. Here, Swedish clubs were amongst the leaders in Europe, with Umeå's victories in the UEFA Women's Cup in 2003 and 2004 as peaks. The recent professionalisation and rapid growth of women's elite football across Europe have transformed the playing field again, and Swedish clubs now face challenging financial conditions in comparison with many European top clubs.

Even though Swedish clubs are struggling to keep up at the European top competitive level, the national teams are still generally performing well. Sweden's men's team is ranked 19th in the world, and the women's team (ranked second in the world) reached the final of the Olympic Games in Tokyo in 2021 (rankings from March 2022, fifa.com).

Sweden's impact on elite football is more evident when looking at international organisations. Following a long Swedish tradition of assuming leading roles in international organisations (e.g., IOC, UN and World Athletics), it was Lennart Johansson (UEFA President 1990–2007) who oversaw the introduction of the Champions League and the economic transformation of European club football. Lars-Christer Olsson was Secretary General of UEFA from 2003 to 2007 and in 2017 Karl-Erik Nilsson became UEFA's first vice-president.

Historically, football has been the largest sport in Sweden and has continued to attract large crowds to the stadiums. However, it was not until the 1970s that more organised supporter groups entered the scene. Inspired by the British supporter culture, the fans of major clubs like Hammarby IF, IFK Gothenburg, Malmö FF and AIK began to separate themselves from the rest of the crowd by singing and chanting in ways that had not been seen in Swedish football before.

In order to understand the English influence, we need to return to a muddy pitch in Wolverhampton. In November 1969, Swedish TV premiered the football show Tipsextra with the Wolverhampton vs. Sunderland game. British matches have been televised in Sweden ever since and this has contributed to the rise of a British-influenced supporter culture. In the 1990s, parallel to the decline of Swedish club football's international success, attendance numbers dropped, although since the late 1990s interest has again risen. A well-organised, vocal and numerous supporter's movement and many new stadiums have been important in this development. Swedish domestic league football has been portrayed as an alternative to the hyper commercial international leagues, and the fact that Sweden has a 51% rule (i.e., that clubs cannot sell more than 49% of their shares, effectively keeping them membership owned) has made Swedish football less interesting for foreign investors but seemingly more interesting for domestic supporters. Both the men's and women's first divisions have benefited from the fact that they are rather open and uncertain, with many clubs having a realistic chance of winning the title. However, many issues remain, especially those relating to the differences in resources and media coverage.

Present and future

The popularity and societal relevance of football show no signs of diminishing. At present, football is by far the largest sport in Sweden with increasing activities at both the elite and grassroots level. Its greatest successes have been achieved by the women's teams, and in the 2000s the national team has won medals in the Olympics, World Cups and European Championships. In addition, during the late 1990s and early 2000s the Swedish premier division, *Damallsvenskan*, was arguably Europe's leading league (UEFA, 2022a). However, due to diminishing financial resources, Swedish clubs have now been surpassed by clubs in France, Germany, England, Spain, and the Netherlands (UEFA, 2022b).

Swedish football has reached its position through hard work, often by voluntary leaders in local clubs. As a response to society's demands for accessibility and inclusion, phenomena such as walking football, futsal (indoor football) and football on artificial turf have been introduced. Football is now a year-round sport, which causes difficulties for smaller winter sports such as bandy at youth levels. Swedish football seeks to build legitimacy through several initiatives as an integration arena and, not least, by engaging numerous migrants and asylum seekers in recent years (see also Peterson, 2000). Additionally, football, together with other sports, is a democratic platform in so-called "segregated areas", where sport activities ideally become a key part in the shaping of individual identity and local community (Svenska Fotbollförbundet, n.d.).

Football's dominant position is maintained with the help of commercial interests; interests that often go hand in hand with increased professionalisation, media attention and societal significance. This position also creates conflicts and is a challenge when the football association's interest does not always align with other federations in the Swedish sports movement (Ljunggren, 2020). Swedish sports are based on a model in which solidarity and distribution between traditional, voluntary, non-profit ideals and commercial market interests are essential (Norberg, 2014). The 51% rule is probably the most evident example, where Sports-Ltd receives a maximum of 49% of the votes at annual meetings, which means that all sports associations continue to be governed by their members. Strictly speaking, this limits the Swedish clubs' opportunities to keep the best players, who instead go abroad where they can earn more. On the one hand, this shows the potential of the Swedish sports model and the 51% rule's ability to balance sport performance with other objectives. On the other hand, it limits owners in their ability to invest and govern clubs, which ultimately also limits the competitiveness of Swedish football clubs internationally.

Recently, another conflict has flared up which in the long-term risks threatening the Swedish sports model. Despite the fact that Swedish children's and youth football account for 46% of the number of active people aged 7–25, SvFF, in a spirit of solidarity, has long "accepted" a 14% share of state support. However, in May 2021 a new ceiling rule was introduced, voted on and democratically won by a majority of federations in the Swedish Sports Confederation. This rule means that a single special sports federation can receive a maximum of 10% of the state's financial support. In short, it means that the boundaries of solidarity have been crossed and SvFF is now investigating the possibility of "own" state funds, which in the long run would disconnect football from the rest of the Swedish sports movement (Svenska Fotbollförbundet, 2022).

Conflicts between major and minor federations have always existed in Swedish sport (Ljunggren, 2020). The Swedish sports model, based on solidarity between federations, now has a new challenge, this time driven by its largest federation. How this conflict is managed, and whether it can be resolved in a satisfactory manner by the involved parties, will be crucial for the future of Swedish football and the entire Swedish sports movement. It also makes the conflict between elite and grassroots sport in the Swedish sports model visible. However, there are some signs of democratic "health" in this model, where democratic issues repeatedly need to be raised and discussed in deliberative dialogues. Historically, conflicts have been resolved whilst maintaining community and solidarity. Such tensions often indicate an unwavering desire to commit to what is best for football and for sport in general, but not always. SvFF appears to be playing a hazardous democratic game that could disconnect it from the Swedish sports movement, thereby ending the Swedish sports model and the solidarity between federations. King or not, at present Swedish football is navigating choppy waters.

References

Alsarve, D. (2014). *I ständig strävan efter framgång? Föreningsdemokratins innehåll och villkor i Örebro sportklubb 1908–89* [The everlasting endeavours for success? The contents and conditions of associative democracy in Örebro Sportklubb 1908–89]. Örebro universitet.

Andersson, T. (2002). *Kung fotboll: Den svenska fotbollens kulturhistoria från 1800-talets slut till 1950* [King Football: the cultural history of Swedish football from the end of the 19th century until 1950]. Symposion.

Andersson, T. (2011). *"Spela fotboll bondjävlar!": En studie av svensk klubbkultur och lokal identitet från 1950 till 2000-talets början* ["Play football peasant shits!" A study of Swedish club culture and local identity during the 1950–2000s]. Symposion.

Annerstedt, C. (2000). Kropp, idrott och hälsa: Dåtid, nutid och framtid [Body, sport and health: Past, present and future]. *Idrott, historia & samhälle*, 20(1), 10–26.
Botelho, V., & Skogvang, B. O. (2013). The pioneers – early years of the Scandinavian emigration of women footballers. *Soccer & Society*, 14(6), 799–815.
Brus, A., & Trangbæk, E. (2003). Asserting the right to play – women's football in Denmark. *Soccer & Society*, 4(2–3), 95–111.
Cox, B. (2012). The rise and fall of 'The Girl Footballer' in New Zealand during 1921. *The International Journal of the History of Sport*, 29(3), 444–471.
Dahlén, P. (2008). *Sport och medier: En introduktion* [Sport and media: An introduction]. IJ-forlaget.
Ericsson, C. (2004). *Fotboll, bandy och makt: idrott i brukssamhället* [Football, bandy and power: Sport in the industrial community]. Carlsson.
Ericsson, C. (2013). *Bandybaronen i folkhemmet: Familjen De Geer, bruket och folket* [The bandy baron in the people's home: The de Geer family, industry and the people]. Carlsson.
Ericsson, C., Horgby, B., & Sund, B. (2019). *Fotboll, kommersialisering, demokrati.* [Football, commercialisation, democracy]. Bokförlaget idrottsforum.org.
Hedenborg, S., & Kvarnström, L. (2009). *Det svenska samhället 1720–2006: Böndernas och arbetarnas tid* [The Swedish society 1720–2006: The time of the farmers and the workers]. Studentlitteratur.
Hjelm, J., & Olofsson, E. (2003). A breakthrough: Women's football in Sweden. *Soccer & Society*, 4(2–3), 182–204.
Horgby, B. (2012). *Kampen om facket: Den socialdemokratiska hegemonins förändringar* [The struggle for the union: Changes in the social democratic hegemony]. Boréa. Umeå.
Janzon, B. (1978). *Manschettyrken, idrott och hälsa: Studier kring idrottsrörelsen i Sverige särskilt Göteborg, intill 1900* [White-collar labor, sports and health: Studies of the sports movement in Sweden, especially Gothenburg, until 1900]. Göteborgs universitet.
Jenkel, L. (2020). The FA's ban of women's football 1921 in the contemporary press – a historical discourse analysis. *Sport in History*, 41(2), 239–259.
Ljunggren, J. (2020). *Den svenska idrottens historia* [The history of Swedish sport]. Natur & Kultur.
Macbeth, J. (2002). The development of women's football in Scotland. *The Sports Historian*, 22(2), 149–163.
Peterson, T. (1993). *Den svengelska modellen: Svensk fotboll i omvandling under efterkrigstiden* [The Swenglish model: Swedish football in transition in the afterwar period]. Arkiv, Lund.
Peterson, T. (2000). Idrotten som integrationsarena? [Sport as an arena for integration?]. In G. R. o. S. Lundberg (Ed.), *Att möta främlingar* [To meet strangers] (pp. 141–166). Arkiv, Lund.
Sjöblom, P. (2006). *Den institutionaliserade tävlingsidrotten: Kommuner, idrott och politik i Sverige under 1900-talet* [The institutionalised competitive sports: Municipalities, sports and politics in Sweden in the 20th century]. Almqvist & Wiksell.
Sund, B. (1997). *Fotbollens maktfält: Svensk fotbollshistoria i ett internationellt perspektiv* [Football's fields of power: Swedish football history in an international perspective]. Svenska fotbollsförlaget.
Sund, B. (2007). *Fotbollsindustrin* [The football industry]. Nomen förlag.

Svensson, D., & Oppenheim, F. (2018). Equalize it!: 'Sportification' and the transformation of gender boundaries in emerging Swedish women's football, 1966–1999. *The International Journal of the History of Sport, 35*(6), 575–590.

Svensson, D., & Svensson, R. (2021). 'Science says': Swedish sports coaching and science during the twentieth century. In D. Day (Ed.), *Sports coaching in Europe* (pp. 56–75). Routledge.

Svensson, R. (2019). *Från träningsoverall till trenchcoat: Tränarpositionens förändring inom svensk herrelitfotboll mellan 1960- och 2010-talet* [From tracksuit to trench coat: The changing position of the Swedish male elite soccer coach between the 1960s and the 2010s]. Örebro University.

Svenska Fotbollförbundet. (n.d.). *Mångfald – Organisation och samhälle* [Diversity – Organisation and society]. Retrieved November 25, 2022, from https://svff.svenskfotboll.se/samhallsnytta/mangfald/ett-steg-framat/

Svenska Fotbollförbundet (SvFF). (2004). *100 år: Svenska Fotbollförbundets jubileumsbok 1904–2004* [100 years: The Swedish FA's anniversary book 1904–2004]. Stroemberg Media Group.

Svenska Fotbollförbundet. (2022, March 1). *Takregel i RF-stödet: SvFF:s talan lämnas utan bifall* [Ceiling rule in the RF-support: SvFF's claim is left without approval]. Retrieved November 25, 2022, from https://svff.svenskfotboll.se/nyheter/2022/02/takregel-i-rf-stodet-svffs-talan-lamnas-ted%20tnt-update-recent/

Tolvhed, H. (2015). *På damsidan: Femininitet, motstånd och makt i svensk idrott 1920–1990* [On the women's side: Femininity, resistance and power in Swedish sports 1920–1990]. Makadam.

UEFA. (2022a). Women's association club coefficients, 2003/04. Retrieved November 24, 2022, from https://www.uefa.com/nationalassociations/uefarankings/womenscountry/#/yr/2004

UEFA. (2022b). Women's association club coefficients, 2020/21. Retrieved November 24, 2022, from https://www.uefa.com/nationalassociations/uefarankings/womenscountry/#/yr/2021

Wikberg, K. (2005). *Amatör eller professionist?: Studier rörande amatörfrågan i svensk tävlingsidrott 1903–1967* [Amateur or professional? Studies of the amateur question in Swedish competitive sports 1903–1967]. SISU idrottsböcker.

Williams, J. (2003). *A Game for Rough Girls? A History of Women's Football in Britain.* Routledge.

Yttergren, L. (1996). *Täflan är lifvet: Idrottens organisering och sportifiering i Stockholm 1860–1898* [Competition is life: Sportification and organisation of sports in Stockholm 1860–1898]. Stockholmia.

Yttergren, L. (2012). *Träna är livet: Träning, utbildning och vetenskap i svensk friidrott, 1880–1995* [Training is life: Training, education and science in Swedish athletics, 1880–1995]. idrottsforum.org.

Zethrin, N.-O. (2015). *Mellan masskonsumtion och folkrörelse: Idrottens kommersialisering under mellankrigstiden* [Between mass consumption and popular movement: The commercialisation of sport in the interwar period]. Örebro universitet.

Part II

Specific Issues and Themes

Professionalisation and Changing Practices

Chapter 6

Football Companies in Sweden and Their Democratic Framework

Björn Horgby and Christer Ericsson

Introduction

Democratic voluntary organisations have played an essential role in the formation of modern Sweden. Historically, the sports clubs are organised within a democratic structure in the same way as other national voluntary organisations, governed by nationally accepted by-laws. Based on this, previous research claim that there is a special Swedish sports model based on the democratic principles of the popular movement (Lindroth & Norberg, 2002; Norberg, 2016). However, as a result of the commercialisation of football clubs, ran as corporations challenge their democratic foundations. In recent decades, especially male elite football clubs have become at an ever-faster pace commercialised. Among other things the sport activities sometimes are conducted as joint-stock companies; companies who buy and sell athletes. Many sports clubs have been professionalised, resulting in a considerably weakened membership influence. The commercialisation affects the democratic concept (Horgby & Ericsson, 2020). In the present chapter – with the focus on male elite football – we discuss such processes and its impact on the democracy of the football clubs.

First, we specifically analyse changes in the governing patterns from the 1960s to 2010 in two historically successful male clubs AIK from Stockholm and IFK Norrköping from the industrial town Norrköping. How did these clubs change their governance and how did the members react? How did the power relations change between the elected trustees and the professional officials? How did they pursue a well-articulated structure of responsibilities and decision-making? Seen from the perspective of the modern elite football expansion in Europe, there are mainly two ways of organising activities – either as democratic associations or as company-run clubs. However, the challenges of commercialisation forced the democratic concept to change and adopt new standards.

Governance models and logics

Based on the overall democratic sports model, it is possible to distinguish four governing models for how Swedish football associations are governed. In these, the

DOI: 10.4324/9781003280729-10

democratic foundation plays a key role. According to a democratic framework, members govern themselves by means of a representative democratic process – as in the Swedish voluntary associations – which implies proposals are discussed and approved by a governing assembly. The trustees are elected by the members in an annual meeting. The trustees can delegate deciding power and the decision-making can be confirmed by the members. The members govern the organisation directly or indirectly through the elected trustees. The organisation is governed by rules and norms. In a representative democracy association, there are rules on how to elect representatives; how the trustees shall act on behalf of the association and its members; and how their responsibilities will be expressed through elections and freedom from liability. Governance is built on democratic values and norms, including principles such as equality amongst members, non-discrimination of minorities by the majority; the right to express opinions and get their points of view tested democratically at member meetings (Alsarve, 2014; Dahl, 1999; Horgby, 2012). In addition to the democratic governance model, a more patriarchal variant has also developed, where one or a few leader's rules, but "their" club is based on the same basic democratic premises as in the democratic governance model.

The company governance model developed as football became professionalised. The organisation is managed as a company based on necessary professional skills. This governance model is also fenced off by the premises of the democratic model. So far, the Swedish Sports Confederation (RF) demands that governance will be based on representative democracy and on the charter adopted by RF. The sports clubs cannot be owned by individuals or companies, such as in the English Premier League. Finally, the fourth governance model, the supporter-influenced one, is a reaction to the undemocratic tendencies of the corporate-governed model and means supporter groups besides the democratic system tries to influence the governance (Horgby & Ericsson, 2020).

The relationship between the governing models is influenced by three logics: one democratic, one competitive and one commercial. The goal of democratic logic is to establish, preserve and sometimes re-establish democratic conditions in the clubs. The short- and long-term goal of competition logic is to win success on the football field. Based on the logic, the clubs try to create a more efficient organisation. The need to succeed makes clubs strive to strengthen their financial resources, to become better equipped when they must invest in players and coaches in an increasingly competitive market.

Finally, the commercial logic is a consequence of the competition logic. According to this, players and clubs become actors in a commercial market and need to adapt to its conditions. This leads to the development of the business model. According to the logic of competition the clubs who have been governed based on the principles of democratic logic, are increasingly becoming commercial companies. Regardless of logic, however, the control must be perceived as legitimate. Success creates legitimacy, but within the framework of the Swedish sports model it is necessary to appear as a democratic association. In commercialised football, the democratic and the commercial logic interact (Dahl, 1999; Horgby & Ericsson, 2020).

In the democratic governance model three types of actor's exercise power within the club – the elected representatives, the employed functionaries, and the members. In the commercialisation process, parts of the organisation are professionalised and power is transferred from the elected representatives to the employed functionaries, who govern without a clear democratic mandate (Horgby, 2012; Horgby & Ericsson, 2020). The internal governance conflicts with the democratic logic and the democratic governance model. In the business model membership is weakened and partially replaced by a "supportership" – with no difference between members or supporters. Now dissatisfied supporters can act both within and outside the democratic framework.

According to our underlying thesis, the governance is based on the actual power relations. Among other things, the power resources are built by the access of the necessary knowledge of governing. Here we use the sociologist Pierre Bourdieu's concept of capital – economic, social and cultural capital. Three important forms of capital in running a football club are the "football capital", namely the knowledge of playing and leading the club; the "association capital" needed for the management of a democratically organised club; and the "corporate capital" defined as the knowledge needed to lead and administer a company (Bourdieu, 1993).

The task of the leadership is mostly to solve *problems of governance* such as insufficient economic or personal resources in order to keep up with a competitive market. Other kinds of problems are organisational. Actions to solve these problems can be analysed as governing strategies. Even though, the ways of solving the problems of governance are historically dated. These strategies are changed as the male elite football is commercialised and professionalised, and as the logic of competition induced a need for more effective organisations. As an effect of these changes, a corporate model becomes predominant (Horgby & Ericsson, 2020).

The specific logic that is predominant within a club influences the distribution of power. In this sense the Bourdieuan concept of different kinds of capital is especially useful to understand the differentiation of knowledge and power resources within such organisations. For example, the association capital is useful in the democratic practice and the corporate capital in the governing of corporate clubs (Bourdieu, 1993).

The impact of commercialisation on two Swedish football clubs

In the 1960s, live football audiences significantly decreased and as a result the clubs' revenue. The financial needs of the elite clubs grew by the professionalisation of the player market and by a growing competition between the clubs, which meant they had to pay higher salaries; make sure the players trained more and better; and organise the game as well as the activities around the team in a more efficient way. Initially the solution was bingo and lotteries. It took some time before sponsorship and advertising became a significant source of income. AIK had most members of the male elite football clubs in Sweden. Despite this the club had weak finances. The costs expanded as the players became professionally employed. It was necessary to find new financiers (Bolling & Johrén, 2012). Strong leaders from the business world tried to strengthen the network of sponsors and AIK funded a joint stock company managing sponsorship money. Bingo still provided most income in an increasingly commercially governed club (Bolling & Johrén, 2012).

A new problem of governance emerged in the early 1990s. Hooligans disorderly behaviour lowered the income of sponsoring. As a solution of the economical and organisational problems of governance, the club leadership tried to create a more effective organisation and mobilised the members and the supporters in envisioned AIK becoming the leading elite football club in Sweden. This goal-driven vision guided the club in the creation of continuity and stability. Strict economic controlling and the professionalisation of the organisation formed a more effective governance, a significant element in a company-driven model (Andersson, 2016; Bolling & Johrén, 2012). Football successes, growing audience, rising incomes from sponsors and television and the sale of players improved the economic situation. In 1997, the team was for the first time composed of solely professional players.

In 2000, the club formed a joint-stock company, to which it transferred the brand and the football business. But the profits disappeared as the club spent too much, paid higher salaries and bought expensive players. In 2000, the association founded a joint-stock company, who ran the business and owned the trademark. It resulted in SEK 50 million SEK (EUR 4.6 million) gain as sponsors, members and supporters bought the stock shares. But still the annual accounts showed between SEK 30 and 40 million (EUR 2.74 million and 3.66 million) in red figures. The board had to slim the organisation and reduce costs. In 1999, the national sports movement (RF) allowed the formation of joint-stock companies for sport associations. RF decided the members still had to be the majority shareholders. The association AIK owns 51% of the stock share. The rule of the 51% was supported by the members and the supporters but was challenged by some leaders. Notably, the hooligan organisation The Black Army made threats supporting the rule. The formation of football corporations illustrates how clubs adapted their structure to the conditions of the market (Bolling & Johrén, 2012). The Danish club Bröndby was the prime role model in such transition (Andersson, 2016).

In AIK, the company-controlled model was introduced in several stages. Leaders were recruited with company capital. They could develop sponsorships and a more company-like organisation. Soon, they began to target the business and professionalise the organisation, by transferring non-profit work to employees with professional skills. A later step was to transfer parts of the business to joint-stock companies and introduce the share on the stock exchange.

From a democratically governed club to a company-governed

At the same time, the power in IFK Norrköping was centralised to the board; the member democracy was handled as a communication issue. During the 1970s, the club began to seek support from the business community. The logic of the competition made it necessary to find new ways of achieving success (IFK, 1970). Initially IFK sought to solve the organisational problems by creating a hybrid between a company and the democratic organisation in a project organisation based on non-profit working members (IFK, 1975). In the end of the 1970s, some businessmen entered as the elected representatives. Another step was the registration of the club badge as a brand (IFK, 1978–1979). As a third step IFK started goal governance – with a goal document. This was a typical business model also used in public activities (IFK, 1980–1982).

The logic of the competition meant that these steps were insufficient. The big change was to professionalise the organisation where football was separated from the economy. A banker was first hired as chairman and then as club director (IFK, 1987). In 1990, advertising and marketing issues were outsourced to a club-owned limited company. The next step was to organise the business based on a customer/executor model, where the board made overall decisions about goals and strategies while the salaried employees performed them. This kind of separation between client and contractor was becoming more and more common in both public operations and in the business world (Ericsson et al., 2016). In order to deal with the hooligan problems, it was ensured – just like in AIK – that the organised supporters created a positive arena culture. Thus, the grandstand culture was made part of the governance model (IFK, 1990–1994).

In the mid-1990s, IFK used corporate strategies to develop the business. The democracy was no longer seen as a governance problem. It was all about being successful and improving the results by increasing economic turnover (IFK, 1997–2002). In 2011 IFK was not just a football club but a company group. Linked to the association was the venture capital company, which owned many of the players. When the club communicated, it used management terms and talked about football as a product (IFK, 2009–2013).

The company-governance model was introduced in IFK in several stages. First, the club sought to develop the organisation with the help of project management. Non-profit forces worked in this hybrid organisation. Leaders with company capital were soon recruited and began to target the business and professionalise. The non-profit forces were replaced by employees with professional skills. The transition to a customer/executor organisation was another step in the development as well as the spin-off of the business to a joint-share company (Horgby et al., 2020). The road to the business model thus looked quite similar, but also featured some differences; among other things, IFK Norrköping does not conduct football in the form of a stock-share company.

Some comparisons

In the 1980s Djurgårdens IF tried to solve economic problems through corporate practices. The club established the brand "Stockholms Stolthet" (The Pride of Stockholm) and outsourced the management of the brand and the commercial business to a joint-stock company. As a corporation director without football capital governed, the club did not achieve the goals and the financial problems continued to the turn of the century (Andersson, 2016). Some venture capitalists and the formation of a company turned the economy of the club around. In the beginning of the millennium the club won the first league three times. Then, the trend ended. Players emigrated to more lucrative leagues. The company's vision was also too large to fit their economic framework (Andersson, 2016).

The patriarchal leader Eric Persson governed Malmö FF 1937–1975. Under his leadership the democratic logic was the guiding-star. From the late 1960s, he changed and saw the corporate governing as a possibility and probably a precondition for being successful as huge resources was needed to professionalise the players. He recruited a bank manager as his successor. Already in the 1970s, Malmö formed a corporate governed leadership. Persson also recruited a professional manager. The club introduced the distinction between the club director and the sports director. The board of trustees, the team leader and the players lost their power previously granted in the selection of team members and the definition of football tactics and strategies. In the creation of a more effective and successful football, the club solved a central problem of governance. In 1989, a totally professional troupe was introduced to strengthen the training and the schooling of the players. The efforts to professionalise football combined with the development of a corporate model including a more effective economic governance and a professional organisation was the path taken (Andersson, 2011).

The corporate model and democracy

The processes of professionalisation and commercialisation greatly affected the democratic conditions when the logic of competition led the clubs to develop a company-governed model in which the association democracy was ignored. It was more important to create an effective organisation to achieve sporting success than to ensure that members' democratic demands were met. The Bosman verdict and the "shock globalisation" accelerated the process of organising the clubs in a global food chain, where Swedish male football became part of a commercial wheel (Andersson, 2011). The competition logic thus challenged the democratic logic and made it more difficult to maintain the democratic governance model.

When the organisation was professionalised, the marketing department became responsible for the sponsor contacts. The sports organisation optimised the team's conditions. Further, the leaders needed new skills. The club was organised vertically in an organisation governed by leaders with the necessary business management skills. The previous forms of association capital lost its validity. This would have been significant for leaders who dealt with democratic challenges in the popular movements. In addition to the business capital, the business leaders' social skills became important in creating good relations with sponsors and advertising buyers.

As another consequence of the commercial logic parts of the power transferred to senior officials with a similar position as their counterparts in business. In addition, large parts of the membership were transferred to a small group of members with the capital resources used in the management of successful companies. Now the value of membership was devalued both democratically and as an identity. The democratic shortcomings reinforced the need of creating success in order to legitimise the business. But when the democratic logic and its value system came into conflict with the leadership failing to create enough success, the leadership power eroded by the conflict with dissatisfied members and supporters.

Reactions to the corporate model

The disgruntled members and supporters both acted in conflict to and according to the democratic logic and value system. During the 1990s, many supporters organised themselves into supporter organisations. A small part of the dissatisfaction was threatening and violent and was directed at individual leaders and players. The supporter activities could also be directed at corporate governance and at undemocratic phenomena (Green, 2009; Horgby et al., 2020). The problems of the organised hooligans were greatest in Stockholm but also occurred in Scania and Gothenburg (Andersson, 2011; Green, 2009; Radman 2013). Violent supporters have tried to gain influence over the organisation, but the mobilisation of members has partially curbed these attempts. On the other hand, threats and violence have led several leaders to leave their posts (Andersson, 2016; Wahlberg, 2017). Players have been threatened if they have considered leaving the club (Andersson, 2016; Billing et al., 1999; Green 2009).

The Swedish Football Supporters' Union has nationally and internationally defended the democratic rules of the modern football – including the 51% rule. The defence of the rule distinguishes Sweden from many other European countries. Therefore, the Swedish model has become a notable example (SvD, 2005; Wahlberg, 2017). Organised supporters have also defended the rule and the democratic model locally when clubs sought to circumvent the regulations. In 2017 AFC Eskilstuna played in the *Allsvenskan*, the men's premier division. The supporters in the other clubs treated AFC as undemocratic. The "owner" is also chairmen of the club, elected for ten years. The cost of membership is also much higher than in other clubs (Wahlberg, 2017).

The popular movement democracy based on democratic norms and values creates trust in the democratic institutions, as well as trust in the associations are governed in a legitimate way. Violent supporters change the conditions through threats and violence, which leads to the undermining of the basic trust in the associations and their democratic foundations. The possibilities to follow a democratic logic are weakened. When supporter organisations mobilise their democratic power, they counteract this tendency. Therefore, the clubs have urged the supporters to act.

Women in commercial football

The establishment of women's football took place between the years 1965 and 1980. After a tentative start women's football in Sweden has expand rapidly. However, male elite football has and has had a hegemonic position in relation to women's football. It has affected the media and the public interest, as well as the commercial and organisational conditions (Hjelm, 2004). In brief, we discuss women's football club as their processes of commercialisation is much slower and the democratic framework stronger.

In 1978, the Elite Women's Football Association (from 2013 Elitfotboll Dam, EFD) was formed to pursue the women's football associations' issues of interest, with the main task of developing the first league (*Damallsvenskan*) and the second league together with the member clubs. The specified goals were Damallsvenskan would become a world-class series; the Swedish women's football would develop its talents to become world class; and the talent and player development would contribute to the success of the various national teams. Since the end of the 2000s, Swedish women's football club has had a hard time maintaining its high level. The commercialisation processes are likely to contribute to Swedish football having developed more slowly than competing countries. For example, several major continental clubs with men's soccer on the programme have invested heavily in women's football. Economically women's football is far smaller scale than men's football, which means the financial conditions of the women's clubs look completely different.

A contributing reason is probably the commercialisation processes have developed more slowly in Swedish football than in the competing countries. The women football has lived in the shadows in the media and struggles with low audience figures. Which in turn affects the opportunities of sponsorship and advertising revenue. The financial conditions of the women's clubs have been limited. As a result, player remuneration is much lower in the women football and the professionalisation processes are of much later date. As we noted earlier the male hegemony will diminish when the larger male clubs will hook on the international trend to start and develop female teams as Paris SG, Juventus, Chelsea, and Barcelona. The differences between men's and women's football have meant the commercialisation processes have been of a much smaller extent and the democratic governance model is stronger than in the male football. Based on this assumption, let's look on some women's football clubs.

In the late 1990s, Umeå IK became one of the leading women's football clubs in the country. During the 2000s, the club won the First League seven times and the Champions League two years in a row (Horgby et al., 2020). The club built its finances on audience and sponsorship income, which generated enough resources to strengthen the player squad. During the successful years, the club tripled its annual turnover and some of the best players became professional players in the club. At the end of the 2000s, the successful period ended. Costs increased rapidly when the women football in Sweden became more business-driven, at the same time as Umeå's revenues weakened significantly, mainly due to reduced sponsorship revenues (Andersson, 2016; Horgby et al., 2020). The club was threatened with bankruptcy. (DN, 2015; Horgby et al., 2020). One part of the reorganisation of the economy and a way to solve the emerging organisational governance problems was to leave the democratic governance model, where the work was largely done non-profit by the elected leaders and instead organise the association according to a business model with an employed club director (Horgby et al., 2020). Umeå was not the only club in the first league that had major financial problems during the 2010s. Although the salaries were low, the players were professional and there was fierce competition on the player market for the most skilled players.

The question we ask based on the example Umeå is whether the introduction of the corporate governance in a sports club based on professional skills presupposes that there are enough financial resources. One possible answer is that the financial support needs to be enough to hire professional resources with the needed organisational company capital and the ability skills to build a successfully functioning business organisation, which can both manage the club and be able to create a stable economic base. A complementary answer is that a corporate governed club also needs the non-profit leadership with the organisational capital necessary to solve governance problems arising in a club, where the financial conditions in the association are on the brink of the abyss. After the successful years and as the domestic competition increased, the democratic model of governance no longer worked. There was also no financial or organisational space to develop a successful corporate model.

In contrast to Umeå and some other clubs such as Eskilstuna United DFF slowly developed a more resistant model. When the team took the step up to Damallsvenskan in 2013, the club was well prepared. The club had conducted a long-term and continuous improvement work and strived to be professional. Compared to Umeå, Eskilstuna United appears to be a more successfully managed club, where corporate governance has not taken place with the help of corporatisation, but by combining the non-profit and the professional work in a goal-oriented organisation. Based on its democratic foundation, it has succeeded in creating a company-controlled organisation.

Regarding women football, the following observations can be made. In recent years most women leagues in Europe have become more professional. In comparison with the male teams, however, the women clubs have very few resources. The economic conditions – understood as the conditions for developing a pure business model – have been less sufficient in women's football than in men's football. The clubs have been hybrid organisations that combine democracy and corporate governance. The economy has not allowed it to be possible to develop a completely professional organisation, which is governed by a business model. The biggest problem is that the audience figures are still too low, which means that the clubs cannot create a stable financial basis.

Towards a new corporate model?

The supporter organisations around Sweden reacted against the democratic conditions in AFC Eskilstuna. The club tried to circumvent the association democratic rules of the game, even though the Swedish football teams need a democratically functioning membership activity to be granted elite license. The club then did not resemble any other club in the Swedish elite football (Horgby & Ericsson, 2020). The supporter organisations thought the club did not want to include members and lacked the democratic standards of the Swedish football clubs (Horgby & Ericsson, 2020). However, the case of AFC is not unique. We believe it is a sign of a distinct and growing problem within the Swedish football family.

In recent years businessmen in some small- and medium-sized clubs have in practice taken control of "their" club by the virtue of extensive financial support. These clubs often have few members, high membership fees and control over who may become members, which in practice is contrary to the RF statutes, according to which everyone should have the right to become members. For the "owners" the purpose is to be able to govern at their own discretion. One such club is the women football club Kopparberg/Göteborg. It was run by a beverage manufacturer who even named the club. After the club won the Damallsvenskan, he lost interest in the club, which was taken over by BK Häcken. The members, however, received insufficient information about the club. In 2019, Kopparberg applied for municipal grant. The City of Gothenburg rejected the application as the club did not fulfil the democratic framework, such as the overall right to become member and the right to participate in the activities of the club (Aftonbladet, 2021). The club probably did not want any members. Or as the Swedish Football Association, SvFF, puts it, "the club has not handled the membership applications in the right way and those who have become members lack influence which significantly deviates the RF charter template" (Aftonbladet, 2021).

The top league club Östersunds FK (ÖFK) – relegated from Allsvenskan in 2021 – has developed a variant of this form of business model. Here it seems as if the power has been transferred to the club director, who runs the club as a company with a weak member influence. The millions the club earned on its successful European game have flowed out of the club and the elite license has been chronically threatened. Today the situation is urgent again and, in the attempt, to save the club, it decided to outsource parts of its operations. The club dismiss faithful servants and are planning to outsource their tasks. Private companies' interest for profit will handle the club's activities such as the events, the security and the sponsorship sales – the core businesses of a football club. Critics claim that this kind of change creates risks of conflict and corruption (Aftonbladet, 2021). The managing of the outsourcing business of ÖFK raises some questions of the club's democratic orientation.

Another example of the twisting of the model is Tyrsö FF, which qualified to the first league in 2010, and shortly afterwards, in 2012 and 2013 the team became Swedish champions. The success story ended 2014 when the team lost the women Champions League final against Wolfsburg (Horgby & Ericsson, 2020). The short-lived success story began as an entrepreneur joined the club and began to transform the club into a company. This required a completely different financial strength. To develop the economy, the club created a company-run organisation with a network of sponsors. With the sports company, the women team got its own finances. But already in the winter of 2014 it turned out the club had major financial problems, which ended in SvFF announced on financial grounds Tyresö FF was not granted the elite license for the next season (Horgby & Ericsson, 2020; Aftonbladet, 2014). In Tyresö a small group of entrepreneurs took over the club and ran it based on a vision. The member influence was extremely limited. The successes legitimised the governance. Tyresö is not an example of a developed corporate governance, but instead an example of what can happen as entrepreneurs could govern without taking a corresponding responsibility for the entire organisation. Consequently, the association and its company took too great financial risks in the attempts of reaching sport success.

What these clubs have in common is the ruler or rulers want to be at peace when exercising power. They want to be business leaders who control their businesses. The democratic logic, however, means that they have been noticed as deviations in the Swedish sports model.

Conclusion

The Swedish welfare model developed as a contract between civil society and the strengthening state. In the 1980s, this contract began to weaken, and a new more corporate driven model of governing arose, with less civic influence of government-controlled businesses as privatisation and professionalisation transferred democratic power to capital interests. The same kind of processes changed the sport model as the leading football clubs became corporations especially in male football, but it is also a growing tendency in women's football (Ericsson et al., 2016).

Historically the voluntary associations in Sweden are based on representative democracy – so are the elite football clubs. The logic of competition forced the clubs as well as their teams to become more efficient, professional and commercial. The democratic logic was outflanked by the commercial logic in the formation of a corporate model of governance. The economy was the main problem of governance, solved by creating a more effective and professional organisation and by developing the trademark, sponsorship, public incomes and by refining and selling players on the globalised market. The commercial logic forced the clubs to re-organise themselves as companies framed by the democratic framework. The latter was a prerequisite for the participation in the national football leagues. The clubs had to balance the democratic preconditions and the need of using the necessary corporate tools. The act of balancing also implied that the members and the supporters referred to the democratic logic in order to act against corporate governance. Some of these supporters became hooligans who discouraged the audience and the sponsors.

In 1999, the national sports movement allowed running the football business in joint-stock companies if the members owned 51% of the stock share. It created a hybrid corporate democracy with lack of democracy. Even earlier, clubs outsourced parts of the business such as transports, marketing and the financing trade of players in venture capital companies. Branding and goal governance were other ways of solving the problems of governance. The division between the buyers and the executive power of the employed professionals resulted in a weakening influence of members. The transformation from the democratic to the corporate model also needed leaders with new competences – from organisational and football capital to corporate and social capital. The lack of success undermined the power of the leadership. The organised supporters counteracted hooliganism and created a positive atmosphere around football. A rather new problem related to the corporate model is the intent to stretch democratic rules and values. In the ambition of being successful, some entrepreneurs govern their clubs as their own companies without considering the members. SvFF has not reacted against this form of corporate model. The reactions have rather come from the media and the supporter unions.

References

Aftonbladet. (2014, March 4). *Tyresös damer riskerar konkurs* [Tyresö's women's team are at risk of bankruptcy]. Retrieved November 28, 2022, from https://www.aftonbladet.se/senastenytt/ttsport/sport/a/qnQlMO/tyresos-damer-riskerar-konkurs

Aftonbladet. (2021, February 15). *Klubben är ute på farligt vatten* [The club is out in dangerous waters]. Retrieved November 28, 2022, from https://www.aftonbladet.se/sportbladet/fotboll/a/weKxl1/klubben-ar-ute-pa-farligt-vatten

Alsarve, D. (2014). *I ständig strävan efter framgång* [In the constant pursuit of success]. Örebro studies in History.

Andersson, T. (2011). *"Spela fotboll bondjävlar!"* En studie av svensk klubbfotboll och lokal identitet från 1950 till 2000-talets början, Del 1 ["Play football bloody peasants!" A study of Swedish club football and local identity from 1950 to the early 2000s, Part 1]. Symposion.
Andersson, T. (2016). *"Spela fotboll bondjävlar!"* En studie av svensk klubbfotboll och lokal identitet från 1950 till 2000-talets början, Del 2 ["Play football bloody peasants!" A study of Swedish club football and local identity from 1950 to the early 2000s, Part 2]. Symposion.
Billing P., Franzén M., & Peterson T. (1999). *Vem vinner i längden?* [Who wins in the long run?] Arkiv förlag.
Bolling, H., & Johrén, A. (2012). *De första 116 åren* [The first 116 years]. AIK fotboll AB.
Bourdieu, P. (1993). *Kultursociologiska texter* [Cultural sociology texts]. Brutus Östlings förlag.
Dahl, A. R. (1999). *Demokratin och dess antagonister* [Democracy and its antagonists]. Demokratiakademin.
DN. (2015, June 4). *Ekonomisk kris i Umeå IK* [Economic crisis in Umeå IK]. Retrieved May 18, 2022, from https://www.dn.se/sport/fotboll/ekonomisk-kris-i-umea-ik-kan-ta-slut/
Ericsson, C., Horgby, B., & Ishihara, S. (2016). *Faderliga företagare i Sverige och Japan* [Fatherly entrepreneurs in Sweden and Japan]. Carlssons Bokförlag.
Green, A. (2009). *Fotboll och huliganism* [Football and hooliganism]. Stockholms universitet.
Hjelm, J. (2004). *Amazoner på plan* [Amazones on the field]. Borea bokförlag.
Horgby, B. (2012). *Kampen om facket* [The fight for the union]. Borea bokförlag.
Horgby, B., & Ericsson, C. (2020). *Football corporations and democracy in Sweden*. Retrieved June 3, 2022, from https://idrottsforum.org/horgby-ericsson200615-in-english/
Lindroth, J., & Norberg, R. J. (Eds.). (2002). *Ett idrottssekel. Riksidrottsförbundet 1903–2003* [A sports century National Sports Confederation 1903–2003]. Informationsförlaget.
Norberg, R. J. (Ed.). (2016). *Föreningen, laget och jaget* [The association, the team, and the self]. Centrum för idrottsforskning.
Radman, A. (2013). *Huliganlandskapet* [The hooligan landscape]. Malmö högskola.
SvD. (2005, April 6). *Sveriges- största -klubbar tar tag mot huliganerna* [Sweden's biggest clubs take on the hooligans]. Retrieved May 23, 2022, from https://www.svd.se/a/20e82de3-5a82-3a90-b7ce-093dd7ebd89e/sveriges-storsta-klubbar-tar-tag-mot-huliganerna
Wahlberg, M. (2017, July 25). AFC Eskilstuna bör bekämpas [AFC Eskilstuna should be fought]. *Aftonbladet*. Retrieved November 28, 2022, from https://www.aftonbladet.se/sportbladet/fotboll/a/BQa0G/afc-eskilstuna-bor-bekampas

Norrköpings stadsarkiv (Norrköping city archive)

IFK Norrköping arkiv: Styrelseprotokoll 1920–1993 [IFK Norrköping archive: Board minutes].
Mötes- och årsmötesprotokoll 1960–1993 [Meeting and annual meeting minutes 1960–1993].
Årsberättelser 1940–1996 [Annual reports 1940–1996].
Årsberättelser 1997–2016 [Annual reports 1940–1996].

Chapter 7

The Professionalisation of Finnish Football from the 1970s to 2000s
From Amateurs to Professionals

Jouni Lavikainen

Introduction

Tensions between amateurism and professionalism affected international football throughout the 20th century. When the popularity of football grew in Europe and South America in the interwar period, local sports elites, clinging to the ethos of amateurism, tried in vain to suppress commercialism and professionalism rising from the masses of working-class players, for whom the British ideal of a gentleman amateur held no appeal. Professionalisation followed often – but not always – similar pathways in different societal settings. From the 1920s Hungary (Molnar, 2007, p. 300) to mid-1900s Hongkong (Lee, 2013, pp. 604–607), the legalisation of professionalism was preceded by a period characterised by shamateurism, featuring "the usual panoply of under-the-table payments, inflated expenses, and invented jobs" (Goldblatt, 2007, p. 197).

The process was similar in the Nordic countries, albeit late by international comparison. The Nordic sports model was based on voluntary activity of sports associations and ideological commitment to amateurism (see Andersson & Carlsson, 2011; Peterson, 2008; Wikberg, 2005), not shared by FIFA or most of its member associations. Instead of establishing openly professional leagues, Nordic football associations safeguarded amateurism with policies similar to the International Olympic Committee (see Llewellyn & Gleaves, 2016). For example, in 1934, 36 of Malmö FF's players and leaders were banned from taking part in Swedish football because of financial compensations that had been paid to players. Although most bans were later revoked, Malmö FF was relegated to the second division (Wikberg, 2005, pp. 161–164). The amateur rules were overturned in Sweden, Denmark and Norway only in 1967, 1978 and 1984, respectively. Fully professional structures were not, however, immediately created, and remnants of the amateur era influenced Nordic elite football until the 1990s (Andersson & Hognestad, 2019).

In Finland, the amateur rules were incorporated into the national rules of football in 1907, and were nominally in effect until the 1970s. By this time, elite clubs had for decades paid players small under-the-table rewards based on points won in matches. Amateur regulations were dropped from the national rules

DOI: 10.4324/9781003280729-11

of competition in 1978 (FA of Finland: Rules of the Association, Rules of Competition, Rules of Punishments, October 1978, Hc1 Domestic Rules of Competition, FA of Finland's archive, Sports Museum of Finland's archive). This simple rule change had little effect on professionalisation. Most Finnish football leaders considered the attendances too low to support even a semi-professional league, and were reluctant to try to overcome the juridical obstacles to professionalism that applied also to other team sports in Finland. Players were not employees of their clubs, and their contracts should not be considered legal contracts of employment, it was often argued in the 1980s (see Lavikainen, 2018). This mentality did not stop the professionalisation of sport in Finland, but confined it to a club and individual level, and left the issue of shamateurism unaddressed.

The professionalisation of Finnish team sports has lately seen increasing interest from researchers (Lämsä et al., 2020; Tuikkanen, 2021), with football players so far receiving only limited attention. The aim of this chapter is to follow up on Szerovay and Itkonen's (2015) research by investigating pathways of individual players during a transition from amateurism to professionalism with methods of oral history. Main research questions are: How have elite male football players' sources of income changed in Finland from the 1970s to 2000s? How did players make their living when Finnish football remained outwardly amateur, and how did this change when professionalism became common in the 1990s?

In this chapter, *professionalisation* is defined similarly to Lämsä et al. (2020, pp. 59–60), as a process characterised by increasing rewards and time devoted to football, and football player's transition towards a profession comparable to others in the society. *Amateur* player works in a full-time job alongside playing and gets all or most of his livelihood from that job whereas a *professional* is legally contracted to his club and gets his full livelihood from football. *Semi-professionals* receive equally important shares of income from football and outside jobs. Concept of *shamateurism* will be examined with the help of Dunning's (1999) typology of overt and covert sports professionalism.

Sources and methods

Primary source material contains oral history interviews that were conducted via telephone with former players in 2022. In total, 15 former players were asked to participate in the research, 11 of whom accepted. One interview resulted in another one with the same person, and one interviewee sent additional information via email after the interview. Research participants were chosen based on their long playing careers in the highest division of Finland. One interviewee, "Anon 1", differed from the others in the sense that during the research period he worked as a club official. All interviewees spent most of their careers in Finland, but four of them also played professionally abroad. The oldest two interviewees were born at the turn of the 1950s, the youngest two in the early to mid-1970s and the rest in the 1960s. Most have worked in football also after their playing careers.

All interviews were recorded and interviewees anonymised. Use of the records and goals of the research were explained before interviews, to which all interviewees gave their consent. Interview records will only be used as source material in this chapter. In the text, the interviewees are referred with identifiers based on their age, with Anon 1 being the oldest and Anon 11 the youngest interviewee. As an interview method, a semi-structured interview with a focus in life history was applied. Apart from Anon 1, interviewees were asked to reminisce about the progression of their careers with the emphasis on sources of income. Figures of former Finnish marks (FIM) were converted into 2022s euros with the Bank of Finland Museum's online Money Value Converter.

Complementary sources include football club Ilves Tampere's archive in the Sports Museum of Finland, containing player contracts from the 1980s and 1990s. The use of the archive is restricted to academic research, and it can only be used on permission of the president of Ilves, with good research ethical practice and agreed-on terms, including the obligation to anonymise all personal data in the documents.

Long swansong of amateurism

Amateurs, shamateurs and semi-professionals – Finnish elite football in the 1970s and 1980s

The men's top division in Finland was a full-fledged amateur league in the 1970s with an established practice of awarding point money to players. Most players did not benefit from football much financially, but received important indirect benefits such as jobs, apartments, bank loans and study places from their clubs (Aalto, 2007, p. 81). In the 1980s, semi-professionalism became more common with varying degrees of shamateurism among clubs (Szerovay & Itkonen, 2015, p. 117). One example of what this meant in practice is provided by the playing career of Anon 2, one of the star players of Finnish football in the 1970s and 1980s.

Anon 2's career can roughly be divided into two periods: The first was characterised by a combination of football and studies, and the second, football and work. Both during and after his studies most of his income came from football. Apart from the brief period when he played outside his hometown and had a written contract, all his contracts were orally done. During his breakthrough seasons, he was once recruited into a major club in Finland, which gave him benefits such as a signing-on fee after the move was sealed, a free apartment, two daily meals, tax bills paid by the club and point money that was paid under-the-table. When living expenses were minimal, "point money kept you in first class" (Anon 2).

After completing his studies, Anon 2 combined football with a job that was perfectly tailored to football. Daily working time was usually only five hours, and even that was flexible:

> It was a little bit like playing as a professional, I did not really have to worry about the job very much. I could train as much as I liked whenever I liked, I could rest whenever I liked, and no one ever asked me in work where I had been. (Anon 2)

As his career progressed, he bought his own apartment with the furniture provided by the club, which he had negotiated into his contract. "In all things where you could exploit that [his value to the club], where you could provide a receipt to the club, it all added to the net money you got" (Anon 2).

The prevalence of under-the-table money and other unofficial benefits was a common pattern in also other interviewees' careers. All interviewees apart from Anon 11 got at least some of their rewards under-the-table or as various kinds of expenses compensations. Despite the increasing threat of tax investigations (see Linnakangas, 1984, p. 12) and the emerging practice of written player contracts, oral deals provided players additional rewards that were hidden from club accounts. "There were two contracts. One was for the outside, the other [included] what was really paid" (Anon 4). Even in the mid-1990s, Anon 10's club paid some of his rewards as mileage allowances based on his need to go to another city because of studies.

> There were mileage allowance hassles also in [my club at the time], but this was a fairly kind version [how to mislead the tax officials], because I really had to go there, but whether that had anything to do with working is questionable.

Some interviewees were arranged sinecures to supplement their incomes. Anon 7 had a sinecure in the city of Pori while playing in FC Jazz in the 1990s, and Anon 8 in the national airline Finnair while playing for Finnairin Palloilijat, the club sponsored by the airline.

Finnish elite football in the 1980s and 1990s therefore contained various elements of Dunning's covert sports professionalism. Footballers were "clandestinely paid from money taken at the gate or from funds provided by rich patrons", and provided financial support "through jobs, often sinecures, in private commercial and industrial firms", as well as with sinecures in civil service (Dunning, 1999, p. 115). Players' work conditions and positions differed, though. Most of the interviewees did not have out-and-out sinecures that required no work effort. Anon 5, for example, was an insurance salesman and had to train after full workdays. To lessen the burden of this kind of lifestyle, HJK Helsinki moved training sessions to afternoons in 1984 and started to compensate those players for their losses who had to leave work earlier (Anon 1). This was a rare, early example of overt semi-professionalism in Finland. Another one was the long-standing practice in Yhtyneet Paperitehtaat, a corporation inside which football club Haka Valkeakoski operated, to let players of the club train in work time. By the late 1980s, about a third of the club's players worked regularly in the paper factory. Many also lived in the factory's apartments (Anon 6).

Nearly all interviewees emphasised that when they rose to the first team, they did not yet realise that it was possible to earn money from playing football in Finland – which the clubs took advantage of – but that they eventually learned their ways. After consolidating position in his team, Anon 4 improved his contract by exploiting the interest of other Finnish clubs and his status as a national team player:

> I was in a good position because HJK asked after me nearly every season. I asked them how much they would pay me, and then went to [club president] and [told him] that if you pay me this much, I will not go to HJK.

After playing professionally in Sweden, Anon 4 received a signing-on fee as a reward from his new club in Finland, because he had negotiated a free transfer for himself from the Swedish club.

Most interviewees did not want to or could not remember their earnings from football in numbers, but were able to compare them to salaries from their day jobs. For instance, one-third of Anon 3's incomes came from football and two-thirds from his job in the late 1980s, whereas for Anon 5, the ratio was about 50:50 at the time (Anon 3). Anon 6 remembers having earned about FIM 30,000 during the season 1983 (2022: EUR 11,950) and about FIM 100,000 by the late 1980s. Anon 4's earnings peaked in 1990, when he earned about FIM 150,000 (2022: EUR 41,410), more than what he had earned earlier in Sweden. This indicates that in the late 1980s player rewards in Finland were comparable to Sweden, where semi-professionalism was still the norm. According to Billing et al. (2004, p. 91), the first Swedish club that turned fully professional was Malmö FF in 1989.

When recollections of the interviewees are compared to player contracts in the archive of Ilves Tampere, similar numbers come up. In the seasons 1988 and 1989, the three most valuable contracts in Ilves provided earnings in the region of FIM 100,000. Most contracts in the archive are well below this level, though. For instance, in 1988, only one player earned a basic compensation of nearly FIM 100,000, whereas four players received FIM 40,000 to 50,000 as a season fee, nine players FIM 10,000–25,000, while three players only got money from points, FIM 500 per point (Player Contracts 1988; Player Contracts 1989, Ilves' archive). To put the numbers into context, the average yearly salary in Finland was FIM 78,000 in 1985 (2022: EUR 27,434) and FIM 103,600 in 1990 (2022: EUR 27,606) (Statistics Finland, 1990, pp. 32–33). Various success bonuses in the contracts demonstrate the bargaining power of key players. For example, one contract has an attachment that states that if the player starts both games in the second round of a UEFA Cup-Winner's Cup match-up, and Ilves progresses to the third round, he is entitled to 6% of the home game's net revenue (Attachment to player contract, 13 September 1991, Ilves' archive).

How did earnings of Finnish players compare to foreign professional players, the first of whom moved to Finland in the 1970s? One such player played for Ilves in the mid-1980s, earning initially a monthly salary of FIM 7,000, from April to October, that later increased to FIM 11,000 (Finnish Centre of Pensions' Decision, 3 September 1993, Ilves' archive). He would have then earned initially FIM 49,000 and later FIM 77,000 for a season that lasted six months in Finland, usually beginning in late April and ending in mid-October. Therefore, his earnings were actually lesser than what some of the seasoned Finnish amateurs earned yearly, especially when salaries from their day jobs are added up. Rewards for Finnish players in Ilves were paid in four batches during the season, though, whereas contracts of foreign players included a monthly salary and often a free apartment.

Transition towards a professional league

The men's top division in Finland was rebranded as Futisliiga (Football League) in 1990, known as Veikkausliiga from 1992. The purpose was similar with many concurrent league reforms around Europe; to increase commercial resources of the elite clubs and speed up professionalisation (Nurminen, 1990). In contrast to especially Denmark and Norway (Andersson & Hognestad, 2019, pp. 712–714), little progress was made in the first years of the league. To the public image, Veikkausliiga remained amateurish, with only foreign players considered professional. In the lists of players' professions published in the media and in the football yearbooks in 1990 and 1991, hardly any Finns were marked as footballers by trade.

Yet, in terms of incomes, some Finnish players were almost completely professionals. Anon 8 earned nearly FIM 200,000 both in 1990 and in 1991 while playing in HJK, and the source of income was almost exclusively football. In 1991, he did not work at all in his public profession – he only played football. According to Anon 1, the average monthly salary in HJK in 1991 was about FIM 10,000. In addition to basic salaries, players got point money and training compensations, FIM 49 for each training, which were paid as untaxable expenses compensations and mileage allowances whenever possible. This enabled artificially raising the level of rewards much above to clubs with lesser resources such as Ilves. Anon 9, who played for HJK that season, recalls that "quite a few still had nominal jobs, but the players were already pretty much focused on football. (...) I studied as a hobby. My income came from football and a little hourly work I did on the side". According to the team's public professions, HJK's squad contained nine students and one conscript (Jari Litmanen), but not a single professional football player (Futisliiga, 1991), despite players having aforementioned earnings, the highest of which surely did not necessitate other work.

Professionalisation was stemmed by a recession, into which Finland plunged in the early 1990s. Tensions between players and clubs grew when even the biggest clubs such as HJK struggled to pay salaries, sometimes resorting to lies to maintain peace in the dressing room (Anon 9). Many players were presented with two options: play football full-time with a lower salary, or play and work in a part-time job. Anon 8 opted for the latter when he was offered a contract that was about a third smaller than the previous one. He changed clubs, and his new club arranged him a job in a sports equipment store with four hours of daily work. Two sources of income provided similar total earnings than in the previous season.

Seven interviewees played in Futisliiga in its inaugural season 1990, with the youngest two, Anons 10 and 11, making their league debuts following seasons. Based on their recollections, there was a generational change in progress. Experienced players continued to work and play football, whereas players in their early twenties usually focused only on football. For an older player like Anon 6, combining football with a full-time job made much more sense than becoming a full-time footballer late on in his career. He worked three years as a physical education teacher in an upper comprehensive school in the early to mid-1990s while playing in Veikkausliiga, which was not only "a good combination of two things that did not impair one another at all", but also provided the best earnings of his playing career. In addition to the salary from his club, he received a full teacher's pay including ideal benefits for football such as three months of summer vacation. Both salaries were above Finland's average salary.

Careers of younger players like Anon 9, 10 and 11 were quite different. Anons 9 and 10 initially combined a part-time job with playing, but by the late-1990s, only played football. Anon 11 never had any other jobs. In his debut season in Myllykosken Pallo (MyPa), he was given a monthly salary that provided yearly earnings of FIM 35,000, which "was a huge sum for a junior living at home. I still remember how happy I was when I got that deal. Point money and bonuses from European games were even added to that". After completing the compulsory military service in the mid-1990s, he was a full-time footballer in Veikkausliiga for the remaining decade of his career. He was also among the first generation of players who could rely on the Players' Association's (founded in 1992) support all his career. Despite not having the kind of "problems where the association's help would have been needed", its existence was important for him. During the recession, the Players' Association helped those players who had problems in getting their contractual salaries from clubs (Anon 9).

Traditional low-pay sinecures became gradually redundant. Anon 7 only got about fifth of his income from his sinecure in Pori. When Anon 10 moved to HJK in the mid-1990s, he at first wanted to also work – and had even set that as a condition when coming to the club – but after two seasons decided to focus on football and use the remaining time on studies. This was facilitated by his yearly earnings that had increased to FIM 150,000. When players earned more than FIM 100,000, day jobs were no longer needed as complementary sources of income.

In 1995, two reforms transformed all team sports in Finland. First, the Bosman ruling freed players from bonds to their former clubs, which increased player transfers in all of Europe. Second, the first decree that covered athletes' social security, pensions and insurances came into effect in Finland. Athletes who earned more than a defined amount of taxable incomes yearly (FIM 56,640 in 1995) were now considered professional athletes with legal contracts of employment with their clubs (Lahti, 2009, pp. 61–69). An unintended result from the latter reform were contracts just beneath the legal limit that were offered to especially young players. This way clubs would not have to pay pensions payments. The Players' Association provided legal support for players in these cases (Anon 9). These changes coincided with the commodification and globalisation of international football (Itkonen & Nevala, 2007, pp. 18–20). The strategy of all Nordic clubs changed profoundly: clubs no longer had incentive to prevent players from moving clubs but to sell them to the highest bidder (Andersson & Hognestad, 2019, pp. 711–712). Consequently, more and more Nordic players became full-time footballers who targeted a career outside their home country. Anon 9 describes his situation in the mid-1990s as follows:

> I was a national team player and merchandise for HJK (…) My contract was quite good, I did not need to do anything else than play football and in fact it was not even possible, because it had professionalised so much.

The cadre of professional football players in Finland was enlarged by a rising number of foreign players, and Finnish players who returned to Finland after playing professionally abroad. Among the latter group was Anon 5 who no longer had to work as an insurance salesman. "Then I was professional also in Finland. (…) If before there were job and sports [as sources of income], now I got that much from just sports". By the mid-1990s, professionalism had become commonplace in at least HJK, MyPa and Haka. The latter two relied on backing from their local paper factories. According to Anons 4 and 11, MyPa in Harri Kampman's coaching tenure (1991–1996) strived to build a fully professional team as one of the first clubs in Finland, which was reflected in both the conditions of football and salaries.

HJK's qualification to the UEFA Champions League as the first Finnish club in 1998 is often marked as an important milestone in the professionalisation of Finnish football (see Szerovay & Itkonen, 2015, p. 118). In HJK's case, it was the final step in a process that had been long in the making. Despite defender Markku Kanerva famously working as a schoolteacher, players who worked full-time or part-time were already in the minority in HJK by this time, and next season, only full-time football players remained (Anon 10). This is no wonder considering that the club's coffers were now filled with Champions League money, from which players received a share. In 1999, 13 first team players earned more than FIM 100,000 (2022: EUR 23,739), and six more than FIM 150,000 (2022: EUR 35,608). The highest paid player earned nearly twice as much as the second highest: FIM 427,000 (2022: EUR 101,365), including all benefits. Ten of the first team players also had free apartments and sponsored cars, a much larger number than before (Anon 1).

HJK's Champions League qualification accelerated professionalisation of Finnish football also through their new local rival, FC Jokerit. FC Jokerit was founded in 1999 by businessman Harry "Hjallis" Harkimo, owner of the identically named ice hockey club. Lured by the money in international football, Harkimo aggressively signed players from Finland and abroad. In Harkimo's ownership, full professionalism of players was a self-evident fact that was reflected in salaries.

> Hjallis was a bit different to Ollis [Olli-Pekka Lyytikäinen, HJK president]. If your worth was one euro, Ollis offered you 50 cents. This was the starting point, you always had to negotiate with Ollis. As far as Hjallis was concerned, if you were worth one euro, he offered you one euro and 20 cents and demanded from you accordingly. (Anon 9)

Hjallis Harkimo's foray into football was short-lived, but it resulted in the capital's first purpose-built football stadium, completed in Töölö in 2000, and a general rise of salaries in Veikkausliiga. Professionalism of male Finnish footballers playing at the highest level in Finland became a norm instead of a curiosity. In a survey conducted by the Players' Association in 2002, 85% of Veikkausliiga's players defined themselves as professional footballers (Kanerva & Wallén, 2007, p. 285). Ten years earlier the numbers would have been closer to the opposite. By the turn of the 2000s, the bulk of the league's players consisted of the likes of Anon 11 – not a star player or a national team player, but still a full-time footballer who earned enough to play professionally. In the late 1990s, Anon 11 earned about FIM 120,000–130,000 in a year, which towards the end of his career rose to EUR 35,000, which was neither among the lowest nor the highest in the league. "I got by well. It did not leave any savings, but I can't complain, I was able to live a good life".

Since the 1990s, Finnish elite football has moved gradually towards overt sports professionalism that is financed by a combination of wealthy individual patrons, gate money, commercial sponsors and money paid for the broadcasting rights (Dunning, 1999, p. 115). The transition has been difficult. Somewhat similarly to Sweden (see Andersson & Carlsson, 2011), Finnish club football struggled to develop a commercial model for football after the turn of the 1990s – in contrast to especially Denmark and Norway. As a result, Finnish elite clubs have not been able to finance full professionalism with revenues from broadcasting rights, and construction of new football stadiums has been slow. Andersson and Carlsson (2011) explain the "immature" commercialisation of Swedish club football with sport's ideological roots and poor connections to the market and sponsors (p. 761), as well as with competition with ice hockey that became the "prime mover in the commercialisation of Swedish sports" (p. 765) in the 1990s and 2000s. These explanations apply also to Finland. However, in

Finland, there are no legal obstacles and not much ideological opposition to private patronage of sports clubs – such as the rule of 51% (51-procentsregeln) that remains an important tradition in Sweden (Andersson & Carlsson, 2011, p. 763) – which has often resulted in overreliance on wealthy private benefactors on a club level.

Unlike in Sweden, where both attendances and conditions of football improved significantly in the 2010s (Andersson & Hognestad, 2019, p. 713), elite football in Finland still struggles with the same issues. From the players' perspective, this has resulted in low salaries and semi-professionalism among the smallest clubs in the league. Of the three Veikkausliiga clubs surveyed in Tuikkanen's research (2021, p. 79–80), one had a squad that consisted of 12 professional players and 12 semi-professionals, whereas the other two were mostly or fully composed of professional players. In a survey conducted for the FIFPRO Global Employment Report, 26% of 192 respondents (who played in either Veikkausliiga or the first division) earned a monthly net remuneration of less than 1,000 dollars, 32.3% 1,001–2,000 dollars, 26% 2,001–4,000 dollars and 15.1% more than 4,001 dollars (Koukiadaki & Pearson, 2016, p. 184–185). Salaries in Finland were higher than in Iceland but much below Denmark, Sweden and Norway.

Conclusion

The findings of this chapter shed light on the complexity of the transition from amateurism to professionalism in Finland. In the 1970s and 1980s, gradual increase in rewards propelled footballers towards semi-professionalism featuring elements of shamateurism. Nearly all interviewees actively pursued better pay when playing as ostensible amateurs, while at the same time working in full- or part-time jobs outside football. Two sources of income generated a comparably good standard of living, but also high workload for those players whose jobs were not tailor-made for football. Star players such as Anon 2 had a socioeconomic status comparable to Finnish "shamateur" star athletes in other sports, notwithstanding the very best of international stars.

The formation of Futisliiga in 1990 is often considered as the first marker of systemic professionalisation in Finnish football. From the players' perspective, rebranding the league changed little – even playoffs were not continued after the first season. The fledgling commercialism of the new league was counterbalanced by financial problems caused by the recession, which left lasting memories to the interviewees. In the mid- to late 1990s, the number of full-time players in Veikkausliiga rose when older players who had always worked alongside football, retired, and were replaced by younger players, many of whom had never had other jobs than football. The catalysts of professionalisation were economic revival after the recession, trickle of money from heavily commercialised international football, the Bosman ruling, and HJK's Champions League qualification. By the turn of the 2000s, most players in Veikkausliiga were full-time footballers.

Paradoxically, professionalisation so far has not benefited football players much in terms of earnings. As indicated, players – apart from students – usually had two sources of income in the 1980s: football and their job. When professionalism became a norm, the second source was cut off, and paying rewards under-the-table became more difficult. Because sustainable business model has not developed, most clubs today struggle to pay professional salaries, and professional commitment is required from players without corresponding pay. The club that has been a longstanding exception to this is HJK that has been able to steadily increase its player budget into a level that significantly surpasses all other clubs.

Professionalisation of Finnish football includes lots of potential topics for future research. For example, players' income progression in Veikkausliiga after the turn of the 2000s could be researched based on public tax records. Further research should also be conducted on female players' pathways in football from the 1970s to the present day, and on the professionalisation of youth football and coaching.

References

Aalto, S. (2007). Ajan hermolla. In S. Aalto, E. V. Lehtola, E. Sulkava, & A. Tiitta (Eds.), *Tähtien tarina: Helsingin jalkapalloklubi 100 vuotta* [Story of the stars: 100 years of HJK Helsinki] (pp. 52–90). Helsingin Jalkapalloklubi.

Andersson, T., & Carlsson B. (2011). A diagnosis of the commercial immaturity of Swedish club football. *Soccer & Society*, 12(6), 754–773. 10.1080/14660970.2011.609678

Andersson, T., & Hognestad, H. (2019). Glocal culture, sporting decline? Globalization and football in Scandinavia. *Sport in Society*, 22(4), 704–716. 10.1080/17430437. 2017.1389015

Bank of Finland Museum. Money value converter. https://app.rahamuseo.fi/calculator?lang=ENG.

Billing, P., Franzén, M., & Peterson, T. (2004). Paradoxes of football professionalization in Sweden: A club approach. *Soccer & Society*, 5(1), 82–99. 10.1080/146609705 12331391014

Dunning, E. (1999). *Sport matters: Sociological studies of sport, violence and civilisation.* Routledge.

Futisliiga. (1991, April 18). *Suomen Urheilulehti*, 94(16), 18.

Goldblatt, D. (2007). *The ball is round. A global history of football.* Penguin Books.

Itkonen, H., & Nevala, A. (2007). Jalkapallo, maailma ja Suomi [Football, the world and Finland]. In H. Itkonen & A. Nevala (Eds.), *Kuningaspelin kentät: Jalkapalloilu paikallisena ja globaalina ilmiönä* [Fields of king football: Football as a local and global phenomenon] (pp. 11–20). Gaudeamus.

Kanerva, J., & Wallén, G. (2007). Rahaakin tarvitaan [Money is also needed]. In Y. Lautela & G. Wallén (Eds.), *Rakas jalkapallo. Sata vuotta suomalaista jalkapalloa* [100 years of Finnish football] (pp. 279–285). Teos.

Koukiadaki, A., & Pearson, G. (2016). *FIFPRO Global Employment Report: Working Conditions in Professional Football.* FIFPRO. Retrieved April 23, 2022, from https://fifpro.org/images/documents-pdf/2016-fifpro-global-employment-report.pdf

Lahti, T. (2009). *Ammattiurheilijan sosiaaliturvaan tähdännyt lainsäädäntö poliittisena prosessina vuosina 1993–2000* [Legislation directed to professional athletes' social security as a political process in 1993–2000] [Master's thesis, University of Tampere]. https://trepo.tuni.fi/bitstream/handle/10024/80846/gradu03740.pdf

Lämsä, J., Nevala, A., Aarresola, O., & Itkonen, H. (2020). Ammattilaisuus amatörismin kriisiyttäjänä suomalaisessa joukkueurheilussa 1975–2018 [Professionalism versus amateurism in Finnish team sports in 1975–2018]. In H. Roiko-Jokela & A. Holmila (Eds.), *Urheilun kriisejä. Suomen urheiluhistoriallisen seuran vuosikirja 2019–2020* (pp. 57–85). Suomen urheiluhistoriallinen seura.

Lavikainen, J. (2018). Ammatiksi jääkiekon pelaaja [Professionalisation of ice hockey]. In O. Viita (Ed.), *Koko kansan Leijonat. Suomi-kiekon historia* [History of Finnish ice hockey] (pp. 198–205). Docendo.

Lee, C. W. (2013). From shamateurism to pioneer of Asia's professional football: The introduction of professional football in Hong Kong. *Soccer & Society, 14*(5), 603–614. 10.1080/14660970.2013.792481

Linnakangas, E. (1984). *Urheilu ja verotus* [Sports and taxation]. Suomen Lakimiesliiton Kustannus Oy.

Llewellyn, M. P., & Gleaves, J. (2016). *The rise and fall of Olympic amateurism*. University of Illinois Press.

Molnar, G. (2007). Hungarian football: A socio-historical overview. *Sport in History, 27*(2), 293–317. 10.1080/17460260701437110

Nurminen, K. (1990, April 26). Toimitusjohtaja Kimmo Suomisen toive: Futisliigan avulla yleisömäärät kasvuun [Executive director Kimmo Suominen hopes that attendances will grow by way of the Football League]. *Suomen Urheilulehti, 93*(17), 23.

Peterson, T. (2008). *The professionalization of sport in the Scandinavian countries*, Idrottsforum.org, February 20, 2008. Retrieved August 2, 2022 from https://www.idrottsforum.org/articles/peterson/peterson080220.pdf

Statistics Finland. (1991). Wages and salaries 1989/1990. Tilastokeskus.

Szerovay, M., & Itkonen, H. (2015). Suomalaisten ja unkarilaisten huippujalkapalloilijoiden aseman muutokset 1980-luvulta nykypäiviin [The professionalization of Finnish and Hungarian top-level football players since the 1980s]. In H. Roiko-Jokela & E. Sironen (Eds.), *Urheilun toinen puoli. Suomen urheiluhistoriallisen seuran vuosikirja 2015* (pp. 109–127). Suomen urheiluhistoriallinen seura.

Tuikkanen, T. (2021). *Suomalaisen jalkapallon liigaseurat ammattimaistumisen prosessissa* [Finnish football's league clubs in the process of professionalisation] [Master's thesis, University of Jyväskylä]. https://jyx.jyu.fi/bitstream/handle/123456789/77947/1/URN%3ANBN%3Afi%3Ajyu-202109295013.pdf

Wikberg, K. (2005). *Amatör eller professionist? Studier rörande amatörfrågan i svensk tävlingsidrott 1903–1967* [Amateur or professional? A study of the amateur question within Swedish competitive sport between 1903–1967]. SISU Idrottsböcker.

Archives

Football Association of Finland's archive, Sports Museum of Finland's archive.
Ilves Tampere's archive, Sports Museum of Finland's archive.

Chapter 8

The Professionalisation of Youth Football in Norway

Implications for the "Sport for All" Ideal?

Anders Belling, Frode Telseth, and Pål Augestad

Introduction

The concept of *sport for all* is a well-known ideal in Nordic societies and sport movements. Sport for all is a natural consequence of a democratic system where voluntary associations are an integral part of the foundation of the Nordic model (Peterson, 2008; Tin et al., 2020). Participating in voluntary organisations is an important feature in cultivating democratic citizenship, and therefore it is also essential that such participation is open to all. The numbers show that the model works for youth participation, with more than 90% of children in Norway involved at some point during their childhood in a sport club organised by the national sporting body, the Norwegian Confederation of Sports (NIF). Importantly, children are also protected from talent identification and development until the age of 13 via the Children's Sports Regulations (NIF, 1987).

Another characteristic of Nordic sport is the strong connection to amateurism. Andersson and Carlsson (2009) highlight the tradition of amateurism as probably the defining characteristic of Scandinavian sport, and Peterson (2008) finds that professionalism was alien to Nordic sports until the end of the twentieth century. A consequence of these two features is that voluntary grassroots sport and elite sport have been strongly integrated in the Nordic model.

Norway experienced surprisingly strong results in international elite football in 1990s, but the Norwegian national teams and the leading clubs have enjoyed little success since the year 2000. This has prompted several initiatives in Norwegian football that have primarily aimed to strengthen the commercial value and competitiveness both nationally and internationally. The two most comprehensive innovations, and the focus of this chapter, are both related to developing the most talented players in youth football.

One initiative was launched in 2014 by the Norwegian Football Federation (NFF) under the name *Landslagsskolen*, literally "the national team's school", an initiative for all players. Landslagsskolen followed the player development model that the NFF initially introduced in the late 1970s and that worked with greater emphasis from 1991 due to more activity and a more holistic national talent model (Morisbak, 2020). A central element in this national player development model has been a strong regional influence in the identification of the talents and the talent development processes. The other innovation this chapter will focus on, the Academy Classification scheme, was initiated in 2017 by *Norsk Toppfotball* (Norwegian Elite Football, NTF, the interest organisation of the male elite clubs). This initiative is directed at improving the talent development taking place at the elite clubs' youth academies.

Increasing professionalism has been documented in previous work on Nordic elite sport (Andersen & Ronglan, 2012; Augestad et al., 2006) and on Nordic elite football (Telseth & Halldorsson, 2017), and it has been identified as a significant feature for improving international results. This chapter will not analyse whether these professionalisation initiatives will improve talent development or results. Instead, we ask what consequences the professionalisation and academisation processes in youth football have for the ideology of sport for all, or more specifically to the NFF's vision of *football for all?* With the two above-mentioned talent development models in mind, we will discuss the processes that challenge the fundamental values of the Norwegian sports model and the integration between elite and grassroots sport, specifically with a focus on the three key dimensions of elite–grassroots, centralisation–regionalisation and commercialisation–democratisation.

Empirical and methodological context

The main aim of Landslagsskolen is to identify, stimulate and develop the most promising players aged 12–16. In the identification process, the responsible coaches in every region search for players who take ownership of their development and show the potential to develop into elite players at a national and international level (NFF, 2021). The "school" contains not only the football principles and the curriculum for activities run by the regional teams, but also the overall framework, core player characteristics, core coach characteristics and game model(s). This school is presented in a 178-page document that is publicly available online (NFF, 2021). The initiative points out that it is the NFF's player development model, but that ideally every club in youth football should use the curriculum for inspiration and development work (NFF, 2021).

The other initiative, the Academy Classification scheme, is a systematic evaluation and grading of the quality of the elite clubs' academies and talent development. It assesses and grades each club's work and philosophy in ten primary areas and about 200 sub-criteria.[1] The classification evaluates the academy's standards on a scale from one to five stars. NTF's chief executive Leif Øverland defined the classification scheme as a benchmark for how professional the elite clubs' academies work, which will help raise the standard of clubs and the national teams (NTF, 2017, 2019). In 2017, the NFF and NTF completed a media coverage deal, of which roughly EUR 30 million was allocated to talent development in the elite club's academies. This pot also covers the development, implementation and administration of the Academy Classification scheme, as administered by NTF-Sport, which is NTF's sport department (Thoresen, 2018).

NTF-Sport is a decisive factor in strengthening the elite clubs' talent development. NTF-Sport was established in 2008 as a national centre working on research, documentation and competence development in key areas, with the aim of helping the potentially biggest talents improve their development (NTF, 2017). When preparing the classification scheme, NTF-Sport comprehensively reviewed the world's leading talent development environments and visited the most competitive nations and academies. The categories and factors in the Academy Classification scheme reflect this preparatory work.

In recent years, Norwegian youth national teams, especially the male ones, have improved their results. For the four-year period 2016–2019, UEFA recognised Norway as the nation with the greatest progress. In 2016, Norway ranked as having the 29th-best male youth national teams (U16–U21) but climbed to tenth after 2019. The NFF highlights the improved commitment to the Landslagsskolen and the elite clubs' academies as the most important success criteria. "Professionalisation" and "systematisation" are the most frequently used words used to explain the progress, for example by the NFF's then director of elite football Lise Klaveness (Hellenes & Herrebrøden, 2021).

Methodologically, documents concerning the above-mentioned initiatives have been examined, along with previous research on football, elite sports in general (as cited above), and talent development in Norwegian youth football (Augestad & Telseth, 2020; Augestad et al., 2021). Furthermore, the authors' real-life experience from various roles in the field of football, such as coach, player developer, coach developer, parent and board member, have been considered in the reflections. Finally, this chapter has also drawn upon the extensive data collected on the two talent development initiatives implementation in the Norwegian region of Telemark in conjunction with a previous article (Augestad & Telseth, 2020).

When analysing these documents and texts, this chapter will situate them in the context of the Norwegian sports model with its three key dimensions of elite–grassroots, centralisation–regionalisation and commercialisation–democratisation. It asks how the professionalisation initiatives, within the context of talent development, challenges and disturbs the balance between these dimensions. It is necessary to emphasise that the choice of documents must be perceived as purposive and not representative. Selected documents have been chosen because they explicitly deal with the talent development initiatives for a limited and recent period to reveal regularity in the use of concepts and argumentation (Andersen, 1999, p. 13). A more comprehensive collection and review of documents from the NFF and NTF would probably reveal other ideas and values.

Theoretical context: Habermas' colonisation thesis

Habermas' colonisation thesis (Habermas, 1987) will be used to reflect upon the consequences of the talent development initiatives in Norwegian youth football. In Habermasian terms, the public sphere is the place where people meet to discuss openly and freely (Habermas, 2012). Habermas exemplified this by the coffee houses of the late nineteenth century, and club houses and online coach forums could be contemporary examples within sports.

When reasoning, an actor can follow either instrumental reasoning or moral deliberation. With instrumental reasoning, the actor views other people more as objects that can be used to reach a goal, thus to a certain extent disregarding their agency. With moral deliberation, on the other hand, all actors are seen as having an inherent value that you must treat with integrity and respect (Heath, 2014). When it comes to action, it is important to keep in mind that Habermas contends that all actions can be seen as goal-oriented (Habermas, 1998, p. 217), whether the more-desired communicative action or the less-desired strategic action. Communicative action aims to reach consensus and understanding between actors (Habermas, 1987), as opposed to strategic actions, where an actor uses purposive-rational actions to mislead and utilise the other actors for own gain (Fultner, 2014). A speaker, when performing communicative action, must also adhere to Habermas' validity claims: normative rightness, truthfulness and sincerity (Fultner, 2014).

In Habermas' view, the communicative action is an action type that primarily belongs to the context of the lifeworld (Habermas, 1987); the lifeworld as a concept is defined as the place where values guide our life where we try to understand and lead an ethical life of integration and shared values (Heath, 2014). Furthermore, the lifeworld is signified by a common language and value system which allows for community and the possibility of argumentation and critique (Nørager, 1985). On the other hand, the system world is the rationalised world where production and efficiency are key concepts, with specialisation, centralisation and standardisation being the main goals (Heath, 2014). In the system world actions can be coordinated with disregard to common value sets (Habermas, 1984). The point is not that one is better than the other, but that both serve their purpose; it is only when the system world influences the lifeworld too strongly that Habermas talks about a colonisation, which brings about pathologies (Habermas, 1987). The colonisation is completed when the rationalised system world has limited the space for communicative actions and does not allow for its cultural, integrative, socialising and identity aspects to flourish, in which case the system world's pathologies will cause people to feel alienated (Heath, 2014). The colonisation thesis will be the analytical tool used to shed light on the effect of the professionalisation process on the three key dimensions of the Norwegian sports model.

Findings

Professionalisation and the market logic

The elite clubs compete for money and attention, which depends on how they perform nationally and internationally, which again relates to money and attention. The money primarily comes from the media deals, sponsors and player sales, all three obviously being interconnected and central to talent development in the clubs. Clubs with lower budgets need to work intensely to develop homegrown players for their senior elite team. This means the club must make a substantial effort to develop its talented young players and prevent them from dropping out along the way. They can, for example, adapt the school schedule to the training sessions, accept that players sometimes lose their motivation and progress slowly, and provide mental support to those players who are struggling. Clubs do not purely develop players for their own first team but are also dependent on selling to larger clubs in Norway or internationally, earning the club both direct transfer revenue and funding from the NTF. To ensure an efficient talent development, the tendency is that several of the elite clubs are pushing for earlier selection and for taking control of the development process themselves, and this adaption is indirectly supported by NTF's Academy Classification scheme (Augestad & Telseth, 2020).

The funding model used by the Academy Classification scheme is widening the competence gap between the elite clubs and the grassroots clubs in relation to player development. The presence of full-time development coaches and specialists at elite clubs could also easily persuade talented young players, and their ambitious parents, to leave their grassroots clubs in favour of the elite academies. At the same time, the increased focus on developing homegrown players will give elite clubs and their development coaches an incentive to attract the most promising and dedicated young players, which will in turn spur elite clubs to speed up the development of their young talents. Specifically, this means that the players train more frequently, with the clubs facilitating the dual career paths of formal education and football from when the football talents are 13 years old.[2] Furthermore, the clubs initiate a more specialised elite athlete education with, for example, dietary courses, physical training and mental training.

The Academy Classification scheme potentially disturbs the traditional balance between the grassroots and elite in Norwegian football, by changing the elite clubs' incentive to engage in player development. This system means the elite clubs receive classification points and financial resources for productively developing talent. A high score not only affords prestige, but a financial reward is also allocated to the clubs' academies. This means the clubs can hire more coaches, specialists and scouts, allowing them to systematise and intensify the talent development even more and increasingly facilitate the dual career system so their young talents can combine education and football. The intention is to streamline the development of the players and one day promote them to the elite squad, and secondarily to the national team. NTF rewards clubs that achieve a grade of three or more stars with additional funding for coaches, further enhancing the incentive (NTF, 2017). In this way, the rewarded clubs upgrade their competence and their staff, but at the same time jobs will depend on this specific funding. This also points to a market where the leading clubs are further strengthened, thus cementing their position in the hierarchy, rather than one where greater quality is generally dispersed.

In other words, the professionalisation of talent development is linked to an increasing performance and market orientation in elite clubs. The entry of this market logic also leads to strategic actions and instrumental reasoning dominating the discourse, to use Habermasian terms (Habermas, 1990). With this logic, the talented young footballers are viewed as raw materials to be processed into tradeable products and then sold to the highest bidder. In other words, there is an inherent danger of objectifying the young talents, given the eagerness of the clubs to create development, success and player sales. Clubs become so preoccupied with assessing, mastering, shaping and measuring the athletes' bodies, movements and mentality that they could easily forget they are dealing with real persons and not objects.

National talent development curriculum

The purpose of the Landslagsskolen initiative is to systematise the development of footballing talent in all the country's regions, ensuring that everyone works with the same principles and speaks a common language no matter the region or club. This work resembles the development of curricula in education, meaning that on each level the coaches know what to teach and the players know what they are assessed on. Landslagsskolen is a formative process for regional and national talents aged 12 to 16, but it also offers schooling towards a professional football career. This includes schooling for performance in the Norwegian youth national teams, which links back to the way the reward system in the Academy Classification scheme is set up. Elite clubs are rewarded productivity points if their players make the youth national teams, with a multiplier the longer they have been at the club.

A clearly defined schooling system of specific roles limits the number of options and will increase confidence and predictability in performing these roles. A result of early role specialisation, in a defined system, is the standardisation of the training process. By using all available knowledge (the "curriculum"), coaches can control the training process and its execution. Questions about who, when, and how are pre-determined by creating principles for the distinct phases of the game. It is decided in advance what information is relevant to whom, and how this information should be processed and executed. Training tasks are standardised in the form of unambiguous principles and procedures, so that players can achieve the optimal effect of each training session (Augestad & Bergsgard, 2007). This means increasingly that the development consists of performing a pre-determined programme. The training process becomes to a lesser extent an individualised and personal process and more a question of testing whether the individual fits the system.

In his famous book *Homo Ludens*, Johan Huizinga describes the basic characteristics of games and playing. One such characteristic is the profound independence of play from other modes of living, especially work – play as a task and as part of a compulsory syllabus is not real play. Huizinga also placed sport under the concept of play, but he claimed that "with increasing systematisation and discipline" the content of play is lost and transformed into work (Huizinga, 1938/1993, p. 199). In this sense, Huizinga anticipates Habermas' claim that sport imitates the rationality and norms that are characteristic of wage labour, and thus does not represent an alternative to labour (Morgan, 2002). Landslagsskolen's curriculum means that football is formed by a rationalist logic from the age of 12. Talent development is a relentless requirement for the footballers who want to succeed in becoming a professional player. Modern industrial production involves the extensive use of knowledge and instrumental application of science to develop a more rational and efficient production process. The current system for elite sports is conspicuously similar to how industrial production is organised, and it is more focused on work and school than on play and joy.

Centralisation or dispersion

An academy model that emphasises early specialisation will intensify the football-specific training at an early age. To facilitate the talent development, systematic and regular training is conducted with several meeting points during the week. Adhering to the early specialisation pathway, these academies will seek to select the players they deem the most talented as early as possible. A few elite Norwegian clubs have started to attract players far earlier than the "formal" selection age of 12. They do so by offering extensive football-specific training from the age of seven, also in competition with purely commercial actors. By letting the players and their parents decide on the amount of specialisation at an early age, the clubs avoid violating the Children's Sports Regulations by not selecting certain players over others themselves. Implicitly these clubs operate with two options for players at an early age: one for those who want to go all-in, and another for those who want to have football as a hobby from this age.

Such an academy model means talent development centralises around the elite clubs already from a very young age. In addition, this means children are taken away from their friends and network in the local community for many hours every week at an early age. Many are sceptical to this model, partly because early specialisation can lead to promising young footballers burning out and quitting the sport (Augestad & Telseth, 2020). They want a different model for talent development, a so-called dispersion model. This model strengthens both the regional football associations and the elite clubs' presence in and influence on (selected) grassroots clubs. NFF is also working to improve the dispersion model, in parallel with the Landslagsskolen initiative, and sports plans have also been developed for children and youth football, including initiatives for grassroots coaches and the so-called quality clubs.[3]

From the grassroots perspective, there has been concerns about how the current dispersion model is coming up short in certain regions. They claim that the NFF and the regional associations focus their resources too much on the best performing players in the age groups, rather than focus on true dispersion. The talents already selected by the elite clubs' academies are also the focus of Landslagsskolen activities and doubling down on the same talents only serves to further emphasise the centralisation model. The dispersion model should be able to serve as an alternative, focusing energy on players otherwise left out and allowing different talent pathways to emerge. This would best be achieved by raising the competence of grassroots clubs and helping them develop their up-and-coming footballers themselves.

The elite clubs' commitment to developing their own players acts as a jar of honey on ambitious parents and players, who dream of a future as professional footballers. At the elite club, they meet modern training facilities, competent coaches, and teammates at a high-performance level. At the same time, private secondary education institutions offer specialised football programmes at their school. Admittedly, such schools emphasise versatility for the first two years, but the result is nonetheless that the children and youth begin to identify as athletes and specialise as footballers at an earlier age.

Discussion: Colonisation of Norwegian football?

Concerning the relationship between elite and grassroots sports, researchers point to the existence of several interconnected and competing logics at the different levels of a club (Gammelsæter, 2010). The focus in this discussion will be on the sport-for-all logic, the performance and commercialisation logic, and how these logics influence the other logics at a club. The sport-for-all role is diminishing, partly due to ever stronger market forces and an increased focus on results (Gammelsæter, 2009, 2016; Steen-Johnsen, 2011; Stenling & Fahlén, 2009). Concepts of institutional pluralism, which posit that organisations are operating with several coexisting and competing institutional logics, are relevant when analysing the sport field (Kraatz & Block, 2008; Thornton, 2008). The sports organisations are also characterised by different practices, values and mindsets (Steen-Johnsen, 2011), and the football field is no different, also having different logics at every level (Gammelsæter, 2010; Rasmussen, 2020).

How does the professionalisation of talent development change both the conditions for and attitudes of those involved in youth football? In the terms of

Habermas' colonisation thesis, how does the Norwegian model of player development direct the actors towards a result-oriented logic and stimulate an objectivistic attitude towards the young players? In short, the professionalisation of talent development resulting from the Academy Classification and Landslagsskolen initiatives has changed the outlook on what talent is and how best to develop it. The importance of the professionalisation of talent development is quite different when seen from the perspective of young players than from NTF. For the young players, early selection and competent coaches given them greater hope that they will achieve their dream of becoming professional footballers, but for the elite club it means opportunities for player sales and better performance.

Colonisation, however, is only total when the purpose-rational action limits the space for communicative action for the actors involved. Whether this has happened in Norwegian football remains an open question. The strategic calculation considers the other only as a means, or as limiting conditions for realising one's own individual action plans. The strategic calculation of self-interest removes the space for interaction and mutual understanding. The players, parents, coaches, managers and clubs adopt a results-oriented attitude towards each other, considering others only as resources to realise their individual projects. In this lies the germ of exploiting and manipulating others. The dominant question is "What do I want to achieve, and how can I get it done in the most efficient way possible?" Researchers have also begun critically examining the trend towards strategic interaction and relations at football academies in English professionalisation initiatives (Thomas et al., 2022). This influence is not only an issue within the academies, but there is also a concern that the tendency will spill over from elite youth football into grassroots football.

From a Habermasian perspective, it is about not only the jostling of competing logics, but also two fundamentally different ways of being and of relating to others. Habermas' concern is that what he calls an objectivist attitude becomes dominant in new areas of society. Adopting an objectivist attitude is the key to understanding how this language is crippled and thus becomes incomprehensible: The communicative roles of "I" and "you" are relinquished, and the dialogical "back and forth interaction" is rejected in favour of the monologic perspective of a third person. The absence of "moral deliberation" in the discourse on talent development in football can be explained by the fact that an objectivist approach becomes dominant (Habermas, 1990; Lysaker & Aakvaag, 2007; Morgan, 2002). This objectivistic approach is seen in the classification of academies, which runs the risk of creating a system where players are estranged, becoming merely a commodity that needs to be effectively produced for the clubs to stay in business. This is an important issue to be conscious of and vocal about because if the instrumental reasoning fortifies the position of the elite clubs' academies, it will make it continuously harder for grassroots clubs to maintain a role in talent development. The effect will only be further emphasised down the road when players have spent their formative years in an objectivistic elite system and not been formed by the grassroots club's ideals of community, of "we".

The challenge is to establish arenas where the moral ideals can be expressed and can frame the development of talent within the values that the football movement wants both for the lifeworld of elite football, but also for grassroots football's lifeworld. These ideals can spring out of football's own constitutional and normative rules, that is from the communicative context in which these ideals are created and reshaped. Or they can emerge from what Habermas calls the universal validity claims – truthfulness, sincerity and normative context – that accompany communicative action. In Norway, football is governed by democratic bodies such as club boards, regional boards and the national football congress. Thus, football has already established its own democratic circle of power. Players, coaches, managers, clubs and regions can put various topics on the agenda. The issues that preoccupy the various stakeholders will be brought directly to football's own decision-making bodies. Binding decisions and "laws" can be made here for the organisation of Norwegian football in general and for talent development in particular. Thus, the democratic circuit of power is already in place and completed.

In other words, Habermas' colonisation thesis may shed light on some of the changes that have taken place and could happen in Norwegian football. Key values such as community, play and mastery must give way to the selection, laborious work and competition for the dream of a future career as a professional footballer.

Concluding remarks

This chapter has shown how talent development in Norwegian football has undergone an extensive professionalisation process, and specifically how the Academy Classification and Landslagsskolen initiatives could have such an impact in recent years. A good deal of prestige and resources have been put into developing and implementing the Academy Classification scheme with the aim of enhancing talent development. This scheme challenges the grassroots clubs' player development by stimulating elite clubs to hire development coaches and coordinate the school and training work of young talent. The elite clubs have been more strongly incentivised to pick up players early and to control the whole development process. The Landslagsskolen initiative has also assisted the professionalisation process by creating a national curriculum for talent development in football. This curriculum clearly defines the roles and tasks that players need to learn and perform, thus also streamlining the training process and standardising the criteria for selecting players for further development with the youth national teams.

The consequences of the two initiatives have been analysed through the lens of Habermas' colonisation thesis, not to analyse whether it has made Norwegian football more successful, but to assess how the professionalisation process stimulates a market logic – a market where young players are considered as investment objects more than as adolescents who are to be socialised into independent, responsible human beings who follow their own pathways. Thus, this is a question of what values and ideals that player and talent development in youth football should be based on in the future. This chapter has focused on how professionalisation initiatives influence grassroots football, but another point of view could also be to look at how the ideals force grassroots football to follow a different system of thinking. To add to this process, future research should focus on how the actors experience this development and how they feel the space to perform communicative actions. Furthermore, it could be of great interest to see how actors experienced their encounter with the football world after their careers there ended.

To conclude, the existing democratic bodies in football are encouraged to assume their responsibility for ensuring the moral deliberation and communicative action about the values in Norwegian talent development and grassroots football, while also acknowledging the interdependent and individual lifeworlds of elite and grassroots football as well as the system worlds' influence on both. Whether this takes place via an integrating or more diverse model remains to be seen, but it should above all be one which puts human values first and football second.

Notes

1 The ten primary areas are anchoring in overall philosophy, player logistics, planning, competence, training process, the player's development year, match platform, school/football, collaboration models, productivity, economy and facilities.
2 Elite clubs have started formal collaboration with secondary schools to offer an integrated educational and football talent development package.
3 NFF certified grassroots clubs in a sports and organisational project started in 2014.

References

Andersen, N. Å. (1999). *Diskursive analysestrategier: Foucault, Koselleck, Laclau, Luhmann* [Discourse analysis strategies: Foucault, Koselleck, Laclau, Luhman]. Samfundslitteratur.

Andersen, S. S., & Ronglan, L. T. (2012). *Nordic elite sport: Same ambitions - Different tracks*. Universitetsforlaget.

Andersson, T., & Carlsson, B. (2009). Football in Scandinavia: A fusion of welfare policy and the market. *Soccer & Society, 10*(3–4), 299–304. 10.1080/14660970902771365

Augestad, P., & Bergsgard, N. A. (2007). Norway. In B. Houlihan & M. Green (Eds.), *Comparative elite sport development: Systems, structures and public policy* (pp. 194–217). Taylor & Francis Group.

Augestad, P., Bergsgard, N. A., & Hansen, A. Ø. (2006). The institutionalization of an elite sport organization in Norway: The case of "Olympiatoppen". *Sociology of Sport Journal, 23*(3), 293–313. 10.1123/ssj.23.3.293

Augestad, P., Bruu, M., & Telseth, F. (2021). 'You create your own luck, in a way' about Norwegian footballers' understanding of success, in a world where most fail. *Soccer & Society, 22*(3), 280–292. 10.1080/14660970.2020.1815009

Augestad, P., & Telseth, F. (2020). *Telemarksmodellen – En analyse av talentutviklingsmiljøet på Skagerak arena* [The Telemark model – An analysis of the talent development environment in Skagerak arena] (no. 46). S. f. U. i. Sørøst-Norge. https://openarchive.usn.no/usn-xmlui/handle/11250/2655976

Fultner, B. (2014). Communicative action and formal pragmatics. In B. Fultner (Ed.), *Jurgen Habermas: Key concepts* (pp. 54–73). Taylor & Francis Group.

Gammelsæter, H. (2009). The organization of professional football in Scandinavia. *Soccer & Society, 10*(3–4), 305–323. 10.1080/14660970902771373

Gammelsæter, H. (2010). Institutional pluralism and governance in "commercialized" sport clubs. *European Sport Management Quarterly, 10*(5), 569–594. 10.1080/16184742.2010.524241

Gammelsæter, H. (2016). *Poeng, penger og politikk. Et institusjonelt perspektiv på ledelse* [Points, money, and politics. An institutional perspective on leadership]. Cappelen Damm AS.

Habermas, J. (1984). *The theory of communicative action, volume 1: Reason and the rationalization of society*. Beacon Press.

Habermas, J. (1987). *The theory of communicative action, volume 2: Lifeworld and system*. Polity Press.

Habermas, J. (1990). *Moral consciousness and communicative action*. MIT press.

Habermas, J. (1998). *On the pragmatics of communication* (M. Cooke, Ed.). MIT Press.

Habermas, J. (2012). The public sphere: An encyclopedia article. In D. Kellner & M. G. Durham (Eds.), *Keyworks in cultural studies* (pp. 75–79). Blackwell.

Heath, J. (2014). System and lifeworld. In B. Fultner (Ed.), *Jurgen Habermas: Key concepts* (pp. 74–90). Taylor & Francis Group.

Hellenes, A., & Herrebrøden, Ø. (2021, November 16). Norge er mest fremgangsrike nasjon: Det har skjedd en revolusjon [Norway is the most improved nation: A revolution has happened]. VG. Retrieved February 12, 2022, from https://www.vg.no/sport/fotball/i/7djxqw/norge-er-mest-fremgangsrike-nasjon-det-har-skjedd-en-revolusjon

Huizinga, J. (1938/1993). *Homo ludens: A study of the play-element in culture*. The Beacon.

Kraatz, M. S., & Block, E. S. (2008). Organizational implications of institutional pluralism. In R. Greenwood, C. Oliver, & R. Suddaby (Eds.), *The SAGE handbook of organizational institutionalism*. SAGE Publications Ltd. 10.4135/9781849200387

Lysaker, O., & Aakvaag, G. C. (2007). *Habermas: Kritiske lesninger* [Habermas: Critical readings]. Pax.

Morgan, W. J. (2002). Social criticism as moral criticism: A Habermasian take on sports. *Journal of Sport and Social Issues, 26*(3), 281–299. 10.1177/0193723502263005

Morisbak, A. (2020). Spillerutvikling/talentutvikling i et historisk perspektiv [Player-/talent development in a historical perspective]. *Fotballtreneren, 34*(3), 18–22.

NFF. (Ed.). (2021). *Landslagsskolens fagplan* [The school of national team's curriculum]. Norsk Fotballforbund. https://740c073d.flowpaper.com/Landslagsskolen2021/#page=1

NIF. (1987). *Barneidrettsbestemmelsene* [Regulations for children's sport]. Norges idrettsforbund

Nørager, T. (1985). *System og livsverden: Jürgen Habermas' konstruktion af det moderne* [System and lifeworld: Jügern Habermas' construction of the modern]. Anis.

NTF. (2017). *Akademiklassifiseringsrapporten 2017* [Academy classification report 2017]. N. Toppfotball. https://www.eliteserien.no/tjenestekatalogen/sport/akademiklassifisering

NTF. (2019). *Akademiklassifiseringsrapporten 2019* [Academy classification report 2019]. N. Toppfotball. https://www.eliteserien.no/nyheter/akademiklassifiseringsrapporten19

Peterson, T. (2008). The professionalisation of sport in the Scandinavian countries. Retrieved April 30, 2022, from http://www.idrottsforum.org/articles/peterson/peterson080220.html

Rasmussen, S. (2020). *Idrettsglede for alle? Et institusjonelt perspektiv på tilrettelegging av topp- og breddeidrettsaktivitet i den norske idrettsmodellen* [Joy of sports for all? An institutional perspective on the facilitation of top- and grassroot sports activities in the Norwegian sport model]. NIH. Oslo. https://hdl.handle.net/11250/2660772

Steen-Johnsen, K. (2011). Særforbund i en brytningstid: Mellom byråkrati, kommersialisme og frivillighet [Special sports associations in changing times: between bureaucracy, commercialisation, and volunteerism]. In D. V. Hanstad (Ed.), *Norsk idrett - Indre spenning og ytre press* (pp. 241–257). Akilles.

Stenling, C., & Fahlén, J. (2009). The order of logics in Swedish sport – feeding the hungry beast of result orientation and commercialization. *European Journal for Sport and Society*, 6(2), 121–134. 10.1080/16138171.2009.11687833

Telseth, F., & Halldorsson, V. (2017). The success culture of Nordic football: The cases of the national men's teams of Norway in the 1990s and Iceland in the 2010s. *Sport in Society*, 22(4), 689–703. 10.1080/17430437.2017.1390928

Thomas, R., Hall, E. T., Nelson, L., & Potrac, P. (2022). Actors, interactions, ties, and networks: The 'doing' of talent identification and development work in elite youth football academies. *Soccer & Society*, 23(4–5) 420–431. 10.1080/14660970.2022.2059870

Thoresen, I. (2018). Her er akademiklassifiseringen [Here is the academy classification]. *Fotballtreneren*, 32(1), 43–44.

Thornton, P. H. (2008). Institutional logics. In R. Greenwood, C. Oliver, & R. Suddaby (Eds.), *The SAGE handbook of organizational institutionalism* (pp. 99–128). SAGE Publications Ltd. 10.4135/9781849200387

Tin, M. B., Telseth, F., Tangen, J. O., & Giulianotti, R. (Eds.) (2020). *The Nordic model and physical culture*. Routledge. 10.4324/9780429320187

Chapter 9

Football Fitness
More of the Same, or a Path-Breaking Concept?

*Søren Bennike, Morten B. Randers,
Peter Krustrup, and Laila Ottesen*

Introduction: Football is a health enhancing activity

In 2011, the Danish Football Association (DBU) is launching Football Fitness (FF), as a completely new way of organising football for adults where flexibility and health are key. A press release (DBU(a)) states that the FF project will "profile football as a health-enhancing activity" and aims to develop and offer football in a "completely new way in sporting and organisational terms, breaking with the traditional organisation, administration and membership structure". Before moving further, we wish to highlight an article by Karp et al. (2014) titled *More of the Same Instead of Qualitative Leaps: A Study of Inertia in the Swedish Sports System*. Karp et al. focuses on the Swedish initiative by the name of "Idrottslyftet", the primary aim of which is to develop youth sports (for young people aged 7–25). We have drawn inspiration from this paper, emphasising that the activities launched under this initiative do not lead to development and change as intended, but instead help to create inertia. Following on from this, we ask the question: Is Football Fitness more of the same, or a path-breaking concept?

The following begins with a section that explores the context from which FF originates. As such, we present selected research below that highlights how playing football is an activity with broad health effects. This is followed by an analysis in which we pursue the claim that FF is a completely new way of organising football for adults as described above. This is done by analysing how FF differs in terms of organisation and play from recreational football and professional football – two other forms of football organised under DBU – as well as highlighting the momentum leading up to the launch of FF applying the idea of path-breaking concepts (Sydow et al., 2005).[1] In conclusion, the local organisation and implementation of FF is discussed, and the analysis is challenged.

Football Fitness, which was presented in 2011 as stated above, can be seen as a reaction to several trends in Danish sport. Following a steady increase in adult (people aged 16 and over) sports participation in voluntary organised sport clubs since this was first measured in 1964, we saw stagnation between

DOI: 10.4324/9781003280729-13

2007 and 2011. Despite this, the total number of people actively involved in sports increased over the same period. This is due to the increasing popularity of self-organised sports, including running, and gym activities in for profit fitness facilities (Laub, 2013). What these activities have in common is their flexibility and, arguably, their focus on health (Thing & Ottesen, 2013). The latter is a very central part of FF, which will be elaborated further. At the same time, it was also clear that older people were becoming more active. In the past, there was a clear correlation between age and participation in sport and physical activity: The older the person, the less activity. Clearly, the 2011 analysis of Danes' sporting habits shows that this pattern is changing over time, with a steadily increasing proportion of the population active for most of their lives (Laub, 2013). In football, which is the focus of this chapter, the 2011 analysis found that the proportion of adult footballers (aged 16 and over) fell from 10% in 2007 to 9% in 2011. Besides changes in sporting habits, another trend was an increasing political desire to involve voluntary organised sport in public social and health-related tasks (Ottesen & Jakobsen, 2011). In the field of sports policy, the seminar "Football Fitness as Prevention and Treatment" organised by the National Olympic Committee and Sports Confederation of Denmark (DIF), the Danish Football Association (DBU) and the Copenhagen Center for Team Sport and Health, is a good example. Preben Staun, then Vice President of DIF, welcomed delegates by asking "How can Football Fitness be incorporated into municipal health policy?"

The understanding of Football Fitness as prevention and treatment and as a potential element in municipal health policy is related to evidence from a large number of scientific studies and meta-analyses showing that football organised as small-sided games with friendly teams can lead to significant improvements in the health profile (Krustrup et al., 2009, 2010, 2018; Milanovic et al., 2015, 2019, 2022). Most of this evidence was available at the launch of FF and has since been enhanced. For example, it has been shown that just one hour of football training per week is enough to provide some positive effects on cardiovascular fitness and health profile, such as an improved fitness rating and lower blood pressure. This is partly because the average heart rate is high, with periods of near-maximal heart rate regardless of participants' age, gender and football experience (Randers et al., 2010). There are a large number of intense runs, changes of direction, sprints, shoulder tackles and specific intense actions (Randers et al., 2010), which together lead to a versatile form of training (Krustrup & Krustrup, 2018). The intensity is high whether playing 3-a-side, 5-a-side or 7-a-side or playing on a large or small pitch (Randers et al., 2014, 2018). There is therefore good evidence to indicate that the training can be adapted to specific needs and the specific composition of participants, which allows flexibility while maintaining the health benefits.

Introducing methodology

The empirical backdrop for the following analysis is based on four documents from 2010 and 2011, all issued by the Danish Football Association: (DBU(a), DBU(b), DBU(c) and DBU(d)). These have been strategically selected as they can shed light on why FF is being presented, and the framework in which it should take place. DBU(b) is an internal document aimed at recipients with decision-making powers who can decide whether or not FF should be launched. The other three are documents where the potential recipients are individuals, non-profit football clubs, municipalities and other parties with an interest in FF. The documents have been collated and coded according to pre-defined themes (Creswell, 2007) generated from the general question as set out in the introduction and the theoretical perspective, which is elaborated upon as follows.

The idea of path-breaking concepts

To present the idea for unlocking paths suggested by Sydow et al. (2005), it is necessary to present the concept of path dependence (Campbell, 2004; Mahoney, 2000; Sydow et al., 2005). In slightly simplified terms, this means that the decision taken today is influenced by the decision taken yesterday. Over time, a certain path, and a certain way of doing things become ingrained. An often-used example of path dependence is the QWERTY keyboard, which are used by computers all around the world. The alternative and (to be discussed) more efficient Dvorak design never gained foothold due to path dependency (Mahoney, 2000). Once something is implemented it is extremely difficult to change direction. There may be many explanations for this (Campbell, 2004; Mahoney, 2000; Sydow et al., 2005), several of which are likely play their part simultaneously. Firstly, it has often been difficult to create the path, which inhibits the inclination and desire for change. Secondly, there are regularities in many cases that often make change difficult. And thirdly, knowledge of how to behave within the existing path is created and acquired. Sydow et al. (2005) illustrate the classical understanding of path dependence as a sequence consisting of three phases. In the first phase, called the preformation phase, a choice is not influenced by past actions. But when this choice is made, a process is initiated in which the degree of freedom of choice is slowly narrowed down. This point is referred to as a critical juncture, which creates the transition to the second phase – path formation. The fact that this is described as critical underlines the fact that when this choice is put into practice, it becomes difficult to return to the starting point and the path is reinforced over time. A lock-in is experienced upon entering the third phase, marking the transition to path dependence. Now the path is locked, and it will be followed, like a train following the tracks in a certain direction.

Sydow et al. (2005) criticises this understanding as being too deterministic and suggests a model for achieving path-breaking and change. The lock-in, which marks the transition to path dependence, should not be understood deterministically in the sense that it is not possible to break the path that has been established. Instead, the marking should be referred to as a restricting corridor illustrating the fact that choices seem limited and restrictive when going this way. Yet path-breaking is possible by means of un-locking, creating a process where choices are gradually opened up again. Sydow et al. (2005) states that "the unlocking of paths may be brought about intentionally, but it can also simply occur" (p. 20).

In line with the above, it is crucial to ask the question; How does un-locking happen, and how is momentum generated for a new path? Sydow et al. (2005) identifies four foci: a cognitive focus, an emotional focus, a social focus and a resource focus with different approaches for unlocking the path. These are examined further.

The cognitive focus includes self-reinforcing blind spots that make it difficult to be critically reflective of the prevailing discourse. People can find it difficult to see what they cannot or do not want to see. This is referred to as the reflection trap. It is beneficial here to gain new perspectives on the situation and acquire new knowledge – perhaps by involving a third party. This is exemplified as external consultants and new knowledge/perspectives. The emotional focus relates to behaviours linked to emotions, engagement and identity that are created by routines. For example, the energy created by engagement can become an identity; and the greater the engagement, the stronger the identity. This is the commitment trap. It is beneficial here for behavioural routines based on emotions to be irritated. The social focus is close to this and involves creating a self-reinforcing norm and an assumption that the way in which things are done is the right way, because that is the way things have always been done. This is referred to as a normative trap. It is beneficial here for this norm to be repeatedly challenged and irritated. The resource focus relates both to the fear of losing resources and the need to possess and/or reallocate resources. This is referred to as the sunk cost trap. It is beneficial here not to be ruled by this fear, and at the same time to be aware that breaking the path costs resources. Overall, the aim is to create a change-based momentum based on these elements that is strong enough to unfreeze fixated patterns and routines.

Analysis: Football fitness – a new path?

The term recreational football, as used here, refers to a practice whereby people train in their leisure time and participate in a tournament structure with matches at weekends. The game is organised by clubs holding an associative structure, meaning that the organisation behind it is non-profit, receives public funding and has a democratic organisational structure where participants pay a membership fee. As players, people are part of a team that is part of a tournament structure with regional/national rules, often closely linked to the international rules of the game.

Depending on the level, the tournament structure and the focus on this will often mean that the game involves a competitive element and focus on game performance optimisation. The advantageous legal conditions for formation of associations in Denmark, together with strong amateur ideals, have helped to establish a particularly strong path of recreational football that has existed for more than 130 years (Bennike et al., 2019).

Professional football – the creation of a new path

We are seeing a break with recreational football nearly 100 years after the game was first organised. The year 1978, when DBU – after a long period of pressure – abandoned the amateur ideal, was key (Bennike et al., 2019). The clubs that competed at the highest level then gradually changed their organisational system, and several clubs formed professional structures in the form of profit-oriented limited companies. Today, clubs that manage professional football at the highest level are market-oriented and privatised and have a hierarchical organisational structure (Bennike et al., 2019; Gammelsæter & Senaux, 2011). The players are employed, and the matches follow internationally defined rules. The game partly resembles the one played in recreational football, but the organisation behind it is significantly different. These differences in characteristics are summarised in Table 9.1.

Based on the ideas by Sydow et al. (2005), there was change-based momentum at the introduction of professional football, where all four foci were continuously challenged and irritated to a relatively aggressive degree. DBU's view of the amateur ideal was heavily criticised in the run-up to 1978, particularly with regard to the international competitiveness of Danish football. DBU was well aware of these challenges, and they were aware of the opportunity to professionalise football. They were not victims of what are known as blind spots. That said, it was difficult to break with the emotional

Table 9.1 Three types of organised football

Three types of organised football	Professional football (1978)	Recreational football (1879)	Football Fitness (2011)
The club's organisational form	For-profit Private funding Hierarchically organised No membership fee (job)	Non-profit Public funding Democratically organised Membership fee	Non-profit Public funding Democratically organised Membership fee
The sporting form of the game	Improve skills International rules Tournament	Improve skills (Inter)national rules Tournament	Improve health Local rules No tournament

and social focus on path dependency attached to the amateur ideal, which held back the decision for a number of years. For example, DBU regarded players who accepted money for playing football abroad as "traitors to their country" who did not fit the Danish mentality (Grønkjær & Olsen, 2007), and so they were allowed to play for the Danish national team. Later, DBU allowed a maximum of five professional players on the national team, and they introduced gift regulations so that division clubs could reward their players with consumer goods. The gift regulations can be viewed as a crucial event in relation to a point of critical juncture towards a lock-in and hence consolidation of the professional path in 1978. At the same time, as an organisation DBU had become professionalised to such an extent that the resources to make a break with recreational football were in place. Gradually, therefore, a momentum was generated which was strong enough to create a new path in which the organisational form of the club distinguishes between recreational football and professional football.

Football fitness – a new path?

An internal document dated 2010 (DBU(b)) dealing with the development of FF states that its primary objectives are to:

> recruit more adult recreational footballers for the organised clubs, raise the profile of football as a health-enhancing activity (…), create interest in using football for training (no tournament structure) (…) and support clubs in creating more flexibility in what they offer to adult recreational footballers.

This description is further elaborated in the first FF folder (DBU(c)) in early 2011:

> DBU is now introducing FF, which is inspired by the sociable and fun aspects of football and the flexibility of gyms. (…) Football is the best form of combined training, and very effective in preventing lifestyle diseases. (…) It (FF) is fitness football with like-minded people, at times to suit you, and the emphasis is on exercise, fun and teamwork. FF should provide an offering at existing football clubs to people (…) who would like to play football but who have neither the time nor the inclination to play as part of the traditional framework, with training several times a week and matches at specific times. (…) (FF is) always played with a ball and on small pitches, so each player gets more touches of the ball and is a bigger part of the game. A dedicated trainer is not necessary, and playing football can be combined with fitness exercises, for example, if participants want a whole-body workout. Football is an effective form of exercise for improving health and fitness and offers better combined exercise than running or weight training.

Moreover, relationships are formed on the football pitch which makes it easier to keep up the new habit.

Three aspects should be highlighted as characteristic of FF if we are to understand the activity in relation to recreational football and professional football, respectively. Firstly, it should be organised by existing clubs (associations) that already organise recreational football. Secondly, there is an articulated health perspective. And thirdly, there is no tournament structure.

It is worth noting that FF is not rooted in the same explicit desire from the surroundings, as was the case with the introduction of professional football, which, as stated, DBU fought against for a number of years. However, DBU itself is presenting the idea for the introduction of FF. However, this does not mean that FF is coming from nothing, as several conditions can be observed as elements that have challenged and irritated the existing path (recreational football) towards unlocking. This includes changes in the sporting habits of Danes, which necessarily includes football. The following quote from the Danish Institute for Sports Studies (Idan, 2010) is presented in the internal paper (DBU(b)) dealing with FF:

> Danish football clubs need to start developing adult football. (…) after the early childhood years, football clubs are world champions at developing talent – and getting rid of the less talented players. Teenagers and adults are leaving football clubs in droves and hitting the running tracks and gyms so that they can pursue activities. (…) first and foremost, this must be explained by the fact that football clubs are unable to organise football training that the population has the opportunity and desire to get involved in after the first years of childhood and adolescence.

In combination with numbers showing that football is a highly popular children's sport, after which its popularity is lost, Idan's quote above can be viewed as an external consultant reveals critical issues in the existing organisational discourse. Regarding the "anchors" of applying the path breaking concepts model, this perspective is situated as a cognitive focus. Moreover, the internal paper (DBU(b)) also mentions commercial "pay 'n' play" scenarios, where a group of players pays a private stakeholder for access to a football pitch. These are examples of stakeholders that could take on the role of provider of a flexible form of recreational football. It is emphasised that if FF is unsuccessful, DBU can "look forward to much greater competition from other providers of recreational football on the Danish market in the future"; but if it does succeed, "there are some very large membership gains ahead, with corresponding subscription income for football clubs" (DBU(b)). These factors are helping to challenge the reflection trap. That said, as mentioned at the outset, a large number of studies were published in the years leading up to FF that provides "new knowledge" underpinning the link between football and health (e.g Football as Prevention,

SJMSS, 2010). Moreover, DBU's national strategy for the further development of Danish football from 2010 (DBU(d)) should also be highlighted. This strategy states:

> Football's position as the country's most attractive team sport based on market share must be maintained and expanded. (…) The key word is flexibility when it comes to registering and playing. Attraction, development and player retention must be achieved by providing relevant and contemporary high-quality football activities, regardless of players' individual potential and ambitions. (…) The broad perception of football as a unique team sport (…) must be linked to the health importance of football (and) the importance of football for the development of social skills.

This strategy, which stands as the skeleton of FF to an extent in the quotation above, can be seen as a point of critical juncture. The identity associated with football as a competitive sport, where a self-reinforcing focus is to train with the aim of doing well in the weekend match, is challenged here. The strategy writes explicitly about flexibility and health and suggests that some behavioural routines should be challenged. Regarding the "anchors" of applying the path breaking concepts model this perspective is situated as an emotional focus. The activities of futsal, beach soccer, street football and panna[2] should also be mentioned in this regard as activities in DBU that irritate the self-perpetuating norm that exists in recreational football, in terms of rethinking the form of the game. This perspective holds a social focus. Finally, it should be stressed that the launch of FF does not affect DBU's operating budget. FF is launched with funding from DIF (DBU(a)) and funding allocated for new projects and development. So, in relation to the resource focus, DBU does not have to fear losing or reallocating resources, and so are not victims of the sunk cost trap. Moreover, it should be noted that the idea in the long term is for FF to become self-sustaining at local clubs (Bennike, 2016).

Unlike the professional path, FF does not break with the organisational form of recreational football as activities have to be organised by existing clubs (associations). On the other hand, FF does appear to break with the sporting form of recreational football, where the emphasis is on the tournament element. Instead, the focus is on health, which at the same time allows individual FF teams to play by their own rules (see, for example, Bennike, 2016). No team is locked down by rules related to tournaments. An attempt is made to capture these points in Table 9.1.

Discussion and concluding remarks

As touched upon in the introduction, between 2007 and 2011 the Swedish Sports Confederation was intending to develop youth sport (Karp et al., 2014). Some interesting parallels can be drawn despite the fact that adults form the target group for FF. In an article by Fahlén et al. (2015), the authors note that a scenario was set up in Sweden whereby grassroots sports clubs can apply for funding for initiatives that have the desired focus; in this case, gender and class equality. The authors conclude that this form "pushes" the task of development onto sports clubs, which are left with a responsibility that they have neither asked for nor accepted. In relation to this, several studies paint a picture of a lack of desire to take on such responsibility, as sports clubs are predominantly oriented towards their core activity (see, for example, Nichols & James, 2008). This refers to the activity being pursued; recreational football, for example. Karp et al. (2014) have also focused on the Swedish scenario and conclude that funding is predominantly granted to initiatives that deal with recruitment. Thus, the activities conducted do not contribute to the development of activities, but rather to inertia and consolidation of the existing path. In contrast, FF is an initiative where the Danish Football Association (DBU) does not "push the task on" but intentionally tries to initiate change and thus challenge the established path and its inertia. This is being done in a form whereby DBU is setting the framework for the sporting form of football to develop and change with the desire to involve a new target group and at the same time respond to a potential threat from commercial providers. Interestingly FF is predominantly played by women at the age 25–59 (Bennike et al., 2014), even though the activity does not have a specific gender ideology or focus. Removing the focus on competition, reducing the emphasis on football skills – both tactical and technical – and the fact that FF is mainly played by middle-aged women, represent a distinct break with recreational football.

In relation to the implementation of what are known as top-down initiatives, which FF can be argued to be in some respects (Bennike, 2016), Vail (2007) writes that the needs of the community are essential, not the activity (core activity) in question:

> (…) top-down initiatives that ignore community needs have not succeeded in sustaining sport participation. (…) Traditional strategies to address sport participation ignore the complexity of the problem of declining participation in sport and overlook a fundamental principle of participation – community development. (p. 571)

Vail's point regarding the needs of the local community is interesting in relation to the implementation of FF. The analysis above shows that FF breaks with the sporting path of recreational football (the core activity), particularly as there is no tournament structure. Taking into account that clubs predominantly have the core activity in mind, implementation difficulties could be predicted that are linked to clubs' lack of interest. Here, however, it is essential to note that FF is malleable, in the sense that clubs can organise it in a form that suits them within the framework defined. Here, the needs of the local community are considered to a much greater extent than is the case for recreational football as an ideal type. And the club's needs can be accommodated at the same time. Bennike (2016) have monitored the local implementation of FF at four clubs by means of case studies. In two cases in particular, FF is openly distancing itself from recreational football but not from the needs of the local community, as testified by an increasing number of FF participants. These clubs are just two of many hundreds currently organising FF, which must also challenge a rigid understanding of recreational football as the core activity of football clubs if such an understanding exists. There is some evidence to suggest that the core activity cannot be defined quite so simply, and that this may involve several conventions (Skille, 2011), implying multiple paths. Having said that, the importance of recreational football and the norms and values that exist within it cannot be ignored. This is particularly true in the before mentioned case study, where the FF activity in one case is confusingly similar to recreational football, with the key difference that the team does not participate in tournaments. However, it should be mentioned that several of the players who participate play for other teams at the club that play actively in tournaments. Clearly the sporting form of the FF in this club does not have the nature of the path-breaking that the analysis suggests exists. Arguably this is due to path dependency, where FF in this case is based on recreational football. According to Bennike (2016), this challenge predominates for FF teams where participants already play and/or have played recreational football.

Another example demonstrating that the path is difficult to break is that some clubs have taken the initiative, in cooperation with DBU, to arrange FF fixtures so they can compete against other clubs. Holding fixtures requires uniform rules, and the participating teams (possibly) want to win and will therefore train with the aim of optimising their performance within a specific set of rules. This means that FF is moving closer to recreational football, where the tournament remains a mainstay. This will reduce the break in the form of the game as indicated by the analysis and will potentially result in a "more of the same – situation", with a focus on recruitment rather than development and change. In this light and given the fact that clubs can (if they find the need) organise FF in a form that suits them, they can "decide" for themselves the extent to which the activity breaks with the path of recreational football. Importantly and with reference to Vail (2007), it can be added that the activity will only be successful if it suits the needs of the local community. With FF, DBU has created a framework for clubs to link the needs of the local community with the activities of the club to a greater extent than is the case with recreational football. In some cases, it will break with the path of recreational football, while in others it will not. Skille (2008) writes in his paper Understanding Sport Clubs as Sport Policy Implementers – A theoretical Framework for the Analysis of the Implementation of Central Sport Policy through Local and Voluntary Sport Organizations: "The outcome of a specific programme always depends on the grassroots implementer" (p. 185).

Notes

1 This analysis is also published in Danish by Bennike & Ottesen (2019), which is recognised as a key paper to this chapter.
2 Panna is a street football game, where you (normally) play 1 vs. 1 on a small pitch. You can gain points by scoring in a small goal or by playing the ball between your opponent's legs.

References

Bennike, S. (2016). *Fodbold Fitness – Implementeringen af en ny fodboldkultur* [Football Fitness – The implementation of a new football culture] [Doctoral dissertation. University of Copenhagen, Denmark].
Bennike, S., Storm, R., Wikman, J. M., & Ottesen, L. (2019). The organisation of club football in Denmark – a contemporary profile. *Soccer & Society*, 21(5), 551–571. 10.1080/14660970.2019.1690472
Bennike, S., Wikman, J. M., & Ottesen, L. (2014). Football Fitness – a new version of football? A concept for adult players in Danish football clubs. *Scandinavian Journal of Medicine & Science in Sports*, 24(S1), 138–146.
Campbell, J. L. (2004). *Institutional change and globalization*. Princeton University Press.
Creswell, J. W. (2007). *Qualitative inquiry & research – choosing among five approaches*. Sage publications, Inc.
DBU(a). (2010). *Pressemeddelelse: Fodbold som fitness*. [Press release: Football as fitness].
DBU(b). (2010). *Fodbold Fitness (motionsfodbold)*. [Football Fitness (exercise football)].
DBU(c). (2010). *Fodbold Fitness – Din sunde og fleksible mulighed*. [Football Fitness – your healthy and flexible opportunity].
DBU(d). (2010). *Passion, Udvikling, Fællesskab – Strategi for videreudviklingen af dansk fodbold til 2015*. [Passion, development and community – Strategy for development of Danish football 2015].
Fahlén, J., Eliasson, I., & Wikman, K. (2015). Resisting self-regulation: An analysis of sport policy programme making and implementation in Sweden. *International Journal of Sport Policy and Politics*, 7(3), 391–406.
Gammelsæter, H., & Senaux, B. (2011). *The organisation and governance of top football across Europe: An institutional perspective*. Routledge.
Grønkjær, A., & Olsen, D. H. (2007). *Fodbold, fairplay og forretning* [Football, fairplay and business]. Turbineforlaget.
Idan. (2010). *Over blik – Nyt fra Idan* [Overview – News from Idan], No. 31.
Karp, S., Fahlén, J., & Löfgren, K. (2014). More of the same instead of qualitative leaps: A study of inertia in the Swedish sports system. *European Journal for Sport and Society*, 11(3), 301–320.
Krustrup, P., Christensen, J. F., Randers, M. B., Pedersen, H., Sundstrup, E., Jakobsen, M. D., Krustrup, B. R., Nielsen, J. J., Suetta, C., Nybo, L., & Bangsbo, J. (2010). Muscle adaptations and performance enhancements of soccer training for untrained men. *European Journal of Applied Physiology*, 108(6), 1247–1258.
Krustrup, P., Helge, E. W., Hansen, P. R., Aagaard, P., Hagman, M., Randers, M. B., de Sousa, M., & Mohr, M. (2018). Effects of recreational football on women's fitness

and health: Adaptations and mechanisms. *European Journal of Applied Physiology*, 118(1), 11–32.

Krustrup, P., Nielsen, J. J., Krustrup, B. R., Christensen, J. F., Pedersen, H., Randers, M. B., Aagaard, P., Petersen, A. M., Nybo, L., & Bangsbo, J. (2009). Recreational soccer is an effective health promoting activity for untrained men. *British Journal of Sports Medicine*, 43(11), 825–831.

Laub, T. B. (2013). *Danskernes motions- og sportsvaner 2011*. [Sport and exercise habits among Danes]. Idrættens Analyseinstitut.

Mahoney, J. (2000). Path dependence in historical sociology. *Theory and society*, 29(4), 507–548.

Milanović, Z., Čović, N., Helge, E. W., Krustrup, P., & Mohr, M. (2022). Recreational football and bone health: A systematic review and meta-analysis. *Sports Medicine*, 52(12), 3021–3037.

Milanović, Z., Pantelić, S., Čović, N., Sporiš, G., & Krustrup, P. (2015). Is recreational soccer effective for improving VO2max? A systematic review and meta-analysis. *Sports Medicine*, 45(9), 1339–1353.

Milanović, Z., Pantelić, S., Čović, N., Sporiš, G., Mohr, M., & Krustrup, P. (2019). Broad-spectrum physical fitness benefits of recreational football: A systematic review and meta-analysis. *British Journal of Sports Medicine*, 53(15), 926–939.

Nichols, G., & James, M. (2008). One size does not fit all: Implications of sports club diversity for their effectiveness as a policy tool and for government support. *Managing Leisure*, 13(2), 104–114.

Ottesen, L., & Jakobsen, P. J. (2011). *Idræt og velfærdspolitik* [Sport and welfare policy]. *Forum for idræt*, 27(5–9). https://tidsskrift.dk/forumforidraet/article/view/31609/29054

Randers, M. B., Nielsen, J. J., Bangsbo, J., & Krustrup, P. (2014). Physiological response and activity profile in recreational small-sided football: No effect of the number of players. *Scandinavian Journal of Medicine & Science in Sports*, 24(S1). 130–137.

Randers, M. B., Nybo, L., Petersen, J., Nielsen, J. J., Christiansen, L., Bendiksen, M., Brito, J., Bangsbo, J., & Krustrup, P. (2010). Activity profile and physiological response to football training for untrained males and females, elderly and youngsters: Influence of the number of players. *Scandinavian Journal of Medicine & Science in Sports*, 20(S1), 14–23.

Randers, M. B., Ørntoft, C., Hagman, C., Nielsen, J. J., & Krustrup, P. (2018). Movement pattern and physiological response in recreational small-sided football-effect of number of players with a fixed pitch size. *Journal of Sports Sciences*, 36(13), 1549–1556.

SJMSS. (2010). Football for health – prevention of risk factors for non-communicable diseases. *Scandinavian Journal of Medicine & Science in Sports*, 20(S1): 1–135.

Skille, E. (2008). Understanding sport clubs as sport policy implementers – a theoretical framework for the analysis of the implementation of central sport policy through local and voluntary sport organizations. *International Review for the Sociology of Sport*, 43(2) 181–200.

Skille, E. Å. (2011). The conventions of sport clubs: Enabling and constraining the implementation of social goods through sport. *Sport, Education and Society*, 16(2), 241–253.

Sydow, J., Schreyögg, G., & Koch, J. (2005). Organizational paths: Path dependency and beyond. *21st. EGOS Colloquium*. June 30–July 2, 2005, Berlin, Germany.

Thing, L. F., & Ottesen, L. (2013). Young people's perspectives on health, risks and physical activity in a Danish secondary school. *Health, Risk & Society, 15*(5), 463–477. 10.1080/13698575.2013.802294

Vail, S. E. (2007). Community development and sport participation. *Journal of Sport Management, 21*(4), 571–596.

Equality and Gender

Chapter 10

Five Decades of Women's Football in Finland

Hanna Vehviläinen, Hannu Itkonen, Mihaly Szerovay, and Arto Nevala

Introduction

The year 2021 marked the 50th anniversary of holding the first official women's football series in Finland. By 2022, football has become the most popular team sport for women and girls with over 38,000 registered players. Their growing number in football reflects a change in society, women's position and sports culture as a whole.

The Nordic countries played a significant role when women's football started to grow in popularity. This chapter aims to map how women's football has changed in Finland during the past 50 years. This change is highlighted through historical periodisation, which is a common method in the social sciences, where change is presented as periods of time that follow each other.

The chapter addresses two primary questions: (1) What periods can be identified in the change of Finnish women's football between 1971 and 2021? (2) What are the turning points and key characteristics of the periods? Our secondary questions focus on what the Football Association of Finland (FAF) has done to promote women's football and how the sport has attracted more participants and become more competitive. The research material of the chapter includes FAF's annual reports and its *Football Yearbooks* as well as other texts on Finnish football culture.

Research on women's football has become more active in recent years. In 2022, the Finnish Society for Sport History published the book *Enemmän kuin peliä: Naisten jalkapallo tasa-arvon tiellä maailmalla ja Suomessa* (More than a game: Women's football on the way to equality worldwide and in Finland) by Vesa Vares. Johanna Ruohonen (2022) authored the book *Naisten laji: Kirja jalkapallosta* (Women's sport: A book about football). Both books describe the history of women's football based on extensive literature and interview materials. Several theses have been written on women's football. Hanna Vehviläinen and Hannu Itkonen (2009) presented the periods of change in women's football in Finland, Susanna Elenius (2019) explored women's football as part of FAF's activities, and Anni Väisänen (2019) analysed the differences between women's football in Finland and Sweden.

DOI: 10.4324/9781003280729-15

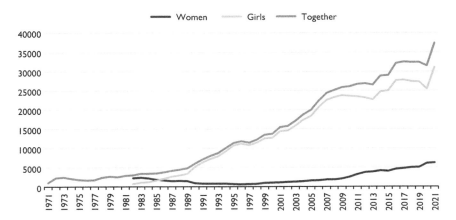

Figure 10.1 The number of registered women and girl players in Finland from 1971 to 2021.

Source: Football Yearbooks (Suomen Palloliitto, 2007–2021) and annual reports of the FA of Finland (Suomen Palloliitto, 2011–2020).

Finnish women's football can be divided into five periods: initial enthusiasm and organisation from 1971 to 1982, stabilisation from 1982 to 1992, the rise of girls' football from 1992 to 2001, a leap into popularity from 2001 to 2010, and differentiation from 2010 onwards, which is still going on. The most essential changes are the growing number of players – which is shown in Figure 10.1 – internationalisation, and differentiation. Besides competitive leagues, Finland now has lower league levels and recreational football. Children start at a younger age, the national teams play more games, and players are more often transferred to foreign leagues.

The early stages

European women took up football during the First World War, particularly in Britain. Female workers now conquered the empty football fields in their leisure time. One of the best-known teams established during the war was Dick, Kerr's Ladies. After the war, men returned to factories and also wanted the football fields back. In 1921, the Football Association (FA) of England took the radical decision to ban women from the fields of the association's clubs. The reason given was that the sport did not suit women. The decision had long-term consequences, as many other European countries established the same rule. Women's football thus disappeared for almost 50 years. Fortunately, despite the bans, many brave and determined women played the sport on a smaller scale, and it got off to a good start again at the end of the 1960s (Vares, 2022).

Along with urbanisation the popularity of team sports, primarily football, baseball and bandy, grew in 1930s Finland. According to Tuunainen (2007), even in Finland football was not regarded as suitable for women for health reasons. However, it was the ideal sport for healthy and vital boys. Despite the opposition, there are signs of women's football activity in Finland during the 1930s and 1940s.

Vehviläinen and Itkonen (2009) pointed out that there are various interpretations about the birth of women's football. The social climate of the 1960s and 1970s undeniably created conditions for women's social equality aspirations. Women's increased free time and better opportunities for education and employment also influenced sport-related goals. Three factors have been highlighted when explaining women's growing interest in football and competitive sports in general. First, women moving from home to employment gained the courage to also break other male-dominated spheres of life. The women's movement claimed gender equality, and breaking gender norms and traditions was part of the spirit of the times. Third, a fitness and health sport philosophy spread in the country, aiming to improve people's mental and physical health.

Initial enthusiasm and organisation (1971–1982)

When women's football grew in popularity in the 1960s, the Union of European Football Associations (UEFA) had to take action. According to UEFA, women were already playing football in almost half of its member countries. In November 1970, UEFA asked the national associations to take women's football under their protection to prevent its uncontrolled development and leadership by shrewd so-called managers.

Similar to the rest of Europe, the activities began in Finland in the late 1960s. Among the Nordic countries, Finland, Sweden and Denmark were active rather early (Vehviläinen & Itkonen, 2009). The kick-off took place in Mikkeli, where women played in a small-scale company league. Women's football had gained more popularity in many Finnish localities, and the first national football tournament was organised in summer 1971, where the female teams of six men's Championship League teams were invited from Helsinki, Turku, Mikkeli, Tampere and Lahti (Tuunainen, 2007).

In 1971, the executive committee decided – in compliance with the recommendations of FIFA (Fédération Internationale de Football Association) and UEFA – to include women's football in the activities of the national association. All competitions were to take place within the association's member clubs. A domestic major competition would be organised in the first year, while the district organisations were responsible for local competitions (Vehviläinen & Itkonen, 2009). Based on the Finnish organisational activity model, the FAF had district organisations, which were in charge of developing the sport and organising competitions in the region (Itkonen & Nevala, 2006).

Despite the fast schedule, 51 teams participated in the first year's competition, including participants from all the 18 district organisations. The first women's final was played at the Helsinki Olympic Stadium on 14 September 1971, and HJK Helsinki won the championship (Vehviläinen & Itkonen, 2009). The first season went better than expected. There were 984 listed female players after the season, and in the second season already 2,252. After the first couple of years, however, playing lost its novelty, and the sport did not spread in the expected way. Elenius (2019) noted that many women quit when the club started to play in the first division and the game became more serious.

The aim of FAF was to develop the national competition system of women's football, to establish regional preliminary stages, and to launch competitive activities for girls. The FAF wanted to be in charge of international activities and the domestic premier division. More extensive organising of competitions and increasing the number of participants were left to the district organisations. Because of their small number of staff, the district organisations were unable to invest in women's football as much as would have been necessary to spread the sport (Vehviläinen & Itkonen, 2009). The number of registered players rose to only 2,830 in ten years. By the end of 1981, all 18 district organisations had included women's football in their programme, but only 11 districts had girls' teams. In many of them, development was slowed down by the low number of teams, as they were not sufficient for competitions. In the 1970s hardly any efforts were made to promote girls' football even though there certainly were girls who were interested in the sport (Elenius, 2019).

Enthusiasm for women's and girls' football caught on slower in Finland than in many other European countries, even though the women's football committee discussed organising the first international game as early as 1972 (Vehviläinen & Itkonen, 2009). In Sweden the number of registered female players exceeded 10,000 already in 1973 (Byström, 1973), whereas Finland had the same amount of registered players only about 20 years later, in 1994. The historic first international match of Finnish female footballers took place in 1973 when Finland challenged Sweden in the Åland Islands. It was the first international match for both countries, broadcast live on Finnish television. The 1,540 spectators at the event were a record for the Mariehamn sports field. The game consisted of two 30-minute halves and ended in a scoreless draw (Byström, 1973).

The Nordic countries played a key role in the growing popularity of women's football in the early years because the sport developed rapidly in these countries. In 1974, Finland hosted the first women's Nordic Championship tournament, attended by Denmark, Sweden and Finland. Denmark was regarded as the top country of women's football because it had won the unofficial 1971 World Cup in Mexico. Norway joined the European Competition for Women's Football organised in 1979 (FIFA World Football Museum, 2019).

Vehviläinen and Itkonen (2009) have argued that Finnish women's team sport culture was still weak in the 1970s. Women's competitive sport history has focused on individual sports, and particularly skiing and athletics have been more popular than team sports. Women played Finnish baseball (*pesäpallo*) in the summer, which was one reason for the slow development of football culture. Finland has lacked the strong handball culture of the other Nordic countries. Furthermore, Finnish women's football did not start at universities, workplaces or other existing communities, like it did in Sweden. Finnish women's football teams had to be created from scratch. Men's football gained a strong foothold in Finland through the school institution. Football was not part of girls' physical education curricula, so they did not play football at school even if they had wanted. It was also challenging to find coaches and background staff for the teams.

Consolidation period (1982–1992)

Finland has closely followed the development of football in Sweden. The Swedish Football Association carried out a survey on the state of women's football; already in the 1970s women's football was mostly taken seriously and gained the attention of the media as well as of spectators (Väisänen, 2019). Inspired by the Swedish example, FAF conducted a survey on the state of football in 1982. The survey highlighted the following key challenges of women's football: (1) the lack of appreciation, (2) the small number of participants and excessive emphasis on southern Finland, (3) the insufficiency and low quality of coaches, (4) poor top level and (5) unsuccessful launching of girls' football (Vehviläinen & Itkonen, 2009, p. 66).

The FAF consequently founded a women's committee to develop women's football, which was active until 1991. Schools were seen as channels to recruit new players. Cooperation increased between FAF, the Finnish School Sport Federation and the National Board of General Education, and in 1985 FAF organised the first national competition between schools (Vehviläinen & Itkonen, 2009). For the first time, the number of girl footballers exceeded the number of women players in 1986 (Figure 10.1).

Year 1991 was named as the theme year of girls' football to engage more players, increase participation in the sport in schools, make the sport better known and improve its image. The theme year was featured numerous events and the cooperation between districts, clubs and schools improved (Tuunainen, 2007). FAF also employed the first part-time employee in charge of female football. Huge plans had been made, but it was not possible to realise all of them. Nevertheless, the number of registered players grew by 1,100 during the year (Vehviläinen & Itkonen, 2009.)

The women's premier division had searched for its final form throughout its first decade. In addition to the premier division, there were also lower divisions (the first division and the regional division). In 1985, there were ten premier division teams, which became the established format until 2008. The present playing time of two 45-minute halves was introduced in 1989 because it was already used in Sweden and Norway (Vehviläinen & Itkonen, 2009). In 1981, women's football received its first major sponsor when the National Workers' Savings Bank (*Suomen Työväen Säästöpankki*, STS) started to sponsor women's Finnish Cup. The competition was accordingly called the STS Cup (Tuunainen, 2007).

FIFA organised the first international football tournament for women in 1988 in Guangzhou, China, and the first official World Championship tournament also in China in 1991. The European countries for the tournament were selected based on the European Championship (Euro) tournament of the preceding year. The Finnish national team played only a few yearly matches during the first years. The women's national team regularly took part in European Championship qualifying games. Even though they put in good performances, usually ended up third in a qualification group of four teams.

The organisation of major international competitions has motivated national sports associations to establish youth national teams. The first European Championship youth tournament was played in the 1997–1998 season and the Youth World Championships in the 2000s (Ruohonen, 2022). The Finnish girls' national team was formed in 1987 by scouting the promising under 16-year-olds, and the under 19-year-old girls started national team activities in 1990 (Vehviläinen & Itkonen, 2009).

The mobility of Finnish female footballers to international clubs was still quite uncommon even among national team players in the 1970s. In those days, players usually moved to neighbouring sports clubs. The first Finnish national team player played in a Swedish club in July 1980 when Åsa Wennström from Åland moved to Hammarby in Stockholm (Itkonen et al., 2014).

The appreciation of the sport clearly grew in the 1980s. People no longer debated whether football suits girls and women (Vares, 2022). The FAF started to consciously improve the attitudes towards women's football. The theme year of girl football (1991) meant the final breakthrough and a change in entrenched attitudes; it anticipated the rise of football to the most popular team sport among girls during the following decade.

The rise of girls' football (1992–2001)

Finland's economy ended up in a profound recession in the early 1990s, which also affected our sports culture. Because of the tight economy, around the mid-1990s, the Ministry of Education adopted performance-based practices for grants allocated to sports associations. The focus shifted on the promotion of physical activity among children and youth as well as adults. Organisations were expected to consider the value basis of the Sports Act, including equality (Vasara, 2004). This also meant that FAF had to increasingly consider girls and women. Its investment now focused on girls' football, and women's premier division and national team were chosen as the sport's flagships. Vehviläinen and Itkonen (2009) reported that the women's committee, which had for almost ten years been in charge of female football at FAF, was suspended in 1991 and replaced by a development group for women's and girls' football. The nationwide *Kaikki pelaa* (Football for all) youth strategy was created in 1999, and it included girls' football right from the beginning.

In the early days women's football was mainly played in Helsinki, Turku, Tampere, Kemi and Kuopio. As the sport grew, it became even more urban. For example, at the beginning of the 1990s, one-third of the players came from the southern part of the country. Because participation in league activities could require long travelling, some clubs gradually became less active (Väisänen, 2019). The FAF was worried about the concentration of the sport in southern Finland simultaneously as the number of licensed players had started to decrease. As a quick remedy, FAF hired an employee to develop women's and girls' football at the club level.

In the early 1990s, the number of over 20-year-old female players was about 900, while the number for girl players had surpassed 5,000. The number of girl players nearly doubled from 1992 to 2001, while no change was seen in that of women (Figure 10.1). There were slightly less than 300 teams taking part in women's competitions, and women's special football clubs were about ten, but there were only about 50 female coaches (Tuunainen, 2007). It turned out to be challenging to make women and girls stay with the sport. As a result of various factors, girls often quit when moving from junior to women's teams. The most concrete factor was having to leave one's familiar team. Young women found that the social aspects of football were important. A problem for women's and girls' football was the lack of an age group for 18- to 20-year-olds because a leap from the U-16 group straight to women's matches turned out to be excessive. In the 1990s, there were no lower age groups at the hobby level. Many young women's motivation for football decreased because other activities became more important.

Regarding international football, the 1999 Women's World Cup in the United States has been regarded as the turning point for women's football. Live broadcasting raised the profile of the event to a broader audience. The final between the United States and China in Pasadena was attended by 90,185 spectators. The United States won the World Championship on penalty kicks. The championship gave a boost to professional football as national associations started to understand that more and more women and girls wanted to play football and needed encouragement (FIFA World Football Museum, 2019).

International connectivity increased along with growing competitiveness and as a result, women and girls played significantly more international matches in the 1990s (Itkonen et al., 2014). This growth was contributed to by the start of European Championship qualifying games in the 1980s, the qualifying games for the World Cup since 1997, and national team activities for girls since the 1980s. Moreover, international tournaments for women's club teams started. HJK Helsinki played for the first time in an international tournament in Taiwan as early as 1978, the Nordic countries organised their own league tournament in the early 1990s, and women's UEFA Cup finally began in 2001 (Tuunainen, 2007). Finland's first international success in football was by the country's youngest national team, the U-16 team, which won the 1994 Nordic Championship in Iceland. The international achievements continued in the following year when the girls of Mäkelänrinne upper secondary school won the World Championship of general upper secondary schools.

A leap into popularity (2001–2009)

The changes in society were bound to be visible in sports culture. The updated Sports Act of 1998 included both the internal development of sports culture and the implementation of social wellness policies through physical activity. The aim was not only to promote equality in sports and physical activity but also to promote equality with the help of sports and physical activity. Along with the legal reform, more emphasis was laid on research related to equality and on information steering (Pyykönen, 2016). At the same time, value-related tensions were identified in the sports culture and organisations among the following three sectors: competitive and world-class sports, physical activity for children and youth, and recreational and health-promoting exercise. Side by side with traditional sports club activities, the aim was to bring new sport activities to daycare centres, schools, afternoon clubs and workplaces (Heikkala, 2000).

The Swedish Football Association had launched a project called *Dam projektilen* in 1998 to promote girls' and women's football. Finland saw a huge potential in female football, so it launched a project of its own following the Swedish example. The goal of this F.U.N. project (2001–2006) was to strengthen the role of girls' and women's football in Finnish football culture. The name of the project came from the Finnish words *futaa, unelmoi, nauti*, meaning "play football, dream, enjoy". During the F.U.N. project, the number of registered female players grew from 13,770 to 22,364 by 2006. The project's initial goal of 25,000 players was achieved in 2009 (Figure 10.1).

There have been various projects and campaigns in female football to increase visibility. The club team HJK Helsinki even progressed to the UEFA Cup semi-finals in 2002. The achievements of the Finnish women's national team, in contrast, lagged far behind the other Nordic countries. When the national team had no success, people were not interested in it and no resources were allocated to it. The visibility of women's football nearly exploded in 2004 when the national team advanced from the qualifiers to the Euro 2005 by beating Russia in the second round of the qualification tournament. This was the first time for a Finnish adults' national team to make its way to a major game. Visibility was also enhanced by the U-19 girls' European Championships played in Finland in summer 2004.

In the Euro 2005 in England, the Finnish national team sensationally advanced to the semi-finals, with more than 400,000 spectators watching the semi-final against Germany on Finnish television (Vehviläinen & Itkonen, 2009).

Anne Mäkinen was nominated as the best player of the entire tournament (Vares, 2022). There were efforts to take advantage of the boom caused by the team's European Championship success because of the unprecedented media visibility of women's football. In 2006, Finland successfully applied for the right to organise the women's Euro 2009, which were played in Helsinki, Lahti, Tampere and Turku.

The resources of the women's national team were modest, and only their success changed the situation. For example, after the European Championship success and the major games organised in Finland, the team received its first full-time head coach when Michael Käld was hired at the beginning of 2009. Before that, the team's head coach had worked on a part-time basis, alongside their regular job. Käld, for instance, worked as a class teacher. Väisänen (2019) noted that in Sweden, as a point of comparison, the women's national team received its first full-time coach in 1980. The Euro organised in Finland set the attendance record for the women's national team, which still stands: the opening match between Finland and Denmark at Helsinki Olympic Stadium was attended by over 16,000 spectators. Finland advanced from its own group to the next round but lost against England in the semi-final played in Turku. Germany won the Euro 2005 by defeating England 6–2 at Olympic Stadium (Vares, 2022).

Hosting a major tournament in Finland had no direct impact on participation in football (Figure 10.1). Despite the lack of impact, hosting the tournament was useful in other ways: media attention had a positive impact on the image of the sport, and attendance at games was high (Vares, 2022). The Finnish Sports Gala chose the tournament as the sports event of the year, and the national team striker Laura Österberg Kalmari was nominated as the sportsperson of the year. This demonstrated the strengthening of female footballers' position as role models for girls. With its success in the 2000s, the national team had cleared its way to everyday discussions.

The differentiation period from 2010 onwards

The phase that began in the 2010s can be called the differentiation period. An increasing number of girls and women have chosen football as their sport activity. Girls have started to play football at a younger age, and many of them have found a suitable level where to play. Recreational leagues have been established, and the lower levels extend even to the fourth division and in futsal to the first division.

The football domain has broadened so that women are also seen as actors outside of the actual playing field. The level of women's *drop in* has been strengthened, in other words, the aim is for women to remain within the sport after their playing careers as coaches, team leaders, club workers or other volunteers. The COVID-19 pandemic that started in 2020 reduced the number of participants to the 2015 level, but in spring 2021 it started to rise again. The number of women and girl footballers exceeded 37,000 in 2021.

The project *Osoitteena futis* (The address is football) aimed to develop a novel sports culture with the help of its "Princess and Knight models". As a result of the project, the age of the largest girl group starting to play football fell first to 7–8 years and then to 6–9 years. The football clubs participating in the project organised events in schools and day-care centres, where children were encouraged to join football club activities. The project developed new hobby activities for 9–16-year-old players. In addition, football clubs aimed at increasing the number of volunteers working in clubs. The UEFA Playmakers programme was launched in Finland in 2021 in cooperation with UEFA and Disney. In that year, over 2,000 girls from 5 to 8 years old had the opportunity to take their first steps in football through the programme, guided by more than 250 coaches. In women's European Championship year 2022, the programme was extended to enable more girls in different locations to have easy and safe ways to get to know football.

Several national and regional events were organised yearly in recreational football. The number of women's hobby teams has grown every year. The number of registered women players (up to 20 years old) increased over 6,000 from 2012 to 2021 (Figure 10.1).

According to Väisänen (2019) the number of women performing different roles within the football sector can be regarded as essential for the development of the sport because women are more eager than men to actively promote women's football. For example, in Sweden women worked in major positions as early as in the 1970s and actively participated in courses specifically designed for them. In the Finnish football sector, attention was paid to the number of women in relevant positions only in the 1990s, and in 2007 the FAF and the district organisations created an action plan to promote women's engagement in decision-making and the organisation of football activities.

One of the objectives of the Act on the Promotion of Sports and Physical Activity (390/2015) was to promote equality and non-discrimination, and the Ministry of Education and Culture accordingly started to require that organisations create equality plans to be eligible for government aid (Pyykönen, 2016). In 2020 about 24% of Finland's registered football players were women and girls, but women's share in football-related tasks was not at the same level. Women were underrepresented especially in decision-making and managerial tasks. The target was now that all expert and decision-making groups should have at least 25% of their representatives from both genders (Suomen Palloliitto, 2021). The number of women in different football tasks has been increased through various measures, such as targeted training programmes. Women's role in the decision-making of FAF, the district organisations and football clubs was enhanced by organising the first *Naiset jalkapallojohtajina* (Women in Football Leadership) programme together with FIFA in 2015.

From local games to the global fields

According to Itkonen et al. (2014), when globalisation reaches the local level, new glocal practices arise: for example, in women's football the sharpest top concentrates on a few clubs. Step by step, players move to bigger clubs from their small local clubs, first within their own country and then internationally. Getting to high-level foreign clubs and teams has become a prerequisite for success.

In many ways, the mobility follows the trends and models of migration in general. The examination of the clubs of women's national team players reveals that in the 1980s and 1990s about every tenth player represented a foreign club, most commonly one from Sweden or the United States. In the early years of the 2000s, even nearly a third of our women's national team players represented a foreign club, most commonly a Swedish one. In the Euro 2005, 13 women played in the matches, seven of them based in Finland and six abroad. The Finnish team in the Euro 2009 consisted of 22 players, of whom only five represented a domestic club. In 2020, a total of 22 Finnish female footballers played in foreign premier divisions. Women are no longer transferred only to the Nordic countries but also to England, France, Spain and Italy. It is very unlikely that a woman can play professionally in Finland, but the reason for playing abroad is often development as a player rather than money. Almost all women study in addition to playing, also when playing abroad (Vares, 2022).

In the global division of labour, the Finnish women's premier division has always been mainly a league that trains players and serves as a stepping stone to higher leagues. Nevertheless, at the beginning of the 2000s, Finland also started to receive its first international players. Their number remained small in Finland but it is a demonstration of internationalisation and links to global football (Itkonen et al., 2014). Based on the FAF strategy 2020–2024, a great leap forward was taken in May 2019 when the FAF hired the former national team player Heidi Pihlaja as the first development manager of women's football and the executive manager of the Women's League (*Naisten liiga*). In the following spring, the women's premier division got a new strategy and a new name: the Women's League became the Subway National League (*Kansallinen Liiga*). The word *naisten* referring to women was omitted in order to shake the attitudes prevailing in sports and to act as a trailblazer of equality.

Clubs traditionally focusing their attention on men's football in Finland (e.g., HJK, Kuopion Palloseura) – in line with trends seen in other European countries – have increasingly embraced and invested in women's football. Simultaneously, the number of clubs concentrating solely on women's football (e.g., Kuopion Pallokissat, FC United Jakobstad, Jyväskylän Pallokerho) has shown a downward trend. A key driver behind these changes has been a growing pressure on clubs from many directions – civil society, state and sponsors – to put more emphasis on social equality and sustainability. These changes have provided more visibility and perhaps more resources to women's football, while creating challenges to smaller clubs.

International success

The national teams of women and girls played more international games from 2011 to 2019 than ever before. In 2020, the COVID-19 pandemic interrupted nearly all their activities. Finland has invested more in regional activities and developed training with the help of, for example, talent coaches in clubs. More clubs have hired full-time coaches, invested in girls' daily training, and upper secondary schools' sports-oriented programmes have been an important factor in the development of players. This has reflected particularly on the international success of girls' national teams, which have had regular success in the European Championship qualifiers, and the U-17 national team progressed to the European Championships in 2018 and 2022. National team activities expanded when the futsal national team started in October 2016. In the following year, the women's national futsal team played its first international games. Qualifying for major competitions and achieving success is harder than before because more countries currently invest in women's football. After dramatically defeating both Scotland and Portugal in the final minutes of the qualifying matches, the Finnish women's national team advanced to the European Championships played in summer 2022.

A giant step for equality was taken in 2019 when equal match compensation was introduced in men's and women's national teams. In addition, the players receive an equal percentage of the profits from major competitions. The agreement was highly significant for the players and a strong value statement by FAF. Finnish society strongly advocates for equality, including the principle of equal pay for equal work (Ruohonen, 2022). Norway was the first country to introduce equal compensation in 2017. Another important equality action was the Finnish Government's decision to include women's football matches in the list of socially significant sports events to be televised. The events must be broadcast in Finland so that they can be watched free of charge entirely or partly, either live or recorded (Valtioneuvosto, 2021).

In addition to the national team, Finnish female referees have also been internationally successful. Katriina Elovirta was the referee of semi-finals in the Women's World Cup finals in 1999 and 2003. Kirsi Heikkinen achieved the same in 2011. Lina Lehtovaara, on the other hand, was one of the referees in the UEFA Women's Euro 2022, and in the same year, she appointed to handle the final between Barcelona and Lyon in the UEFA Women's Champion League. From the perspective of gender equality, refereeing has crumbled the borders in international football. In the 2000s, female referees have crossed the line by taking first care first of men's lower division matches and later stepping into the premier leagues. One of the most famous female referees is the Frenchwoman Stephanie Frappart, who has been refereeing top league since 2019 and was also referee in the men's Euro 2020 (organised in 2021) as well as in the World Cup 2022. Surprisingly, the Nordic countries, known world-wide for their equality, come lagging: we have seen a female referee in the premier league matches only as the fourth official.

Discussion

Gender equality is a significant discussion point both in Finland and abroad. Mental images and attitudes towards female sports are changing. In football, the 2019 Women's World Cup is regarded as a turning point where the efforts of FIFA bore fruit as higher media attention as well as more spectators and partners. The visibility also produces role models for girl players, for whom professional football careers are an increasingly realistic dream.

The organisation of women's football started with a clear handicap as compared to men. The periods identified in women's and girls' football for the past five decades demonstrate how rapidly the gender inequalities have been reduced. Women's football has become more professionalised – just like men's football – although on a smaller scale. The professionalisation is visible as female players' transfers to high-level international clubs and as higher player wages. Many of the major men's football clubs, especially in England, France, Italy and Spain, have started to invest in women's football, which offers women opportunities to create a football career.

Professionalisation in Finnish women's football is also manifested as success. The national team has often made its way to international major tournaments. Finnish players have drawn interest within the global football system. Futsal has also taken its first steps when the national team activities have been enhanced and the domestic division system has been extended. The successful players of women's teams have served as positive role models for girls.

The goal-oriented activities of the Football Association of Finland (FAF) have enabled the success of women's football. FAF has supported girls' football through various projects. The role of women has simultaneously been strengthened at all levels of the football organisation. These actions have made football the most popular team sport among Finnish women and girls. More general equality efforts in Finnish society and the guidance policy of the Ministry of Education and Culture have also contributed to equality in football. Moreover, the improved training and playing conditions are a significant factor, even though full equality has not been achieved in this area either.

In Finnish football culture, women's and girls' football will encounter certain challenges despite its favourable development. As a result of lower birth rates, continuously shrinking age groups are a challenge for team sports, particularly in smaller localities. The organisers of women's and girls' football therefore also face competition with other sports. The struggle for new participants will become more intense, especially because new sports and forms of physical activity are continuously created. However, the positive development of girls' and women's football, our effective organisations, and the large number of participants suggest there will be enough female players on Finnish football fields also in the years to come.

References

Byström, B. (Ed.). (1973). *Fotbollboken: Med Svenska fotbollförbundets tävlingskalender* [The football book with the Swedish Football Association's competition calendar]. Svenska fotbollförlaget.

Elenius, S. (2019). *"Alku on aina alku ja siitä lähetään nousemaan" – Suomen Palloliiton rooli suomalaisen nais- ja tyttöjalkapalloilun kehittämisessä 1971–2009* ["The beginning is always a beginning and from there we begin to rise" – The role of Football Association of Finland in developing girl's and women's football 1971–2009] [Master's thesis, University of Eastern Finland]. http://urn.fi/urn:nbn:fi:uef-20190835

FIFA World Football Museum. (2019). *FIFA Women's World Cup official history: The story of women's football from 1881 to the present*. Carlton Books.

Heikkala, J. (2000). Liikunnan järjestökentän muutokset ja toimintaympäristö [The changing field of sport organisations and operating environment]. In H. Itkonen, P. Koski, K. Ilmanen, & J. Heikkala (Eds.), *Liikunnan kansalaistoiminta – muutokset, merkitykset ja reunaehdot* (pp. 119–134). Liikuntatieteellisen seuran julkaisu nro 152.

Itkonen, H., & Nevala, A. (2006). Suomalaisen jalkapalloilun kaudet ja urheilukulttuurin muutos [The phases of Finnish football and changes in sport culture]. *Liikunta & Tiede, 53*(6), 69–75.

Itkonen, H., Nevala, A., & Giulianotti, R. (2014). Paikallisilta kentiltä kansainvälisille viheriöille: Suomalaisten naisjalkapalloilijoiden liikkuvuus [From local pitches to global fields: Migration patterns of Finnish women footballers]. In H. Roiko-Jokela & E. Sironen (Eds.), *Urheilu ja Sota* (pp. 155–174). Bookwell Oy.

Pyykönen, T. (2016). *Yhdenvertaisuus- ja tasa-arvotyö valtion liikuntapolitiikassa* [Non-discrimination and equality in the sport administration of the government]. Valtion liikuntaneuvoston julkaisuja 2016:1. Retrieved May 15, 2022, from https://www.liikuntaneuvosto.fi/wp-content/uploads/2019/09/VLN_YT_FINAL.pdf

Ruohonen, J. (2022). *Naisten laji: Kirja jalkapallosta* [Women's sport: A book about football]. Kustantamo S&S.

Suomen Palloliitto. (2011–2020). *Toimintakertomus* [Annual Report]. Suomen Palloliitto. Retrieved June 15, 2022, from https://www.palloliitto.fi/palloliitto/missio-visio-ja-strategia/toimintakertomukset-ja-tilinpaatokset

Suomen Palloliitto. (2007–2021). *Jalkapallokirja* [Football Yearbook]. Suomen Palloliitto.

Suomen Palloliitto. (2021). *Yhdenvertaisuussuunnitelma* [Non-discrimination plan]. Retrieved June 22, 2022, from https://www.datocms-assets.com/62562/1655846477-yhdenvertaisuussuunnitelma_2021–2022.pdf

Tuunainen, S. (2007). Naisjalkapallon seuratoimintaa 1970-luvulta lähtien [Sport club activities in women's football since the 1970s]. In Y. Lautela & G. Wallén (Eds.), *Rakas jalkapallo. Sata vuotta suomalaista jalkapalloa* (pp. 235–253). Teos.

Väisänen, A. (2019). *Vertaileva tutkimus naisten jalkapallon kehityksestä ja nykytilasta Suomessa ja Ruotsissa* [Comparative research of the development of women's football and its current state in Finland and Sweden] [Master's Thesis, University of Jyväskylä]. http://urn.fi/URN:NBN:fi:jyu-201906243380

Valtioneuvosto. (2021). *Naisten ottelut yhteiskunnallisesti merkittävien tapahtumien televisiointilistaan.* Retrieved June 27, 2022, from https://valtioneuvosto.fi/-/naisten-ottelut-yhteiskunnallisesti-merkittavien-tapahtumien-televisiointilistaan

Vares, V. (2022). *Enemmän kuin peliä: Naisten jalkapallo tasa-arvon tiellä maailmalla ja Suomessa* [More than a game: Women's football on the way to equality worldwide and in Finland]. Jyväskylän yliopistopaino.

Vasara, E. (2004). *Valtion liikuntahallinnon historia* [The history of the government's sport administration]. Liikuntatieteellinen seura.

Vehviläinen, H., & Itkonen, H. (2009). *Mimmiliigasta maailmalle: Tutkimus suomalaisen naisjalkapalloilun muutoksesta* [The change in the women's football in Finland]. Ilias.

Chapter 11
Breaking Barriers in Norwegian Women's Football

Bente Ovedie Skogvang

Introduction

Women's football has met huge resistance during history in Norway. There are several areas and periods of the history, which are under-researched by historians and other researchers, due to that the focus has been put on men's football. However, the largest organised sport for girls and women continues in breaking barriers with the women's national teams' abroad, better professional opportunities inland and abroad, as well as increase in media attention and attendance in the clubs. Several players are playing in professional leagues, i.e. the first *Ballon d'Or* winner Ada Hegerberg (Olympic Lyon), Caroline Graham Hansen (Barcelona), Maren Nævdal Mjelde and Guro Reiten (Chelsea). The earlier years of huge resistance and discrimination of women's football in Norway has neither stopped women from playing, nor coaching, leading, nor refereeing football. Here, I address how women's football in Norway developed from entertainment in men's eyes, with pressure from the women's movement to inclusion in the Norwegian Football Federation (NFF), international successes, stronger league organisation and professional opportunities domestic and abroad.

The chapter is built on academic research in Norwegian football. Researchers have studied football in Norway, but research which highlight the perspective of women themselves is scarce. The focus at the development of the sport has received attention from historians (Fretland, 1996; Goksøyr & Olstad, 2002; Hansen, 1994; Lippe, 1997) and others (Fasting, 2004; Skogvang, 2006). The football magazine *Jossimar* celebrated 100 years of women's football in Norway presenting history, role models and on-going challenges (Johnsen & Lien, 2019). Scraton et al. (1999) underline that "It's still a man's game?" in their study of top-level European women footballers' experiences, and the gendering of media addressed by Hovden and von der Lippe (2017). Fasting (2004, p. 160) concludes that

> … the development of women's football in Norway can be looked upon as a clear example of how girls and women can succeed in 'invading' a

DOI: 10.4324/9781003280729-16

traditional masculine sport. By doing that, female footballers may contribute to a transformation of the concept of "femininity" and gender in society in large.

Several areas within Norwegian elite football among men and women focussed in "Elite football – field of changes" (Skogvang, 2006): Attitudes and values of male and female players were analysed according to gender differences, important values for the players, coaches and team officials. Professionalisation and commercialisation in Norwegian elite football and the role of the media in this process, and how the varying conditions affecting player's participation, quality of the coaches, conditions of the training and playing arenas, wages, voluntary work and equipment support were other topics. Melkersson (2017) interviewed Scandinavian female footballers and concludes that because men's football has had the advantage of preceding women's football this advantage still is visible in most aspects of contemporary football where women has been given a less equitable chance compared to men.

A recent study carried out with key persons (players, coaches, leaders and referees) in the development of women's football in Norway (Skogvang, 2022, 2023). Themes focused are the participants' experiences of the frame factors, commercialisation, professionalisation, spectatorship and media attention in the past, and, in the last 20 years and reflections about the future of women's football. The findings show that female teams have closer collaboration with top male clubs than before, and some of them have emerged into male top clubs, which has attracted more sponsors and larger support (i.e. medical, economic, volunteers). In general, women footballers have more and better professional opportunities, attract more spectators and sponsors, and the media attention has exploded the last period.

Here, I address the following vital factors in football and society which have influenced the development of women's football in Norway:

1. Playing for charity, entertainment and fun for the men's eyes;
2. Women's movement and the struggle for inclusion and acceptance in the governing bodies;
3. Female pioneers and development of national and international competitions and successes;
4. Building of a strong league organisation, the equal-pay-deal, collaboration with the NFF and male elite clubs and league organisation.

Development of women's football in Norway

The development of women's football in Norway has been considerable, and the earlier years of huge resistance and discrimination has neither stopped women from playing nor coaching, leading, nor refereeing in football. 1975 was the first year with registered players with about 1,500 registered players (75 teams), which rapidly increased to 52,000 players in 1980 (Skogvang, 2006). Since 1995, football has been the largest organised sport for girls and women in Norway, and it still is with 113,036 players and 8,416 teams in 2019 (NFF, 2019), and with a small reduction during the pandemic to 108,962 female footballers (NFF, 2021, p. 88). From the 1990s the Norwegian women's national team has had significant success both in European Championships (winner 1987, 1993, silver 2001, 2005, 2013), World Cup (silver 1991, gold 1995) and in the Olympic Games (bronze 1996, gold 2000). The national team has continued to qualify for major tournaments, but the top results, except for a silver medals (2005, 2013), have declined for a period since 2000. In Euro 2022, they were eliminated at the group stage, but in September 2022 they as group-winners qualified for World Cup in New Zealand and Australia 2023 with nine wins and a draw and a goal difference of 47-2.

Thus, at club level the players still struggle with acceptance, inclusion and support from their own club, stadium owners, local community, etc., and the top clubs have never been successful in Women's Champions League (WCL). The two best teams in Norway at the time of writing Brann and Rosenborg recently lost their matches in the second round of WCL. Due to lack of professional opportunities, several Norwegian key players earlier years (and today) are playing in professional leagues abroad as full-time professionals (Botelho & Skogvang, 2014). One example is Ada Hegerberg who is breaking barriers internationally as the first women winning the *Ballon d'Or* (2018) and top scorer of Olympic Lyon and in WCL. Hegerberg withdraw from playing at the Norwegian national team for nearly five years after the European Championships in the Netherlands 2017, but she came back again in March 2022.

Built on the historians Goksøyr and Olstad (2002), who wrote the 100 years history of the NFF, the early development of women's football described in three phases: Show matches and curiosity (1920s–1960s), struggle for acceptance (1970s–1980s) and increased popularity and international successes (1980s–2000s) (Skogvang, 2006). Later development with increased commercialisation and professionalisation necessitate a fourth phase (Skogvang, 2019). The women's elite league *Toppserien* established (2007), *the equal pay-deal* for men and women playing at Norway's national A teams signed in 2017, and the interest organisation for women's two top leagues; *Toppfotball Kvinner (TFK)* (established in 1987 as *Serieforeningen for kvinnefotball*) assumed responsibility of the sale of sponsor and marketing rights for the women's elite clubs in 2017 (Skogvang, 2023). From 2022 a debatable knock-out league system introduced at elite level to make tighter matches with the six best club teams competing during the second period of the competition.

Playing for charity, entertainment and fun for the men's eyes

Women's football in Norway started out as a curiosity on celebrations, i.e. at Norway's national day and other feast days. It seems to be the Østfold county with border to Sweden, which was the pioneering area from 1919, during the

1920s and the 1930s (Johnsen & Lien, 2019), and in general the capital area (Oslo) started later than in the regions (Goksøyr & Olstad, 2002). Matches played for entertainment against men's teams with the purpose of providing extra spectators interested mainly by the entertainment and unusualness. In 1922, the NFF Executive Board member, Per Christian Andersen, described "football as a game for strong men and powerful boys and men" with any notion of women as players being regarded as something strange and monstrous (Skogvang, 2022).

However, there was initial interest in women playing organised football and one of the earliest recorded matches featured *Moss Ladies Team* who played against a men's team in 1921, and against a fellow female team from *Askim* later the same year. Further recordings of matches involving women are quite sketchy but nonetheless in 1928 Crown Prince Olav attended a match between Sonia Henie's team (a famous ice-dancer and actor) and a men's team. The match was not viewed seriously as can be seen in the emphasis on novelty but, nevertheless, it inspired the formation of *Hamar Idrettslags Ladies Team*, and sources show that women played football all over Norway (Goksøyr & Olstad, 2002; Hansen, 1994). A match between *Aurland* and *Kapp Idrettsforening* women's teams also took place that year and this match is regarded as a "real match" as it was formally officiated by a referee.

The situation summed up by an example regarding the women's team from the club Fløya in Tromsø, northern Norway, in 1931: The newly formed women's team decided to organise a match to raise funds for a club banner and Harald Rønne, an instrumental figure in football in the region, wrote to the NFF seeking permission as it was generally not seen as appropriate for women to take part in football or any other physically demanding activities. By reason of the slow mail system at the time the reply from the NFF in Oslo arrived Tromsø after the game had taken place. It took a long time before the NFF answered the letter. Because the match was announced, the *Fløya Ladies* played without the permission from the NFF. According to Hansen (1994, p. 28):

> It was a great match between two teams of players from Fløya's Ladies department. As expected, a lot of curious spectators attended the match. The girls played in "ski boots" and long "stretch pants", and the spectators got a historical and adventurous football experience. Not all the movements were gracious and controlled. It was a tough game, and the girls left the pitch with blue marks both here and there after kicks which were both controlled and uncontrolled. But it had been fun, and it brought money to the banner and there was a strong wish for a repeat match.

When planning for another game, Fløya received a letter from NFF with the following instruction: "Ladies should not play football!" This sport was unsuitable for women, and the ladies, could also get injuries which might destroy their reproductive organs, and "... football was for boys and men!" (Hansen 1994, p. 29). Fretland (1996, p. 98) comments that during this period

> ... many people in Norway spoke against women's sports in general. It was not medically defensible for women to take part in competitive sport. She could not stand the same pain as the man and must be saved from health injuries. Neither was it aesthetic to see sweaty female bodies.

All together it was against the healthy ideal for women to do hard sports, and injury risks, challenges of menstruation, problems with getting pregnant and giving birth afterwards highlighted (Lippe, 1997). Football was thus considered too tough and physical for women to partake in with gymnastics and handball more preferred for women.

Women's movement and the struggle for inclusion and acceptance in the governing bodies

The subsequent development of women's football must be viewed in relation to the development of Norwegian society in general and the progress of the women's movement towards the end of the 1960s and early 1970s (Fasting, 2004). *The Gender Equality Council* was established in 1972, and the *Gender Equality Act* with an Ombudsperson to enforce it came into force striving to achieve gender equality in Norway (1979). The philosophy of equality stresses that equal opportunity is not enough and that active efforts are required to promote the status of women. In 1981, a gender quota with the "40%-rule" incorporated which required that any committee of at least four people had to have at least two members of each sex as members (Norwegian Government, 2021).

The anti-authoritarian wave in Norwegian society inspired women to give a flat refusal to oppression, and merely act as supporters of men's sport. Women of this era "... wanted to take part, move borders, and break barriers" and playing football was part of this mandate (Pettersen, 1985, p. 126). There was resistance within the NFF to include women's football as part of development plans arguing that football made women more masculine, it affected their reproductive organs (Pettersen, 1985) and it encouraged "lesbianism" (Lippe, 1997). There was also the view that if the NFF formally accepted women it would make football a "frøkensport" – a sport for wimps (Goksøyr & Olstad, 2002). Even though there was clear desire by women to play football, the view of the NFF remained the same between the 1920s and 1960s: Women should not play football, and women held behind for several years. Still, women continued playing against boys, with boys, and in "unofficial" leagues and tournaments outside the governing bodies. Pioneers as Målfrid Kuvås, Ellen Wille and Sif Kalvø played on boys' teams. Kuvås, often named as the *Mother of Women's Football in Norway* played with boys until the age of 16 years old, because there were no girl's teams. Kuvås was influential for the development of women's football, as leader and organiser of a large tournament for girls and women-only, *BUL Cup*, and the first women honoured with NFFs *Golden pin* (2002).

UEFA asked their national associations members to take control over women's football and include it in the national FA's in 1971, and when the first women, *Unni Hole* met at the NFF's general assembly in 1973 the visibility of football-playing women increased in Norway. A *Women's Committee* established in 1975 with Ellen Wille (Frigg), Grete Einarsrud (Ullensaker/Kisa) and the NFF General Secretary Nikolai *"Nikken"* Johansen (leader). In 1978, the national team played the first match with former elite player, *Per Pettersen* as the first manager (1978–1982). At NFF's General Assembly in 1976 Pettersen underlined the need for real inclusion and acceptance (Pettersen, 1985), and women wanted to follow the same laws of the game as men with 2 × 45 minutes and ball-size five. In principal speeches the NFF presidents spoke friendly about women's football, but the reality was that football playing girls and women were met with fear and harassment. The same arguments as earlier years were highlighted about creation of masculine women, that football-playing women would create problems with their reproductive organs, and all women footballers labelled as lesbians. In addition, lack of dressing rooms, stadiums, leaders and referees were used to discriminate women in football. Girls could play at boy's teams until UEFA banned it in 1979. The former NFF president and former FIFA executive board member, *Per Ravn Omdal* fought for women's football underlining that the dressing rooms could be used of both genders.

Women played football outside the governing bodies for more than 40 years before the so-called first official matches by Sandviken against Brann, Bergen and Amazons-Grimstad against BUL-Oslo in 1970. Ellen Wille and Frigg started the first in-official cup tournament in 1971 with 16 teams, increased to 57 teams in 1977, and in 1978 the first official cup championship organised by NFF, where BUL-Oslo won 6-5 against Trondheims-Ørn in the final. Concurrent with this, leagues formed for girls and women organised by clubs in the 1970s; Vestfoldserien, Rogalandserien, Østlandsserien and later on Middle-Norway (1981), Vestlandsserien (1983) and North-Norway was the last one in 1985 (Hansen, 1994). The women's movement was a door-opener for starting the international football tournament, Norway Cup in 1972. Both genders included in the tournament, which was an inspiration for many football playing children and youth. Class Q included women between 16 and 19 years old. Fifteen female teams out of 420 teams in total took part and the Amazones of Grimstad won (Goksøyr & Olstad, 2002). A class for girls launched in 1977, and at Norway Cup's 50th anniversary in 2022, eight classes for girls and women with approximately 500 female teams, of 2,100 teams participated. Latest news is to welcome a mixed-sex class in football and include handball teams (Skogvang, 2022).

Sif Kalvø from Ålesund became Norway's first female professional player abroad, playing for Lazio, Roma and Lecce in Italy (1971–1975). Botelho and Skogvang (2014) present the paths for migration of Scandinavian women footballers in three phases. In the first phase (until 1990s), the international transfers of players were sporadic and limited to few countries. In the second phase (late 1990s-mid-2000s), the migration developed into more systematic and intense flux, and from around 2005 onwards women's football got more and more absorbed into the sport globalisation process with new migratory fluxes linking countries across of continents.

Pioneers and development of national and international competitions and successes

The first sponsor contract for women's football with women's sanitary pads SABA in 1982 was the first step to commercialisation. More and more young women choose football as their sport in Norway, and in 1985 the Executive Board decided that there should be at least one woman in all NFFs governing bodies. In 1984, there were classes of ages for girls/women in the same way as for boys/men in Norway, and in 1987, the national team won the European Championship with a 2-1 victory against Sweden in the final at Ullevål stadium in front of 10,000 spectators. The next gold medal came in 1988 at the unofficial World Cup in China (1-0 against Sweden). The goal-scorer *Linda Medalen* together with *Heidi Støre* and *Gunn Nyborg* had a great impact on Norwegian football, and all played professional in Japan (1995–1999). Nyborg played all Norway's 113 first international matches, scored 20 goals and was Norwegian, Danish and Japanese Champion. Støre acted as captain for years, scored 22 goals through her 151 international matches. Medalen stopped playing in 2006, scored 64 goals for the national team in her 152 international matches.

Women became members of boards, committees and councils, and *Ellen Wille* was the first female NFF Executive Board member elected in 1985. Goldman (2021) named her "the Queen of Women's Soccer" because she was the first women to speak at FIFA's annual congress in 1986 in Mexico City, where she suggested a Women's World Cup and women's football in the Olympic Programme. The suggestions resulted in FIFA's first invitational tournament in Guangzhou, China in 1988, followed by the first Women's World Cup in China in 1991. Norwegians elected in roles in international governing bodies UEFA and FIFA. Per Ravn Omdal and *Karen Espelund* became members of the women's committees of FIFA and UEFA, and "the Norwegian Model" introduced, which includes the same skill development programme for both genders. In 1996, girls and women allowed to play at boy's and men's teams at all ages and levels, at the same time as it was forbidden (and still is) in many countries to play at gender mixed teams. Several development and recruitment projects established in clubs, and NFF focussed their aim to recruit more girls and women as players, coaches, leaders and referees. In the NFF Executive Board today (2022) four of eight are women, but among coaches (7%) and referees (6%) the representation is low (Skogvang, 2019).

A more family-friendly profile was an aim for the NFF in the 1990s (Goksøyr & Olstad, 2002). During the 1990s, both the World Cup and the Olympics welcomed women's football into competition. Women were members of boards, committees and councils, and some female pioneers led the path to the global stand with international competitions for women in UEFA and FIFA. One of the pioneers is *Karen Espelund*, who was a member in the NFF's Executive Board from 1988, the first female vice president in 1996 with responsibility and in 1999 she was inaugural once again when employed as the first female NFF General Secretary.

Norway participated in the World Women's Invitational Football Tournament (WWFT) organised in China (10–22 October 1981). The president of Asian Ladies F.C. Veronica Chiu welcomed 14 teams from Europe, America, Oceania and Asia, and it is referred to as the second WWFT in Asia, the first organised in 1978. Among them Norway and Finland from the Nordic countries took part with their national champion teams, HJK Helsinki (Finland) and IL BUL Oslo (Norway). On 1–12 June 1988, the International Women's Football Tournament (IWFT) was played in People's Republic of China at the four venues Guangzhou, Foshan, Jiangman and Panyu. Twelve teams participated in this first FIFA organised women's world cup from Asia (China PR, Japan and Thailand), Africa (Ivory Coast), CONCACAF (Canada and United States), CONEMBOL (Brazil), Europe (Czechoslovakia, Netherlands, Norway and Sweden) and Oceania (Australia). Again, two teams from the Nordic countries were invited, this time Norway and Sweden. These tournaments were building women's football network between clubs and national teams aiming to develop a permanent women's world cup every second or fourth year. From the Nordic countries Norway and Sweden participated in this tournament with 18 players from each country and 12 team officials of whom 2 were women. Norway won 1-0 against Sweden in the final, and Brazil won 4-5 against China in the Bronze final. There were only male referees and assistant referees/linesmen appointed by FIFA, and 12 linesmen were appointed from China. One of the main referees was from the Nordic countries; Egil Nervik from Norway.

The successful tournaments presented above as well as the struggle from women's movement in Norway and the Norwegian woman Ellen Wille criticising FIFA at the FIFA congress in Mexico City in 1986 resulted in *the first FIFA championship for Women's football* organised from 16 to 30 November 1991 in China. The same venues as in 1988 used all in the Guangdong province: Guangzhou, Foshan, Jiangmen and Panyu. Eighteen players from each country plus team officials from China PR, Chinese Taipei and Japan (Asia), Nigeria (Africa), United States (North America), Brazil (South America), New Zealand (Oceania) and Denmark, Germany, Italy, Norway and Sweden (Europe) participated in the first official FIFA tournament. Europe was dominating women's football, and from the Nordic countries Denmark, Norway and Sweden participated. Norway and Sweden qualified due to their great performance in the IWFT in 1988, and both countries' teams manage to qualify to the finals. In addition, the referees were appointed by FIFA with ten male referees, six female "lineswomen" (Ingrid Jonson from Sweden) and four "linesmen".

The Nordic teams performed well, but United States did beat Norway 2-1 in the final, and Sweden lost 4-3 against Germany in the Bronze final. The Bronze match was refereed by women-only: referee Claudia Vasconcelos (Brazil), lineswomen Linda Black (New Zealand) and Zuo Xiudi (China PR). The matches were played 2 × 40 minutes with ball size 5. More than 60,000 spectators watched the final match between United States and Norway at Tianhe stadium. The fight through decades from the Nordic pioneers in close collaboration with other European countries as well as countries in Asia and other continents had come to an end, and women footballers could play in a worldwide tournament organised by the international governing bodies. No matter how, it was not before ten years later in Atlanta 1996 that women's football was included in the Olympic programme. The United States beats China 2-1 in the inaugural Olympic tournament in Athens (United States) in front of 76,489 spectators, where the author was the main referee.

Globally, FIFA and UEFA established several competitions in women's football during the 2000s, which is an inspiration to women who wants to take part in the sport both at local and national level as well as internationally (Skogvang, 2019). When UEFA established the club competition for women *UEFA Women's Club Championship* in 2002, this was of great importance for female clubs all over Europe including Norway. Among the coaches, *Hege Riise*, the former international professional (Japan, United States) and the most capped female player in Norway with 154 international matches made history when recruited as assistant national team coach for United States (2009–2011). Riise and manager Pia Sundhage (a pioneer in Swedish football) led United States to silver medal in World Cup 2011 with loose against Japan on penalty kicks in the final. Riise also was the manager of England women's A team in 2021, and in 2022 she took over as manager of Norway's national team as the first woman in this role.

Stronger league organisation, equal pay deal, collaboration with the NFF and male elite clubs and league organisation

As mentioned above professional opportunities for female footballers from Norway mainly were abroad in the earlier stages, and several development projects for girls and women carried out in Norway. Internationally increased professionalisation, and competition opportunities and well-organised league systems have been crucial in spreading women's football globally and has had great impact also in the national associations. To have playing opportunities inland and abroad influence recruitment of players, leaders, coaches and referees and develop the sport worldwide (Skogvang, 2019). An all-national league, *1st Division, women* was established in 1987, with Northern Norway as the last one included (Skogvang, 2006). When founded in 1987, the women's Elite League was established, followed by an all-national 1st division in 2001 (level two). Since 1996, the league named Toppserien, and the clubs playing at level two *1st Division women*. To build strong leagues and development of a strong league organisation for women's elite football has been a tool for the clubs as well as for NFF, which financed the first employer in the organisation. The league association for women's top football established the same year as the all-national league in 1987 as Serieforeningen for kvinnefotball and had a volunteering board until 1993. Today the organisation is named Toppfotball Kvinner (TFK) working for improvement of the conditions for female players and clubs at the two top divisions in Norway. TFK assumed responsibility of the sale of sponsor and marketing rights for the women's top clubs in 2017. In TFKs strategy document (2020–2023) their aims are (1) increased professionalisation, (2) increased numbers of "proff-days" with football only for the players and (3) increased competence about all levels in women's football (Skogvang, 2023).

At the same time as professional playing opportunities increased in Europe, opportunities opened for playing professional or semi-professional in Norway, and increased numbers of foreign players arrived to play in the top league Toppserien. A huge step for national team players made in 2017 when an "equal pay deal" was signed for men and women playing at Norway's national A teams. The same year Toppfotball Kvinner took over the sale of sponsor and marketing rights for the women's top clubs, and TFK succeeded to sign four large sponsor contracts. The new sponsor contracts made it possible to increase the professionalisation of the women's game, and at least one professional day – "proff-days" were made possible for all female players in the elite league. Despite the positive development, the huge gender differences in wages and full-time or part-time possibilities still exist. The norm is men's football, and it keeps the privileged position in Norwegian as well as international football. The female league organisation TFK put pressure on the NFF and has increased the collaboration with both the NFF and the male elite clubs' interest organisation *Norsk Toppfotball*. In 2022, the three organisations signed a historical co-operation contract for mutual development of football for women and men in Norway. From 2022, a new knock-out league system is introduced in the women's elite league to make tighter matches with the six best clubs competing during the second period of the competition aiming to perform better at club competitions abroad in UEFA WCL. At the time of writing the clubs and Toppfotball Kvinner are arguing against the newly introduced knock-out league system, and a suggestion for change already the coming year is presented. The two best club teams Brann and Rosenborg both lost their matches in round two in UEFA WCL against Rosengård from Sweden and Real Madrid from Spain. As mention, the positive is that Norway's national team has qualified for World Cup in New Zealand and Australia 2023.

Concluding remarks and reflections about the future

Women's football has developed a lot, and the changes in professional opportunities has increased, especially in Europe. Nevertheless, women elite footballers in Norway in general are strongly dependent on enthusiasts and voluntariness at local level in combination with promotion of the sport nationally, as well as in other Nordic countries and globally. The collaboration between women's and men's teams has increased in several clubs, and the last few years some female elite teams have emerged into male premier league clubs also in Norway, some of them successfully, and others not. Each team includes not only the players, coaches and team leaders, but also referees, parents, waffle makers, kit washers, and so on, and the women footballers underline that a larger club might make the work easier, and may attract more sponsors and larger support (medical support, economic, volunteers, etc.) around the team in women's football (Skogvang, 2023). A better co-operation between NFF and Toppfotball Kvinner also pinpointed as crucial for further development. In NFFs strategy (2021–2023) the successful World Cup in France 2019 described as a performance and commercial break-through for women's football. The challenge is to continue the work for improvement of the frame factors for women's football nationally and internationally (NFF, 2021), and the annual general assembly on 8 March 2020 underlined the importance of persist on highlighting women's football in their strategy. One of the challenges today and for the future is to increase the attendance at the elite league matches, which has changed from an average of 274 spectators (2019) to 52,090 and average 578 so far in 2022. The attendance is still increasing with new attendance records in June 2022 Brann-Vålerenga (10,582) and Rosenborg-Brann (11,636). However, this is far from the UWL world records with Barcelona on top, i.e. Barcelona – Real Madrid 30 March 2022 with 91,553 spectators, and then the first leg Barcelona – Wolfsburg with 91,648 spectators (UEFA, 2022).

Several Norwegian women and some "women's-football-loving men", i.e. Per Ravn Omdal, has influenced the professionalisation and development of women's football worldwide. Ellen Wille, Karen Espelund, Sif Kalvø, Hege Riise and Ada Hegerberg are mentioned above as Norwegian pioneers internationally. Thus, the first female president in NFF, *Lise Klaveness* elected at the annual meeting on 7 March 2022, 120 years after the NFF was founded. Klaveness is a former professional player and Norwegian national team player. She has already gained huge media attention through her first speech at the FIFA congress in Qatar 2022 on 31 March 2022. She was criticising FIFA World Cup in Qatar and addressing equality and human rights on and off the pitch. National and local sponsors and support from the media, family and friends continue to be crucial for women's football development in Norway. The newly elected NFF president Klaveness addressed transparency, equality and human rights on and off the pitch nationally and internationally (NFF, 2022). When it comes to equality, the right to play football for women highlighted. Future pioneers as

Klaveness will hopefully bring increased equality for everyone who wants to play, no matter girl or boy, and a more transparent football might increase the income and professional opportunities for women even more.

References

Botelho, V., & Skogvang, B. O. (2014). Leaving the core? The Scandinavian emigration of women footballers. In S. Agergaard & N. Tiesler (Eds.), *Women, soccer and transnational migration* (pp. 117–139). Routledge.

Fasting, K. (2004). Small country – big results: Women's football in Norway. In F. Hong & J. A. Mangan (Eds.), *Soccer, women, sexual liberation. Kicking off a new era* (pp. 149–161). Frank Cass.

Fretland, F. (1996). *Sogn og Fjordane Fotballkrets 75 år 1922–1997* [Sogn and Fjordane Regional football association 75 years 1922–1997]. Sogn og Fjordane Fotballkrets.

Goksøyr, M., & Olstad, F. (2002). *Fotball! Norges Fotballforbund 100 år* [Football! The Norwegian Football Federation 100 years]. Norges Fotballforbund.

Goldman, R. (2021). *The sisterhood: The 99ers and the rise of U.S. women's soccer.* University of Nebraska Press.

Hansen, J. (Ed.). (1994). *I "futtbollens" tjeneste. 75 år med Troms Fotballkrets* [In service of "futtboll". 75 years with the Troms regional football association]. Troms Fotballkrets.

Hovden, J., & von der Lippe, G. (2017). The gendering of media sport in the Nordic countries. *Sport in Society, 22*(4), 625–638. 10.1080/17430437.2017.1389046

Johnsen, L., & Lien, M. (2019). Den lange kampen. 100 år med norsk kvinnefotball [The long battle. 100 years of Norwegian women's football]. *Josimar – tidsskrift om fotball.* 04/2019. Dype skoger.

Melkersson, M. (2017). *(Women's) professional football clubs in Scandinavia – Marketing and positioning in transition* [PhD thesis]. Malmö University.

NFF (Norges fotballforbund). (2019). *Annual Report 2019.*

NFF (Norges fotballforbund). (2021). *Annual Report 2021.*

NFF (Norges fotballforbund). (2022). *Lise Klaveness calls for at change at the FIFA Congress.* Retrieved November 3, 2022, from https://www.fotball.no/tema/nff-nyheter/2022/calls-out-for-change-at-the-fifa-congress/

Norway Cup. (2022). *Om Norway Cup 50 år 1972–2022* [About Norway Cup 50 years 1972–2022]. https://norwaycup.no/om-oss/om-norway-cup/

Norwegian Government. (2021). *Gender and Anti-Discrimination Act.* Retrieved May 25, 2022, from https://www.regjeringen.no/en/topics/equality-and-diversity/likestilling-og-inkludering/gender-equality/id670481/

Pettersen, P. (1985). Damefotball. Idrettshistorie og viktig skanse i likestillingskampen [Ladies Football. Sport history and a crucial bulwark in the gender equality battle]. In E. "Drillo" Olsen (Ed.), *Fotball – mer enn et spill* [Football – more than a game] (pp. 125–141). J.W. Cappelen forlag A/S.

Scraton, S., Fasting, K., Pfister, G., & Bunuel, A. (1999). It's still a man's game? The experiences of top-level European women footballers. *International Review for Sociology of Sport, 34*(2), 99–111.

Skogvang, B. O. (2006). *Toppfotball – et felt i forandring* [Elite football – a field of changes]. [PhD thesis]. Norwegian School of Sport Sciences.

Skogvang, B. O. (2019). Scandinavian women's football: The importance of male and female pioneers in the development of the sport. *Sport in History, 39*(2), 207–228. 10.1080/17460263.2019.1618389

Skogvang, B. O. (2022). Hitos en el desarrollo del fútbol femenino en Noruega [Highlights of the development of women's soccer in Norway]. In A. Janson, J. Branz, B. O. Skogvang, T. Arimoto, & M. Santino (Eds.), *Del jugar por jugar a jugar en serio – La Profesionlizacion en el fútbol femenino* [From playing for fun to playing for real – Professionalization in female football] (pp. 46–87). Buenos Aires.

Skogvang, B. O. (2023). Professional women's football in Norway – a field of empowerment and discrimination. In A. Culvin & A. Bowes (Eds.), *Women's football in a global, professional era*. Emerald Publishing.

UEFA. (2022). UEFA Women's Champions League Records. Retrieved 27 April 2022. https://www.uefa.com/womenschampionsleague/news/025b-0ef163bc672f-4f70d38ff3af-1000-women-s-champions-league-records/

von der Lippe, G. (1997). *Endring og motstand mot endring av femininiteter og maskuliniteter i idrett og kroppskultur i Norge: 1890–1950 – med sideblikk på Tyskland, Sverige og Danmark. En feministisk analyse av et empirisk materiale.* [Changes and resistance against changes of femininities and masculinities in sport and body culture in Norway: 1890–1950 – with a sidelong glance at Germany, Sweden and Denmark] [PhD thesis]. Norwegian School of Sport Sciences.

Chapter 12
Women's Football in Iceland
Don't Wait for Change, Just Do It

Daði Rafnsson and Hafrún Kristjánsdóttir

Introduction

A comprehensive history of women's football in Iceland is recited in the book *Stelpurnar okkar* (Our girls) (Steinarsson, 2017). The first all-female team in Iceland was formed in Ísafjörður in 1914 by women who were not allowed to train with men. Women's football was not recognised as an official sport in Iceland until 1970, and the first official Championships were held in 1972. Iceland lost 3:2 to Scotland in its first national game in 1981 and participated in the first official European Championships (Euro) in 1982–1983. Controversially, due to financial constraints, The Football Association of Iceland (KSÍ) decided not to participate in the next version played from 1984 to 1987, claiming its mission was to build for the tournament to be played from 1992 to 1994. During this period, youth competitions were introduced to strengthen the foundations, but the national team did not play from 1988 to 1992. On its return, it had to use the blue kit of club team Fram as the uniforms were not ready. Still, there were promising signs with a top eight finish in the Euro 1994.

The Union of European Football Nations (UEFA) published its first official strategy document for women's football in 2019. It describes women's football as the most significant growth market in the sport and the development of its foundations as fundamental to its success (UEFA, 2019). UEFA aimed to double the number of female players, female representation on all its bodies, and the reach and value of the European Championships and the Women's Champions League by 2024. Additionally, to improve player standards and safeguarding policies and to change perceptions of women's football in Europe. According to Nadine Kessler, UEFA's head of women's football, the aim was to "transform words into action".

Various social transformation theories are used across academic fields to explain systemic changes, including social practices and knowledge (Hölscher et al., 2018). While transformation can be forced on societies through adverse events, proactively, it can effectively promote sustainability and social prosperity (Feola, 2015). Sport significantly influences the empowerment and motivation of cultural groups and can exalt social transformation by widely sharing its benefits (Gillion & Keim, 2020). Traditionally, gendered nature and leadership in sports are dominated by males (Burton, 2015). Meanwhile, women's football worldwide has traditionally been "invisibilised" and treated as a lesser form of the mainstream men's game by national associations and international governing bodies (Dunn, 2018). Milestones on the road to greater recognition can appear as "watershed moments", as Bell (2019) described the Euro 2005 hosted by England. Changes did emerge at the policy level and with more significant investment by professional clubs in England. Ultimately, the lack of opportunity for young girls in schools and at the grassroots level and the lack of media interest eventually meant that enthusiasm for the 2005 event did not ignite the expected growth. When England won the Euro as hosts of the 2022 tournament, celebrations were followed by calls to seize the moment by increasing access for young girls by the likes of Chelsea manager Emma Hayes (Hamilton, 2022).

Social transformation research also examines how changes in one area can affect others, many small events leading to transformation within and across nations (Castles, 2001). The Iceland women's team that qualified for the Euro 2009 was the country's first senior football team to qualify for a major tournament. Looking back, the qualification and the subsequent interest in the team and its players have not only proven sustainable but transformative. In contrast to the experience of England after 2005, the team inspired a generation of young girls to participate in football (Football Association of Iceland, 2021). While the population of Iceland grew by 14% from 2009 to 2020 (Statistics Iceland, 2022), the number of registered players increased by 46% in the same period. Female players' were 32% of all players in 2009 and 33% in 2020, but the number of female players grew by 48% in this period from 6,470 to 9,551 (The National Olympic and Sports Association of Iceland, 2010; The National Olympic and Sports Association of Iceland, 2021).

The national team players also staked their claim on the national consciousness inspiring greater media interest. Schmidt's (2016) analysis of *The New York Times* found that over 30 years, only 5.2% of all sports news covered women. In Iceland, similar trends were observed; by Daðason (2013) and Ólafsdóttir (2014). But live television coverage of the women's top division in Iceland increased by 53% between 2019 and 2020, and viewership share rose by 105%. The largest football website, *fotbolti.net*, increased its articles on women's football by 26%, and live text coverages from games rose by 35%. In the summer of 2020, three of its top four stories during a single day were related to women's football after a national team game. News site *Mbl.is* increased its coverage of women's football by 55% between 2017 and 2018, and clicks increased by 47% from 2018 to 2019 (Football Association of Iceland, 2021). Gatekeeping theories (Shoemaker & Vos, 2009) explain how people in positions of power in the media decide what is covered. In 2019, the director of sports for the Icelandic Broadcast Service (RÚV), said that men have always made the decisions about investment and coverage. RÚV's new policy on gender equality now mandated that women should be 50% of RÚV's sports journalists, up from 10% in 2015 (Football Association of Iceland, 2021). This resulted in live sports coverage at RÚV growing to 45% for women's sports in 2019.

The relationship between sports, culture and values in society is dynamic and bidirectional (LaVoi et al., 2019). Iceland national team players acquired the status of role models through increased media visibility and actively visiting young girls in their clubs. Aspiring youngsters compare themselves to models similar in prior performance and task-related attributes (Wheeler et al., 1997), and role models can motivate individuals to perform novel behaviours and aspire to attain ambitious goals (Morgenroth et al., 2015). While boys choose athletic superstars as role models, girls explore more to find a role model similar to the self (Ronkainen et al., 2019). The best players enjoy an exalted profile in Icelandic society as spokespersons for major brands and regularly appear in the media. In 2017, Iceland played Brazil at home before a record crowd in its final preparation game before the Euro, then enjoyed a raucous send-off at the airport as 3,000 Icelandic fans descended on the Netherlands (Steinarsson, 2017).

After 2009, the national team qualified for the next three Euros, reaching the quarter-finals in 2013 and exiting at the group stage in 2017 and 2022. After the 2022 tournament, Iceland placed number 14 in the FIFA world rankings (FIFA, 2022). Iceland's top league was ranked number nine at the European club level in April 2022, and Breiðablik qualified for the first Champions League group stages in the autumn of 2021 (UEFA, 2021). Institutional knowledge began accumulating at KSÍ, and several of their national teams have since reached major tournaments. The men's senior team qualified for the 2016 Euros and the 2018 World Cup. The men's U21 team qualified for the 2011 and 2021 Euros, and the U19 women's team in 2009. The U17 women's team reached the semi-finals of the 2011 tournament and hosted the 2015 version. The men's U17 team qualified for the Euros in 2012 and 2019 (J. O. Sigurðsson, personal communication, 2 December 2022).

Research on talent development in sports tends to neglect describing pathways of female athletes (Curran et al., 2019). In Iceland, clubs are multi-sports community clubs governed by a volunteer board. Hrafnsdóttir et al. (2014) estimated that around 10% of Icelanders volunteer for their sports club. Public demand for equality is high, and training, competition structure and career pathways in football run parallel for boys and girls. As part of a prevention strategy aimed at keeping children and teenagers in structured and organised youth activities, municipalities provide parents vouchers to lower participation costs (Milkman & Jonsson, 2019). They also fund the most significant part of the construction of sports facilities (Reykjavík Principal Office for Sport and Recreation, 2012). In return, clubs allow everyone who wants to train and play through the U19 age group. A strong league and appearance at major tournaments have exposed female players to playing opportunities abroad. In 2021–2022, 34 players were under contract with top league clubs in Europe and North America, according to the author of the annual publication *Íslensk Knattspyrna* (Football in Iceland). Most played in Sweden (ten) and Germany (six) (Víðir Sigurðsson, personal communication, 6 May 2022). The CEO of the largest college athlete recruiting service in Iceland estimated that around 100 female players from Iceland will earn scholarships at universities in the United States in 2022–2023 (Brynjar Benediktsson, personal communication, 6 May 2022).

Despite notable changes in visibility and attitude regarding women's football in Iceland, challenges remain in the sport's structure. KSÍ's review of the state of the women's game concluded with a report noting the disparity in qualification payments of ISK 1.1 billion (EUR 7.5 million) for the Men's Euro 2016 and 36 million ISK (EUR 245,000) for the Women's Euro 2017 from UEFA (Knattspyrnusamband Íslands, 2021). A quarter of club executives in Iceland believe football club culture is demotivating for women. Only 7% of handball, football and basketball chairpersons are female (Kristjánsdóttir et al., 2021).

As women's sport rises to prominence in society, women assume roles typically shaped by men (Chinurum et al., 2014). It is important to explore new dimensions in sports through their own narrative (Hall & Oglesby, 2016). The aim of this study is to examine the transformation in women's football in Iceland from 2009 to 2022 through the experiences of five women at the centre of the sport during the period.

Method

A qualitative case-study drawing on semi-structured interviews with five women at the centre of women's football during a transformative period in Iceland. The participants were chosen for their respective roles during the period. From football governance, Klara Bjartmarz, who became the first female CEO of the Football Association of Iceland (KSÍ) in 2015 and still holds the position, and Borghildur Sigurðardóttir, who was elected as the first chairwoman of the top league club, Breidablik, in 2013, and in 2019 became vice-chairwoman of KSÍ and still holds the position. From the media, Mist Rúnarsdóttir is a pioneer of women's football coverage. And from the national team, former national team captain Margrét Lára Viðarsdóttir, whose international career spanned 124 games and 79 goals from 2005 to 2019, and Karólína Lea Vilhjálmsdóttir, who was eight years old in 2009, then a national team player at the Euro 2022.

Original interviews were conducted for this study between 28 December 2021, and 18 January 2022, using a semi-structured method. It obtains subjective responses regarding personal experiences and allows participants to verbally and non-verbally communicate on complex issues (McIntosh & Morse, 2015). Due to restrictions related to COVID-19, interviews were conducted and recorded through MS Teams and Zoom, lasting between 60 and 90 minutes. A study by Gray et al. (2020) found that interviews through online meeting software enhance convenience and accessibility to participants for researchers and a positive experience overall for participants. All participants were eager to share their experiences, and most had prepared themselves with notes, only knowing that the subject was the development of Icelandic women's football since 2009. The interview guide consisted of ten broad questions, with follow-up questions to extract clarity and context if needed. The first two questions asked if the participants had noted any change in women's football in Iceland since the Euro 2009. The following four questions focused on whether Icelandic clubs, KSÍ and international organisations have initiated positive change during this period. Two questions addressed visibility, including media coverage and role models. One question asked whether the participants had to overcome prejudice due to their gender, and finally, they were allowed to add anything they wanted to discuss. A thematic analysis was conducted following the transcription of the interviews, observing if similar themes emerged from the participants' experiences.

Due to Icelandic being a small country, with a population of 376,248 (Statistics Iceland, 2022), the researchers have previous knowledge of all participants. The participants are recognisable due to their profiles in Icelandic football. They all consented to recording the interviews and being named in the research. The study respected the principles of the Declaration of Helsinki.

Results

The participants feel they have fought for their sport's growth. Increased ambition and professionalism at KSÍ have made the Icelandic national teams competitive internationally. Lessons learned from major tournaments have inspired qualifications for youth and men's national teams. Participants talked about gender equality as key to women's success in sport, and sport can, in turn, inspire women in society. Increased visibility in the media has garnered more interest from the public. The impact of role models is presented in the example of a young player ending up playing alongside her hero in the national team. The participants encourage others in positions to enact change to adopt a "just do it" mindset to accelerate the development of the sport in other countries.

Structure: Just do it

Young Margrét Lára Viðarsdóttir saw change arrive with ambitious coach Sigurður Ragnar Eyjólfsson in the autumn of 2006. He found a receptive group of experienced players mixed with young and hungry players, and the culture in the national team changed from social to achievement-oriented. Klara Bjartmarz remembers small things coming together, the quality of the football getting better. KSÍ invested in playing stronger teams. Improvement was made on so-called 1% extra things such as nutrition and physical therapy. Heimir Hallgrímsson, the men's national team coach, was an analyst for the women's team in Sweden in 2013. By the time his team qualified for the European Championship in 2016, he and KSÍ had accumulated valuable knowledge and know-how. Borghildur Sigurðardóttir wondered if the women's team had initially benefitted from an enlarged tournament format but put those thoughts to rest when they qualified again in 2013 and 2017.

Borghildur says it matters who runs football institutions. Around 2009, men still had better facilities, training times, food and training, but people in positions of influence were determined to do better. She says they just went to work and got things done. This is often the Icelandic attitude to things, don't wait around, just do it. Klara and Borghildur emphasise how KSÍ works for the benefit of everyone and does not have different strategies for men and women. While UEFA emphasises separate women's football strategies at its member associations, KSÍ's board and management have implemented a single football strategy. Klara likes to tease UEFA on surveys on how many staff KSÍ dedicates to women's football by answering none. Changes in the national team structure since 2009 include equal daily allowances and bonus payments in qualification games. KSÍ's board has set goals of gender quotas in its committees and conducted an extensive review of women's football. Youth national team committees recently merged, and Klara expects senior national team committees to do the same eventually. National team coaches support each other as analysts for other teams. Iceland has a club licensing process for the top two divisions in men's football and the women's top division, while UEFA only demands it of women's teams in the Champions League.

Klara, whose club disbanded its women's team after a promotion to the top league when she was young, thinks most clubs are now ambitious towards their women's teams. Mist Rúnarsdóttir sees equality statements appearing in club mission statements and communication and says it is easy for clubs to tick off common-sense things. Some clubs actively make players visible, benefitting from attendance and involvement. Their stadiums will have big banners and flags with images of female players alongside male players. Maintaining gender balance on social media, they benefit from becoming "whole clubs" where everyone feels included.

Equality: An excellent place for women to do what they love

All participants agreed that Iceland is at the forefront of gender equality, and this supports their endeavours in football. In turn, their visibility influences gender equality in society. Margrét Lára thinks it is mad to think that a football association should not be at the forefront of progress and says that making the daily allowance of the national teams equal mattered. Karólína Lea Vilhjálmsdóttir mentions that both national teams play their home games in the same stadium, which is a meaningful gesture. She feels fortunate to have grown up in Iceland, not facing prejudice for being herself, and appreciates it as a great place for women who aspire to do what they love.

She says that when KSÍ has been found wanting, it quickly gets berated by not only feminists but also the public. The participants all said that their efforts in their fields had been well received by men, and they had not felt pressure to act up to the masculine norms of football. The exception raised by three participants was a recent rise of football podcasts whose hosts tend to be dismissive and overtly critical of women in football.

Karólína Lea feels that as Icelandic clubs are member-owned and rely on public funding, they should emphasise equality. Official grants should depend on performance on equality milestones. Margrét Lára says that clubs that get things right, like perennial rivals Breiðablik and Valur, are stable in their approach, and the key is genuine respect. Everyone at Valur was behind her to succeed as a player, treating her with the same respect as their male national team players. Karólína Lea echoes the sentiment from her time at Breiðablik, where she felt the respect for her work was genuine. Klara says it matters to have buy-in from top management. Things do not change overnight but can happen quickly if everyone heads in the same direction.

Klara adds that KSÍ's corporate sponsors emphasise and demand equality from the organisation. Most members on the board of KSÍ and its committees demand parity. Fathers of female players, some of whom played at a high level themselves, have gotten involved and do not accept their daughters' opportunities being limited. She emphasises that she does not want to use the word lucky to describe advancements, as women have fought for their rights and earned them in Iceland. She thinks that the reason Nordic countries are at the forefront of women's sports is directly connected to women's rights and does not envy people in some countries trying to fight for women's football.

Media: Tending to the plant that needs attention

Mist says emerging sports must be given exposure to grow. The disposition of media companies changed when they tended to women's football from the point of goodwill and discovered that there was interest. Now they see business opportunities. When Mist attended the 2009 tournament as a journalist, her counterparts at RÚV brought a small team to cover the event. Now journalists fight to cover major tournaments. Margrét Lára claims the national team felt they had truly arrived in the mainstream after the Euros in 2017 when they were criticised with a similar fervour as the men's team. The media cared enough to demand better performances after poor results.

Klara says sport can manufacture interest through good content and that the appearance of Margrét Lára at the TV expert table in men's football in recent years has done wonders. Anyone watching sees that a woman can understand football. Margrét Lára says she might offer a different viewpoint from her colleagues. Mist has been asked to cover men's football but would rather spend it tending to what she calls the plant that needs attention.

Margrét Lára and Karólína explain that social media has bypassed the gatekeepers for women's sports making it easy to create interest and get good content directly to fans and young girls. People can share and comment, and traditional media is now referencing material generated by the players themselves.

Role models: She inspired me so much that now we are team-mates

Mist did not know about Iceland's best female players until they were running rings around her on the field in senior football. Her teenage role model was Dennis Bergkamp. Borghildur had no female role models in football and says it matters that the big European clubs now have women's teams. It gets their attention when people hear Dagný Brynjarsdóttir plays for West Ham. Klara played and coached and had no female role models. She was happy when she recently heard a young female coach describe hers.

Young Margrét Lára did not have female role models. She later played in Sweden for a long time, where the best players were not visible, and says it is unique how recognised Iceland's national team players are now. She appreciates KSÍ's hard work and efforts from 2006 to make players available to the media and advertising and visit young players in their clubs. Closeness is so important in society, and players must give back to their origins.

> When you are young and see someone you can compare yourself to, it is everything. Ásgeir Sigurvinsson [FC Bayern, Stuttgart] came from my hometown, and I thought to myself, why can I not become one of the best players in Europe like him? You compare yourself to those around you, and if they like Ásthildur Helgadóttir can play for a club like LdB Malmö, then one of the best clubs in Europe, I must have a chance if I work hard and remain motivated.

Margrét Lára remembers becoming a celebrity in Iceland. Suddenly, she was known everywhere, appearing on billboards, in television ads, and magazines. This was very different from when she was a young girl, and she thinks this boosted participation. She says signing autographs and talking to young girls had a significant effect. The culture was craving female models, and for players born around 2000, having role models must have been like a shot of vitamin to their careers. To emphasise this point, Karólína Lea tells a heartwarming story about an early moment in her career.

> Young girls mirror themselves in high achieving role models. My role models when I was growing up were Dóra María Lárusdóttir, Sara Björk Gunnarsdóttir, and Margrét Lára Viðarsdóttir. I met all of them when I was small, and I will never forget it. Margrét was my coach at a

Christmas football clinic and took me aside and told me she saw something in me. She said that if I played my cards well, I could go very far. I don't know if she remembers this, but it made me so excited and was a turning point for me. A few years later, I played with her on the national team, and my mind thought back to what she had told me. I thought, wow! She inspired me so much that now we are teammates. It is so important that role models are visible to little girls so that we can peek into their world and see how they are. I hope someday I can be this kind of a role model for someone.

Margrét Lára vaguely recalled this exchange and said it almost brought her to tears.

Future challenges: Women must make decisions for women

Mist feels it can be easy to feel annoyed about any lack of progress instead of being grateful for a few breadcrumbs. More female delegates must attend the annual meeting of KSÍ, where clubs make decisions affecting women's football, many without a woman present or even without having a women's team at their club. Women must make decisions for women and ensure they and other underrepresented groups have voices in governance. Klara agrees. There is no one way to manage football, and it is good to involve people from different backgrounds. According to Mist, all the roles are ready for women to assume, with an expectancy to pick up what was made by men for men. There is potential in many women, and more need to get involved. But clubs should not recruit them by saying they need a woman but an expert.

Karólína Lea extended her contract with German champions FC Bayern at 20. A male player with her profile would be financially set for life, but she knows that her career path is forged through ambition rather than financial incentives. Margrét Lára, a former German League winner, trained in the afternoon while all men playing in the top three or four divisions were entirely professional. She explains the need to change the working environment for mothers in football. She has not accepted coaching or governance offers after retiring as it is hard to be a mother and work until four, pick up the kids, get them to a babysitter and then go to training. If she could concentrate on training, nutrition and recovery like the men, she would have played until she was 40. Karólína Lea mentions maternity leave as a crucial benefit for women's athletes.

Borghildur claims that for Iceland to stay competitive, the next step is to make the domestic league semi-professional. Klara lists issues UEFA has neglected in recent years to bring the structure closer to the men's game, including a club licensing system and player transfer compensations. Clubs must receive transfer compensation for their best players going abroad, and the new Champions League format will improve the league through an extra financial injection if teams qualify for the group stages.

Conclusion

The aim of this study is to examine the transformation in women's football in Iceland from 2009 to 2022 through the experiences of five women at the centre of the sport during the period.

Linnér and Wibeck (2019) described societal transformation as "a deep and sustained, nonlinear change" occurring within a system or culture. Since Iceland's first qualification for a major tournament in 2009, women in football have pushed glass ceilings of participation, exposure and achievement. The team and its members ascended into the national consciousness (Steinarsson, 2017) and provided lessons to other Icelandic teams that would later qualify for major tournaments. Improvements in football's structure have been made by people in governing positions at KSÍ and the clubs. Women's football in Iceland enjoys a bidirectional relationship with mainstream society emphasising gender equality, each inspiring inclusivity in the culture. Similarly, football is not excluded when there is a backlash in the fight for gender equality in society. Such is the nonlinear nature of change that is not driven top-down by society's institutions but, in Icelandic football's case, emerges from ordinary people making decisions in a volunteer culture. One participant said emphasising gender equality makes football clubs in Iceland "whole". The participants in this research encourage people in positions of power not to wait around for top-down strategies and campaigns but rather adopt a "just do it" attitude to accelerate the growth of women's football.

Efforts to increase visibility have paid dividends through increased media coverage and emerging role models for young girls. In the decade examined in this study, Icelandic media discovered that interest grows with exposure. Once invisible, players from the national team suddenly found themselves being criticised by the media, like the men's team. For them, this was a signal that they had arrived in the mainstream. Social media, bypassing gatekeepers, has accelerated the visibility of women's football in Iceland. In their work, Bandura (1986) and Lockwood and Kunda (1999) emphasised similarity, attainability and relevance in role modelling. Making national team players accessible to young girls in their communities grew participation and motivation, as evident by the story told by a national team player of her encounter with her national team hero. She inspired her so much that they eventually became teammates. As opposed to England's experience after 2005, when the interest sparked by the Euros only affected change at the policy and professional level, the change in Iceland appears deep and sustainable because it has stirred emotions in young girls at the grassroots level.

Finally, while progress has been made, the participants warn of complacency. It is easy to check boxes in official documents and pat oneself on the back as a champion of equality. As the participants explained, the best organisations display genuine respect for their efforts.

References

Bandura, A. (1986). *Social foundations of thought and action: A social cognitive theory.* Prentice-Hall.

Bell, B. (2019). Women's Euro 2005 a 'watershed' for women's football in England and a new era for the game? *Sport in History, 39*(4), 445–461. 10.1080/17460263.2019.1684985

Burton, L. J. (2015). Underrepresentation of women in sport leadership: A review of research. *Sport Management Review, 18*(2), 155–165. 10.1016/j.smr.2014.02.004

Castles, S. (2001). Studying social transformation. *International Political Science Review, 22*(1), 13–32. 10.1177/0192512101221002

Chinurum, J., OgunjImi, L. O., & O'Neill, C. B. (2014). Gender and sports in contemporary society. *Journal of Education and Social Research, 4*(7), 25–30.

Curran, O., MacNamara, A., & Passmore, D. (2019). What about the girls? Exploring the gender data gap in talent development. *Frontiers in Sports and Active Living, 1*(3).

Daðason, K. T. (2013). *Sports journalism in Iceland. Sports coverage of men and women in Icelandic web media* [Unpublished Master's thesis, University of Iceland]. Skemman. https://skemman.is/handle/1946/13757

Dunn, C. (2018). Canada 2015: Perceptions and experiences of the organisation and governance of the Women's World Cup. *Sport in Society, 21*(5), 788–799. 10.1080/17430437.2018.1440719

Feola, G. (2015). Societal transformation in response to global environmental change: A review of emerging concepts. *Ambio, 44*(5), 376–390. 10.1007/s13280-014-0582-z

FIFA. (2022, August 9). Women's rankings. https://www.fifa.com/fifa-world-ranking/women?dateId=ranking_20220805

Football Association of Iceland. (2021). *A comprehensive review of women's football: A task force report.* https://www.ksi.is/um-ksi/frettir/frettasafn/frett/2021/02/01/Heildarendurskodun-a-knattspyrnu-kvenna/

Gillion, L., & Keim, M. (2020). Sport, peace, and social transformation. *Peace Review, 32*(4), 441–447. 10.1080/10402659.2020.1921398

Gray, L. M., Wong-Wylie, G., Rempel, G. R., & Cook, K. (2020). Expanding qualitative research interviewing strategies: Zoom video communications. *The Qualitative Report, 25*(5), 1292–1301.

Hall, R. L., & Oglesby, C. A. (2016). Stepping through the looking glass: The future for women in sport. *Sex Roles, 74*(7), 271–274. 10.1007/s11199-015-0572-z

Hamilton, T. (2022, August 1). *England's Euro 2022 success is a platform for the next generation.* ESPN. Retrieved August 23, 2022, from https://www.espn.com/soccer/england-engw/story/4710282/englands-euro-2022-title-success-is-a-platform-to-inspire-the-next-generation

Hölscher, K., Wittmayer, J. M., & Loorbach, D. (2018). Transition versus transformation: What's the difference? *Environmental Innovation and Societal Transitions, 27*, 1–3. 10.1016/j.eist.2017.10.007

Hrafnsdóttir, S., Jónsdóttir, G. A., & Kristmundsson, Ó. H. (2014). Participation in voluntary work in Iceland. *Icelandic Review of Politics and Administration, 10*(2), 427–444. 10.13177/irpa.a.2014.10.2.12

Kristjánsdóttir, H., Björgvinsson, K. B., & Ingvarsdóttir, R. (2021). *Evaluation of Icelandic FA responses and procedures regarding complaints and suggestions that the Icelandic FA has received about gender-based and sexual violence from 2010 to 2021.* The National Olympic and Sports Association of Iceland.

LaVoi, N. M., Baeth, A., & Calhoun, A. S. (2019). Sociological perspectives of women in sport. In N. Lough & A. N. Geurin (Eds.), *Routledge handbook of the business of women's sport* (pp. 36–46). Routledge.

Linnér, B. O., & Wibeck, V. (2019). *Sustainability transformations: Agents and drivers across societies.* Cambridge University Press

Lockwood, P., & Kunda, Z. (1999). Increasing the salience of one's best selves can undermine inspiration by outstanding role models. *Journal of Personality and Social Psychology, 76*(2), 214–228. 10.1037/0022-3514.76.2.214

McIntosh, M. J., & Morse, J. M. (2015). Situating and constructing diversity in semi-structured interviews. *Global Qualitative Nursing Research, 2*, 1–12. 10.1177/2333393 615597674

Milkman, H. B., & Jonsson, G. K. (2019). Perspective – Iceland succeeds at preventing teenage substance use. In M. Stephens, M. El-Sholkamy, I. A. Moonesar, & R. Awamleh (Eds.), *Future governments* (pp. 315–324). Emerald Publishing Limited.

Morgenroth, T., Ryan, M. K., & Peters, K. (2015). The motivational theory of role modeling: How role models influence role aspirants' goals. *Review of General Psychology, 19*(4), 465–483. 10.1037/gpr0000059

Ólafsdóttir, T. (2014). *Comparison of Icelandic web media coverage of men's and women's football* [Unpublished Master's thesis, Reykjavik University]. Skemman. https://skemman.is/handle/1946/19344

Reykjavík Principal Office for Sport and Recreation. (2012). *Sports policy in Reykjavík 2012–2020.* https://rafhladan.is/bitstream/handle/10802/3419/Itrottastefna_2012-2020I.pdf?sequence=1

Ronkainen, N. J., Ryba, T. V., & Selänne, H. (2019). "She is where I'd want to be in my career": Youth athletes' role models and their implications for career and identity construction. *Psychology of Sport and Exercise, 45*, 101562. 10.1016/j.psychsport.2019.101562

Schmidt, H. C. (2016). Women's sports coverage remains largely marginalized. *Newspaper Research Journal, 37*(3), 275–298. 10.1177/0739532916663211

Shoemaker, P. J., & Vos, T. (2009). *Gatekeeping Theory.* Routledge.

Statistics Iceland. (2022, March 24). *Population overview.* https://www.hagstofa.is/talnaefni/ibuar/mannfjoldi/yfirlit/

Steinarsson, S. Ó. (2017). *Our girls.* Football Association of Iceland.

The National Olympic and Sports Association of Iceland. (2010). *Participants by sport 2009.* https://www.isi.is/library/Skrar/Efnisveita/Tolfraedi/Idkendur---Greinar/I%c3%b0kendur%202009%20eftir%20%c3%ad%c3%ber%c3%b3ttagreinum

The National Olympic and Sports Association of Iceland. (2021). *Participants by sport 2020.* https://www.isi.is/library/Skrar/Efnisveita/Tolfraedi/Idkendur---Greinar/I%c3%b0kendur%20%e2%80%93%20%c3%8d%c3%ber%c3%b3ttagreinar%202020.pdf

UEFA. (2019, May 17). *Time for action: First ever UEFA women's football strategy launched.* Retrieved June 19, 2022, from https://www.uefa.com/insideuefa/news/0251-0f8e6ba98884-3dd4ba899f93-1000--time-for-action-first-ever-uefa-women-s-football-strategy-launc/

UEFA. (2021, October 4). UEFA Women's Champions League group stage preview: Breidablik vs Paris. Retrieved June 21, 2022, from https://www.uefa.com/womenschampionsleague/news/026e-136580f3192a-0cc70858fbd0-1000--preview-breidablik-vs-paris/

Wheeler, L., Martin, R., & Suls, J. (1997). The proxy model of social comparison for self-assessment of ability. *Personality and Social Psychology Review: An Official Journal of the Society for Personality and Social Psychology, Inc, 1*(1), 54–61. 10.1207/s15327957pspr0101_4

Supporters, Audiences and Culture

Chapter 13

Historical Rivalries in Swedish Club Football

Torbjörn Andersson

The background

This text will address the most enduring historical rivalries in Swedish men's club football from the turn of the 20th century until today. The focus is on the three major football regions, namely Stockholm (the clubs AIK, Djurgårdens IF and Hammarby IF), Gothenburg (IFK Göteborg, Örgryte IS, GAIS, and BK Häcken) and the county of Scania (Malmö FF, Helsingborgs IF, and Landskrona BoIS). The analysis was part of a research project on the relationship between club football and local identity in 11 different cities during the period 1950 up to the beginning of the 2000s (Andersson, 2011, 2016). The theoretical basis consists of Richard Giulianotti's and Roland Robertson's concept of glocalisation and Manuel Castells' analysis of the emergence of the network society (Castells, 1999; Giulianotti & Robertson, 2009).

Giulianotti and Robertson talk about a world characterised by constant interactions and conflicts between global and local contexts. In the case of Sweden, the glocalisation process of football has been marked by a desire to create a local football culture with a relatively low degree of commercialism. During the late 19th century, football was a global sport that reached Sweden from two directions: Denmark, which influenced Scania in the south, and Great Britain, which influenced the rest of the country. In both countries, amateurism had a strong position among football practitioners from the middle and upper classes. In Sweden, this amateur ideal was transformed to apply to the working class players. Soon after the First World War, the players, as well as the spectators, were mostly from the working class. The game, on the other hand, was controlled by the middle-class in the Swedish FA (Andersson, 2002). The amateur system went through a gradual liberalisation process. And although the amateur rules were abolished in 1967, professionalism was never actually officially introduced on a given date. Indeed, it was not until the turn of the millennium that one can de facto talk about professional football in Sweden. Nevertheless, in many respects Swedish football culture came to resemble English professional football. Many clubs soon became important for local identities, with rivalries becoming fierce both within cities and between

DOI: 10.4324/9781003280729-19

neighbouring cities. Crowd trouble was rife from the 1910s until the 1930s, only to return in a more modern hooligan form during the 1970s (Andersson, 2001).

Manuel Castells, for his part, shows how information technology and globalisation have transformed capitalism and the world in a process that has intensified since the 1970s. The network logic has come to permeate the whole of Swedish society, including Swedish club football. However, the relatively low economic turnover in Swedish club football can make it difficult to relate it to Castells' analysis of capitalism. Throughout history, Swedish football has tried to protect itself from overt commercialism. A 50+1% rule was introduced in Swedish sports in 1999, which prevented private owners from taking over clubs. A strong supporter culture has upheld this rule (Andersson & Carlsson, 2011). In this context, networking has been fundamentally important for Swedish clubs, an aspect of relevance in Castells' analysis. No club has been able to rely on a wealthy owner. Rather, the clubs have seen the importance of establishing and maintaining good relations with local politicians because stadiums have usually been financed by their local municipality. In addition, the clubs have had to work intensively to obtain sponsorship from small, local enterprises. The long hegemony of amateurism has resulted in a tradition where large companies and the super-rich have not supported football. Another important necessity for the clubs has been the creation of good local press relations to ensure positive coverage. Traditionally, Sweden has had many local newspapers with a strong readership. Moreover, social media has been a distinctive part of the network society. However, the most important part of the network has been to attract large attendances: a large loyal fan base provides positive synergy effects to the rest of the network. An important aspect in attracting many spectators has been club rivalry. However, spectators can negatively affect the network in cases where there have been major hooligan problems (Andersson, 2016, pp. 26–31). The project which this text is based on worked with a qualitative method and a source material including literature of various kinds about the different cities and clubs, board minutes from the clubs, newspapers, sports magazines, different kinds of internet material, match observations and interviews.

The start of the rivalries: Gothenburg

The first long-standing rivalry arose in Gothenburg, the city that soon became known as the capital of Swedish football. The background to the rivalry had to do with social class and concerned two clubs: Örgryte IS and IFK Göteborg. Named after an exclusive district, Örgryte IS was a middle-class club from its leadership to its players and fans, and it came to dominate football at the end of the 19th century. From the more central parts of the city came its rival, IFK Göteborg, with a more mixed middle- and working class composition. However, the club was seen as the team of the people as its players were predominantly working class. By 1907, IFK had turned into a major football force. The origins of the rivalry partly concerned Örgryte IS controlling the city's best football ground and denying its rival access to it. Soon, the derby matches were attracting thousands, with Örgryte's supporters occupying the seating section and IFK's the cheaper stands. In the 1910s, the heated rivalry included brawls between clubs' leaders, players and spectators, so much so that there was talk of stopping football in Gothenburg (Persson, 2011, pp. 291–294). In terms of networking, there was a certain dysfunctionalism, as the press wrote negatively about the incidents.

During the 1920s, the situation changed for the better. Now another team had joined the scene: GAIS, located in the central areas with no geographical difference to IFK Göteborg. However, GAIS was more working class with a political leaning further to the left. The city's clubs created a co-operation alliance in 1919, thus mitigating the rivalries. The three teams dominated Swedish football until around 1930, with IFK Göteborg remaining strong thereafter. Gothenburg as a city became famous for its high football attendances, and football enthusiasts could watch all the three teams. Before the 2000s, the city held every possible attendance records – despite Stockholm being double its size. The city's football fans were known for their knowledge, humour, and exemplary behaviour. Now all three teams had the same centrally located home ground, Ullevi, inaugurated in 1916. Moreover, they did not recruit players from each other and helped each other out in economic crises. The networks around the clubs in the interwar period were based on large crowds and enthusiastic press coverage. The proceeds came from the turnstiles as sponsors were not yet anywhere to be seen in Swedish football. Furthermore, all three clubs operated from the centre of town, with no geographical differences. In terms of class, almost all players were working class. As for the boards and the supporters, Örgryte was the more exclusive. IFK Göteborg was the most popular, while GAIS had the deepest working-class roots. As a city, Gothenburg had a strong local identity, nurtured in opposition to the capital Stockholm. In politics, Gothenburg was known for a unifying spirit, with politicians striving for consensus by working for the city's best interests. The same spirit characterised football in Gothenburg from the interwar period (Andersson, 2011, pp. 295–326). Overall, football had a stronger significance for this working-class city compared to the more white-collar Stockholm.

Early rivalry in Stockholm

In Stockholm, AIK and Djurgårdens IF met for the first time in 1899, making it the oldest rivalry. There was no geographical difference between the two as both were centrally located with a leaning towards the exclusive Östermalm. Both clubs had a similar middle-class character; but towards the First World War, they had become popular within a large social span. They were known as the Twin Clubs, a fitting name given that both were founded in 1891 and based in the same areas. The similarities led to immediate discussions about the differences, ultimately developing into an obsession among the supporters. Here we can talk about a narcissism of minor differences, a concept coined by Sigmund Freud about the small – but frequently discussed – differences between e.g. England and Scotland, Spain and Portugal, and southern and northern Germany (Baldwin, 2009, p. 10).

Both Twin Clubs played at Stadion, built for the 1912 Olympics, and located on Östermalm. AIK had higher attendances, though Djurgården's fans were more vocal. AIK became the country's biggest club around 1930 with impressive attendances of 15–17,000. And although it became glamorous, it simultaneously became more unpopular in Stockholm. Many young men who went to the games had migrated to Stockholm, especially from the north of Sweden, and did not identify with their new hometown: Consequently, they went to AIK's matches supporting the away team. Further irritation was caused by AIK being the first club to recruit good players from other teams. Those who disliked AIK came to be known as *AIK-Hatets Vänner* (The Friends Hating AIK), a name that appeared in the press into the 1960s. In terms of class, AIK had greater breadth, with the royal family as patrons since 1907, but also with a stronghold in the poor northern suburbs of the city. Meanwhile, Djurgården, in the interwar years had moved to Traneberg's sports ground, located west of the city centre, resulting in the club having a more extensive geographical base than AIK. During the First World War, Hammarby IF, which become the third major club in Stockholm, started playing football. The club came from Stockholm's poorest parts, Södermalm, an area with a strong local identity. Despite little sporting success before the 1950's, a distinct urban working-class flavour characterised the club. One strength was that the municipality in 1915 built a ground for Hammarby on southern Södermalm (Andersson, 2016, pp. 237–250).

In terms of network, AIK had the strongest in Sweden during the 1930s with its impressive attendances and good support in the press. However, the spectator capacity of its home ground, Stadion, had become too low. Therefore, AIK in 1937 moved to the new Råsunda stadium, which also became home to the Swedish national team. It was located in Solna, a northern district that never was incorporated in Stockholm, but became a city of its own in 1943. AIK thus gained its modern character as the club for central and northern Stockholm (Andersson, 2016, pp. 231–232).

Early rivalries in Scania

Around 1930, Helsingborgs IF became the leading club outside Gothenburg and Stockholm. Its main strength was that the club represented the entire city. Its main rivalry was directed 25 kilometres south towards Landskrona BoIS, representing the small shipyard town of Landskrona. Fuelled by the more working-class Landskrona, a strong rivalry developed during the interwar period. Malmö, Scania's largest city, was represented by the middle-class IFK Malmö, a team of less importance in terms of rivalry. During the 1920s,

Landskrona boasted a higher attendance record than Malmö, and the sporting press wrote of BoIS as having the country's worse behaved supporters (Andersson, 2011, pp. 90–94).

In Malmö, an internal class-based rivalry between IFK Malmö and the working-class club Malmö FF gradually grew. It peaked in 1934 when IFK reported its local competitor to the Swedish FA for violating the amateur rules. Malmö FF was punished with relegation, while players and leaders were banned for a year, resulting in enduring hatred from Malmö FF's side towards its rival. Ten years after this incidence, Malmö FF won its first league title and remained a major club, while IFK stagnated. Malmö, like Helsingborg and Landskrona, was now a city with only one major team, and Malmö FF was to lead the professionalisation of Swedish football (Billing et al., 2004). In terms of networking, it was noteworthy that Landskrona BoIS in 1924 got the country's first major municipal sports ground. Earlier on, the sports grounds were private. But from the interwar period, they turned into municipal projects as part of the welfare society (Sjöblom, 2006, p. 103). As elsewhere, the Scanian clubs' networks were based on good attendances in combination with an enthusiastic local press coverage.

Before moving on to the post-war golden age of Swedish football, it should be noted that no real crowd troubles – except in Gothenburg in the 1910s – permeated the different rivalries. The spectator culture had a glocal character. In connection with the 1912 Olympics, an American cheering squad showed up in Stockholm, with the phenomenon from American university sport soon transferred to Swedish football. Thus, the interwar period became the golden age of organised cheering. A cheerleader led the crowd in chanting various rhymes; the repertoire was gentlemanly and not rivalry provoking (Andersson & Radmann, 1998).

The golden age of football

After the Second World War and into the 1960s, the top-tier Swedish league, *Allsvenskan*, had attendance averages of over 10,000 per match. The peak was in 1959, the year after the World Cup in Sweden, with an average of over 13,000 (Persson, 2004, p. 156). The three Gothenburg teams had especially impressive attendances. The municipality's interest in football was highlighted by the construction of the Nya Ullevi stadium for the 1958 World Cup. It was one of the world's most modern arenas and was centrally located next to the older Ullevi arena, thus testifying football's significance for Gothenburg's local identity. The difference with Stockholm was striking, where Råsunda was inaugurated way outside the city centre in 1937. Despite plans for a new World Cup stadium in Stockholm, the capital was in the end content to upgrade Råsunda. Örgryte IS recorded a Swedish attendance record in 1959 with an average of over 25,000 per match. The three Gothenburg clubs all played at Nya Ullevi, and the good cooperation between them continued. Although Örgryte's players were mostly social democrats, the leadership was connected to the city's strong political liberalism. IFK Göteborg was still the most popular and associated with the social democrats. GAIS, on the other hand, had the weakest network, and the club and its supporters were politically more to the left.

In the golden age all three Stockholm teams played together in Allsvenskan with Råsunda being home to everyone. Now the local derbies, especially between AIK and Djurgården, became highlights. Previously, Stockholm's highest attendances had seldom been recorded at derby matches (Hellspong, 2013, pp. 110–111). The press described the atmosphere at derbies in Stockholm as more fanatical than in Gothenburg. The author Jan Olof "Jolo" Olsson tried, in 1959, to capture the differences between the supporters of AIK and Djurgården. He pitched a trendier and more enthusiastic Djurgården supporter against a shaggier and more critical AIK fan (Erséus, 2007, p. 178). Meanwhile, Hammarby, had a more acute working-class character, and the fans stood out as more patriotic. The working-class identity of Södermalm was built on the bohemian artisan culture (Billing et al., 2004).

The situation in Scania was reminiscent of the consensual mood in Gothenburg. The strong Scanian regional identity was unifying, with its inhabitants preferring a Scanian team as champions rather than a team from Stockholm. The previously intense rivalry between Landskrona BoIS and Helsingborgs IF cooled as the former usually played in a lower division. However, in 1959 Landskrona demonstrated its strong football identity while qualifying for promotion to Allsvenskan: BoIS supporters became the first to wear their team's colours. The inspiration seems to have come from the lively West German fans who showed up in Malmö during the 1958 World Cup (Andersson, 2021, pp. 201–202).

Modern supporter culture and hooliganism

The 1960s marked a decline in interest in the top league, Allsvenskan, reaching lowest attendances of 4,000 spectators per match around 1990. Many Swedes now began to follow English clubs as a result of live televised matches broadcasted since 1969, but English supporter culture inspired the Swedes who still went to football matches. When IFK Göteborg was about to be relegated in 1970, the fans stormed the pitch in a game at Örebro. The episode has been described as the start of modern hooliganism, with the supporters now younger and more subcultural than before (Radmann & Andersson, 2018, p. 151). At the same time, Hammarby's fans started singing at matches, having being inspired by their English counterparts. These supporters were the first to introduce a more confrontational style in songs and cheers. Stockholm as a city had a low sense of self-esteem at this time. Entertainment was meagre, classic neighbourhoods were demolished, and the inner city lost population. A green wave-craze gave a boost to the countryside.

Amid all of this, Hammarby's lively fans appeared with a patriotism for Stockholm – more precisely for Södermalm – of a previously unknown kind in Swedish football (Cederquist & Hagström, 2020).

The next step taken in the creation of a modern supporter culture was by AIK's fans. In Stockholm, ice hockey was popular, and around it a younger and wilder supporter culture was created. The followers came to be known as the Black Army, after Manchester United's Red Army. Punk was a source of inspiration in contrast to Hammarby's more mods- and hippie-inspired fans. With the Black Army, aggression came to the forefront, and the group soon became better known at football matches. Because AIK as a club was in financial crisis, it was happy to finally have vocal supporters, but worried about the negative publicity the group attracted. AIK, which was previously seen as a gentleman's club like old Arsenal, soon resembled Millwall. The Stockholm rivalries became more aggressive at a time when football was in decline (Andersson, 2016, pp. 298–303).

In Stockholm, geography became the major watershed, as the three teams from the early 1970s got different home grounds. AIK played at Råsunda and represented Stockholm north of Slussen, and area between Gamla Stan (Old Town) and Södermalm. South of Slussen and the Old Town was Hammarby's territory, in the workers' district of Södermalm. Hammarby moved from Råsunda to Söderstadion, built by the municipality in 1967, and located just south of Södermalm, thus connecting Hammarby's old core lands with the new child-rich suburbs to the south. Hammarby turned into the team of the southern part of the green metro line. In these new areas, the local identity was weak, and Hammarby became part of a more general southern identity. Meanwhile, Djurgården also left Råsunda in favour of the old Olympic Stadion. At this time, 1972, Djurgården was in crisis. Stadion's surroundings was an area losing population with families moving out and older, wealthy people with no interest in football remaining. Djurgården therefore chose to create football schools outside the inner city, and thereby continuing the tradition of having a scattered fan base (Andersson, 2016, pp. 273–275, 296).

During the 1980s and 1990s, attendances in Stockholm were low, with rowdy fans making headlines. The skinhead culture, with its racism, gained a foothold within all three teams, especially with AIK. The rivalry between AIK and Djurgården was confirmed as the strongest in Sweden, despite the fact that Hammarby's identity clearly differed from the Twin Clubs. In the rest of Sweden, Hammarby's bohemian appearance was popular, while AIK emerged as the main representative of the arrogant side of the capital. AIK's hooligans strengthened this picture. The networks around the Stockholm clubs were weak, attendances dropped, press coverage was low, and sponsors preferred the more friendly sport of ice hockey. However, the arena situation was positive: Hammarby had a small but suitable arena in Söderstadion, AIK played at a modernised (although far too big) Råsunda, while Djurgården played at the old-fashioned and charming Stadion.

IFK Göteborg developed into a major force during the mid-1970s. After a long crisis, its new management quickly built up a strong network. Attendances rose spectacularly, and top players were recruited. Sponsors were involved to an extent never before seen in Swedish football. In fact, the Swedish Sports Confederation, the organisation that brings together all sports, did not officially approve sponsorship until 1978. The lateness underlines the glocalisation process of Swedish sports, resulting in a relatively non-commercial sports model. The golden years of IFK – with UEFA Cup victories in 1982 and 1987, and successes in the European Cup/Champions League – lasted until the introduction of the Bosman ruling in 1995. The triumphs resulting in new fans all over the country, a trend facilitated by Gothenburg's general popularity as a city. Locally, GAIS supporters were annoyed by IFK's stardom; thus, the club, inspired by punk and rock n'roll, developed a more subcultural profile. Nevertheless, Gothenburg football had no greater dynamism than the three teams abandoning the vast Nya Ullevi in 1992 in favour of the more intimate old (Gamla) Ullevi, which the three teams' supporters renovated together. In this respect, the Gothenburg spirit of football continued (Andersson, 2011, pp. 338–348, 369–370).

Although Swedish clubs were still amateur, they were successful, with Malmö FF reaching the European Cup final in 1979. However, the team did not become as nationally popular as IFK Göteborg. The playing style was too boring, and the strong regional identity won few fans outside of Scania. Under Bob Houghton's leadership, Malmö FF had cultivated an identity based on antagonism against the rest of Sweden. Only AIK rejoiced in a similar attitude (Andersson, 2011, pp. 153–167; Peterson, 2000).

2000s football boom

In the new millennium, interest in football exploded. Attendances in Allsvenskan reached averages of 10,000 per game. The atmosphere was now significantly higher than in the golden years. Those who went to the stadiums were passionate, unlike when previous general football enthusiasts attended, many of whom now preferred international televised football. The paradox was that the atmosphere peaked, while the quality of football deteriorated. After the introduction of the Bosman ruling, players flooded out of the country as wage levels were higher almost everywhere (Andersson & Hognestad, 2019). The modern supporter culture paved the way for the renewed interest, with the fans in Stockholm and Malmö being at the forefront, while football's old capital, Gothenburg, failed to keep up. One problem was that Gothenburg did not modernise its arenas to the same extent as in Malmö and Stockholm. Through the intensified passion in the stands, the networks around the clubs strengthened. The press expanded its coverage, and the supporters became deeply involved in the development of social media. The result being that more sponsors flocked in, and finally municipalities and private actors began to renew the obsolete stadiums. However, a Swedish distinctiveness was maintained as a strong supporter culture successfully defended the 50+1% rule introduced in 1999.

There are many factors behind the renaissance of football. An increased interest in football among the middle class and women was one aspect. Swedish fans were open to global impulses and good organisers – note the old tradition of organised cheering. Important was the highly increased urbanisation. Young people moved to big cities, where the football team facilitated them finding a metropolitan identity. The large number of single households increased the search for a community. In addition, alcohol policy was liberalised in the mid-1990s, with the number of pubs increasing dramatically. It became part of a new urban lifestyle to discuss football in pubs. The speed of supporters embracing social media meant that the football debate continued non-stop. The vitalised supporter culture was inspired by Italy's ultras; thus, new influences were added to the British singing and the old organised cheering. These global impulses got a distinct local flavour, with supporters often performing a repertoire with a lot of dialect. This was paradoxical as many fans had recently moved from areas with a different dialect. The people who were drawn to the stands were obviously part of the same subculture. The similarities led to a fixation on the few noticeable differences. In this milieu, the "us against them" narratives were cultivated and rivalries increased markedly.

Only now did Malmö FF and Helsingborgs IF become serious rivals. Helsingborgs IF had during the 1990s turned into a leading club with a strong network, characterised by strong sponsorship. The club had a hooligan problem that far exceeded Malmö FF's, despite the fact that Malmö was a tougher city. Between Landskrona BoIS and Helsingborgs IF, the dormant rivalry was brought to life when BoIS won promotion to Allsvenskan. Even in Gothenburg, the convivial atmosphere disappeared when IFK Göteborg and GAIS became bigger rivals among the fans, despite IFK's superiority on all levels. In Stockholm, the rivalry between all three teams exploded, with AIK and Djurgården as the main opponents. Hammarby grew rapidly as a club – especially the number of spectators – and the team won its only league title in 2001. It became the hipster's favourite club, a process facilitated by the gentrification of the old working-class district of Södermalm. AIK was the epicentre of the growing hooligan culture. When its hooligans formed a well-organised firm in the early 1990s, Djurgården and IFK Göteborg had to catch up with firms of their own (Radmann & Andersson, 2018, p. 151). Soon enough, there were firms around different clubs. The hooligan culture – resulting in two deaths – hampered the networks' growth. The negative writings of the press made sponsors hesitate, especially in the rich and dynamic Stockholm.

The history of rivalries

The supporter movement of the 21st century has been reflexive. The fans have been knowledgeable about global and local conditions, and have worked to find a glocal balance. Rivalries have been deliberately heightened and exaggerated in order to strengthen the "us against them" mentality on which the supporter culture is based. The intensified passions helped to develop the networks around the clubs. Although much has changed, there are continuities in terms rivalries: Class and geography are the two main identity markers. In Gothenburg all three historic clubs in the Gothenburg Alliance – IFK Göteborg, Örgryte IS and GAIS – are centrally located, and without noticeable geographical differences. From the 1970s, IFK has become far bigger than its rivals, and the most popular in all parts of the city. GAIS has a stronger connection to old gentrified working-class areas than Örgryte, which has its base in more exclusive circles. Class (and political preferences) is still the main marker. IFK is the club of the labour movement, but it also has connections to the city's political bourgeoisie. GAIS is more to the left, with a more subcultural profile among fans and the board. Örgryte is still associated with the previously strong Gothenburg liberalism. In recent decades, the club has been dependent on major sponsors, while GAIS lived on contributions from its loyal supporters. The images of the three teams are quite stable over time. In fact, they can be seen as opposites in a number of different ways. Given the differences, the rivalries ought to be tough. Despite the new supporter movement trying to intensify the rivalries, they have not fully succeeded. There is still a unifying Gothenburg spirit that leads to the strongest rivalry being between IFK Göteborg and AIK. A result of the spirit was that the city's three teams getting a new stadium from the city's social democratic government in 2009. Unfortunately, it was a low-budget solution, where the poor sponsorship facilities hampered network building (Andersson, 2011, pp. 402–403).

Another Gothenburg team has been successful during the 2000s: BK Häcken. The club stems from the island of Hisingen on the other side of the Göta River. The fact that Hisingen has been a working-class district – home to the big shipyards and Volvo – should have formed the basis for a strong local identity. Hisingen is, however, a stigmatised part of Gothenburg. It is located beyond the centre and not seen as the true Gothenburg. By running the Gothia Cup, the world's largest youth football tournament, Häcken has built up a stronger economy than the three alliance clubs combined. Still, they have not managed to attract more than a few thousand to the games. In 2007, an attempt was made to merge Häcken, GAIS, and Örgryte into a major force named FC Gothia. The project crashed when GAIS supporters threatened the club's own management. It was not possible to merge GAIS and Örgryte, which were clearly opposites (Andersson, 2011, pp. 355–363, 393–395). The failed merger underlined the conservative nature of Gothenburg football. The city is no longer the capital of football.

The rivalries in Stockholm are based on geography. In fact, AIK and Djurgården are almost inseparable in terms of class. Their identity constructions include accusing the opponent of being more upper-class. In a country with a long political hegemony of social democracy, it has been important to be regarded as the people's team. In reality, AIK and Djurgården have long been clubs covering the entire spectrum of society. Hammarby has been the working class team of Södermalm and the southern suburbs. As Södermalm has been gentrified and Hammarby trendy, rival fans have happily pointed out that they are no longer the people's team. With 49% of Hammarby controlled by a large American owner, AEG, the image of the club has partly changed. The class confusion around the three clubs, has made geography more important. Among the supporters, the geographical differences, imaginary and real, have developed into an obsession. This was made possible by the fact that they from the early 1970s played in different parts of Greater Stockholm: AIK in the north, Djurgården in the centre, and Hammarby in the south. All three clubs built up impressive supporter cultures, with Djurgården's mostly inspired by English singing, while AIK and Hammarby took greater inspiration from southern Europe. Djurgården and Hammarby had the problem that the network's expansion was hampered by old arenas with bad sponsorship facilities, while AIK were better off at the national arena, Råsunda.

When Stockholm finally modernised its arena park, it happened in style. Two new arenas were completed in 2013 for EUR 550 million. The foreplay included that all three teams wanted new arenas in the areas where they played. Now AIK moved into the new national arena, Friends in Solna, not far from Råsunda. In Stockholm, Tele2 Arena was built right next to Hammarby's old Söderstadion, and Djurgården was forced to move there. Hammarby's supporters were upset that Djurgården moved to Hammarby's core land. However, Djurgården's popular ice hockey team had long played their home matches in the neighbourhood. Thus, they already had many supporters in the area. It did not only have to do with football that Greater Stockholm got two large arenas, Friends with a capacity of 50,000 and Tele2 Arena with 30,000. Stockholm wanted to overtake Gothenburg as the event capital in terms of staging major concerts and events (Andersson, 2016, pp. 386–390). AIK's fans complained about the lack of atmosphere in the luxurious Friends, and the team's attendances remained around 20,000, much like at the Råsunda stadium the fans had come to love (Herd, 2018, pp. 144–165). Hammarby, on the other hand, doubled its following in the larger Tele2 Arena, and in 2015 the average of 25,507 surpassed Örgryte's record from 1959. Djurgården slightly increased its average, and landed around 15,000. Hammarby appeared as the largest club, but in terms of sponsorship, they were behind their two rivals, with AIK on top. Stockholm's current football culture is remarkable, considering how internationally weak the teams are. Due to the 50+1 rule – which inhibits investors – and a continued hesitation from many sponsors to enter the frantic scene of Stockholm football, the three teams are still behind Malmö FF – the shining star of the 2000s. In fact, no Stockholm team has ever had a strong network.

In the 2000s, Malmö FF is Sweden's leading club. The basis for the success is the country's best new arena, Swedbank Stadium, built in 2009, right next to the old stadium from the 1958 World Cup. With Malmö FF being the only major team in a rapidly growing city, sponsors have flocked to the club. The network became strong. Through successes in Europe, Malmö FF have superior finances. And it now seems obvious that Malmö FF and the three Stockholm clubs will dominate in the future.

The main Swedish rivalries are old, and it is difficult to see any new ones emerging. The intensified rivalries of recent decades are to a large degree constructed by the supporter groups, a fact that has not prevented Swedish club football from appearing very authentic.

References

Andersson, T. (2001). Swedish football hooliganism, 1900–39. *Soccer & Society*, 2(1), 1–18.
Andersson, T. (2002). *Kung fotboll. Den svenska fotbollens kulturhistoria från 1800-talets slut till 1950* [King Football: The cultural history of Swedish football from the end of the 19th century to 1950]. Symposion.
Andersson, T. (2011). *"Spela fotboll bondjävlar!" En studie av svensk klubbfotboll och lokal identitet från 1950 till 2000-talets början, Del 1* ["Play football bloody peasants!" A study of Swedish club football and local identity from 1950 to the early 2000s, Part 1]. Symposion.
Andersson, T. (2016). *"Spela fotboll bondjävlar!" En studie av svensk klubbfotboll och lokal identitet från 1950 till 2000-talets början, Del 2* ["Play football bloody peasants!" A study of Swedish club football and local identity from 1950 to the early 2000s, Part 2]. Symposion.
Andersson, T. (2021). *Fotbollens Kuriosakabinett. Svensk fotbolls kulturarv i ord och bild* [The Football Cabinet of Curiosities. The cultural heritage of Swedish football in words and pictures]. Arx Förlag.
Andersson, T., & Carlsson, B. (2011). A diagnosis of the commercial immaturity of Swedish club football. *Soccer & Society*, 12(6), 754–773.
Andersson, T., & Hognestad, H. (2019). Glocal culture, sporting decline? Globalization and football in Scandinavia. *Sport in Society*, 22(4), 704–716.
Andersson, T., & Radmann, A. (1998). Football fans in Scandinavia 1900–97. In A. Brown (Ed.), *Fanatics! Power, identity & fandom in soccer* (pp. 141–157). Routledge.
Baldwin, P. (2009). *The narcissism of minor differences. How America and Europe are alike.* Oxford University Press.
Billing, P., Franzén, M., & Peterson, T. (2004). Paradoxes of football professionalization in Sweden: A club approach. *Soccer & Society*, 5(1), 82–99.
Castells, M. (1999). *Informationsåldern. Ekonomi, samhälle och kultur. Band 1 Nätverkssamhällets framväxt* [The age of information. Economy, society and culture. The rise of the network society]. Daidalos.
Cederquist, J., & Hagström, M. (2020). *Hösten 70* [The autumn 1970]. Idrottsförlaget.
Erséus, J. (Ed.). (2007). *JOLO. Allsvensk idyll – texter om och av Jan Olof Olsson* [JOLO: Allsvensk idyll – texts about and by Jan Olof Olsson]. Jolosällskapet.
Giulianotti, R., & Robertson, R. (2009). *Globalization & football*. SAGE Publications.
Hellspong, M. (2013). *Stadion och Zinkensdamm: Stockholms idrottspublik under två sekel* [The Stadion and Zinkensdamm: Sport's spectators in Stockholm during two centuries]. Stockholmia.

Herd, K. (2018). *"We can make new history here". Rituals of producing history in Swedish football clubs.* Lund Studies in Arts and Cultural Sciences 19.

Persson, G. (2004). *100 år. Svenska Fotbollförbundets jubileumsbok 1904–2004, band 2* [100 years. Swedish Football Association's anniversary book 1904–2004, volume 2]. Stroemberg Media Group.

Persson, L. K. (2011). *Den hårda kampen: fotboll i Sverige, särskilt Göteborg, före första världskriget* [The hard fight: Football in Sweden, especially in Gothenburg before the First World War]. Bricoleur Press.

Peterson, T. (2000). Split visions: The introduction of the Svenglish model in Swedish football. *Soccer & Society, 1*(2), 1–18.

Radmann, A., & Andersson, T. (2018). Sweden. In J.-M. De Waele, S. Gibril, E. Gloriozova, & R. Spaaij (Eds.), *The Palgrave international handbook of football and politics* (pp. 139–161). Springer International Publishing.

Sjöblom, P. (2006). *Den institutionaliserade tävlingsidrotten: Kommuner, idrott och politik i Sverige under 1900-talet* [The institutionalised competitive sports: Municipalities, sports and politics in Sweden during the 20th century]. Acta Universitatis Stockholmiensis.

Chapter 14

The Development of Supporter Cultures in Norwegian Football Since 1990

Arve Hjelseth and Hans K. Hognestad

Introduction

From the early days of the game in the Nordic region, reports show that football spectators behaved differently than other sports audiences. A Norwegian sport reporter, visiting Copenhagen around 1920, complained that spectators had yelled and screamed, rather than applauding politely (Goksøyr & Olstad, 2002). Football spectating was also more partisan than in most other sports. The atmosphere at games could take on a hostile nature. This was also the case in Norway. It was not, however, until the 1970s that these ways of supporting a team gradually formed into more distinct *supporter cultures*. We will define the term more thoroughly in the next section.

In this chapter, we shall discuss the emergence and developments of supporter cultures in Norwegian club football since 1990. The analysis is restricted to men's football, mostly at the elite level. Only men's elite football clubs have enjoyed followings large enough to form supporter cultures in the way we define the term here. Currently, women's football undoubtedly enjoys a surge in popularity that requires investigation in its own right. This chapter, however, is based on previous research (see, e.g., Andersson & Hognestad, 2019; Armstrong & Hognestad, 2006; Giulianotti, 2002; Goksøyr & Hognestad, 1999; Hjelseth, 2006; Hognestad & Hjelseth, 2012; Reim, 2012), which makes men's elite football the point of departure.

We start by offering a brief sketch of previous and current research on football supporters in Europe, to identify some key issues and concepts. Particular attention is paid to supporter research from the 1990s, when commercialisation challenged the traditional cultures of support. Thereafter, we give an account of the rise of organised supporter cultures in Norway. Then, we discuss the changing international influences on Norwegian supporter cultures, particularly the increasing influences from Latin and German traditions. While aspects of the rituals supporters are involved in are discussed in that section, we shall discuss examples of supporter activism in the subsequent section. Finally, we attempt to outline briefly the possible futures of supporter cultures in Norway in the concluding section.

DOI: 10.4324/9781003280729-20

A brief overview of research on football supporters

The research on supporter cultures emerged in England in the 1970s. A major motivation was to understand and handle the hooligan issue. A new form of so-called hooliganism had emerged during the 1960s and increased in the following decade (Giulianotti, 1994, p. 9). Around 1990, the focus of research gradually changed, partly as the result of changes within football itself. The globalisation of football implied that questions concerning identity and meaning were increasingly addressed by a growing number of researchers from the early 1990s. The much-cited *taxonomy* of football spectators, developed and published in an article by Richard Giulianotti (2002) is a case in point, as are issues of the interactions between local and global influences in shaping current football identities and practices (Giulianotti & Robertson, 2004; Giulianotti & Robertson, 2009; Sandvoss, 2003).

The changes in football also reflected wider societal changes (King, 2002). While the "traditional" supporter cultures of the 1970s and 1980s reflected industrial societies, the changes after 1990 reflect post-industrial or post-modern societies. Giulianotti (1999) identified a particular figure called the "post-fan" to describe a new category of spectators that emerged as football became an integral part of popular culture: Knowledgeable and often enthusiastic, yet characterised by at least a minimum of ironic distance towards the development of the game.

Such concepts gave rise to distinctions between "traditional" and modern, "consumerist" ways of supporting a team (Giulianotti, 2002). This chapter explores and discusses the tensions between supporter groups and the ruling institutions of Norwegian football, the Norwegian Football Federation (NFF), *Norsk Toppfotball* (Norwegian elite football), UEFA, FIFA, sponsors, and the media. However, tensions are also rife between different groups of supporters, where some are less opposed to the modern, media-driven "hypercommodification" (Giulianotti, 2002) of the game, similar to the spectators defined as *new consumer fans* by Anthony King (2002). Interestingly, it is not difficult to find examples of adaptations to the commercialised game, also among the critical and activist sections of supporters, as leaving the game altogether is rarely seen as an option.

Research on Norwegian football supporters has been inspired by these perspectives (Hognestad & Hjelseth, 2012). Of particular interest in Norway has been the strong connection to English football (Goksøyr & Hognestad, 1999; Hognestad, 2003), and the complex and multi-faceted issues of identities that follows. Supporter activism has also been addressed more specifically (Fossum, 2012; Hjelseth, 2006; Reim, 2012). It is on this background that we now turn to an overview of Norwegian supporter cultures.

The rise of organised supporter cultures in Norway

Since the 1990s, football supporters in Europe are known for their activism regarding the development of football as a sport. Pan-European campaigns such as "against modern football" is, at its core, a political movement with the explicit aim of "defending" football against the consequences of its popularity. Issues include protests against the European Super League proposed in 2021, the dislike of unpredictable and ever-changing fixture hours, criticism of ticket pricing, the hostility towards football's governing bodies and the sceptical approach to the influences of sponsors and the media, all adds to the picture of supporters as a body of ideologically conscious actors, aiming to influence the further development of the game. The dawn of such activism can be dated back to the late 1980s. In England, the Football Supporters' Association was launched in 1985, in the aftermath of the Heysel disaster (Football Supporters Association, 2014). Later, the establishment of the English Premier League in 1992 became a symbol for a form of unbounded commercialisation that supporters have – at least partly – opposed.

While the dawn of a more activist kind of supporter practice may be traced back to Britain in the 1980s, organised support itself can be traced back to the origins of the game when supporter clubs were set up to organise travels and the distribution of tickets to games (Giulianotti, 1999). Culturally, football support evolved out of gatherings which exceeded that of mere spectating: Singing, the use of club colours and collective behaviour gradually became an integral part of the football ritual. For the later activists, "modern" commercial football represented a threat to these rituals.

We define supporter cultures as forms of support for a football team that transcend the mere spectating and sympathy for a team, by expressing the support orally and/or visually, and by the forming of formal or informal groups, which also enjoy the socialising with fellow supporters. Supporting in this sense involves some sort of *collective action*, a joint effort to produce an attractive atmosphere. Both singing and the displaying of *tifos*[1] are dependent on quite sophisticated levels of coordination. Most often, these kinds of coordination are more informal than formal.

It is noteworthy that Norwegian supporter cultures emerged parallel to the gradual professionalisation and commercialisation of the game. While commercial interests were regarded as a threat to supporter cultures in many countries, and partially as the backdrop to which such cultures were organised, the emergence of supporter cultures and professional football in Norway evolved simultaneously, starting modestly in the 1980s and flourishing in the 1990s and 2000s. Norwegian supporter culture was not activist from the start, but supporters soon positioned themselves as critical voices of both their own clubs, of the NFF and various commercial stakeholders in the game.

Prior to the late 1980s, supporter practices and cultures were more ad hoc and sporadic, often linked to big events, such as cup finals and other decisive games. Some clubs had official supporter clubs, which the emerging independent supporter club tended to distance themselves from. Bodø/Glimt, for example, had a supporter club and a "colourful" – supporters dressed in club colours – following in the 1970s, but this did not sit comfortably with the styles of support which gradually emerged 10–15 years later.

The changes that took place during the 1990s consisted of several parallel processes. In Norway, the Norwegian Sports Federation (NIF) finally abolished amateurism as a principle for the organised game in 1990. This paved the way for the opening of the first professional football league in 1991. With it, the number of televised games in the top league increased. Arenas were built or upgraded to accommodate spectators who were expecting more comfort, while sponsors became crucial to the financial well-being of clubs. Some clubs were also in fact controlled by businessmen. This undoubtedly helped to pave the way for a flourishing supporter culture, but as mentioned earlier, they were not political from the start. When, for instance, Valerenga of Oslos supporters established *Klanen* (The Clan) as an independent supporter organisation in 1991, a main aim was simply to provide for transport and tickets to away matches. However, the development of a modern, professional football simultaneously provoked resistance and opposition. Like in most of Europe, fractions of such supporter groups became more activist from the late 1990s. We will return to this later.

International inspirations and the cultural positioning of football support

The early inspirations of the modern supporter culture came from Britain, and England in particular. For instance, it has been reported that at some clubs, the early chants by loosely organised supporter groups around 1990 were chanted in English, and more or less directly imported from what some had experienced during travels to England (Goksøyr & Hognestad, 1999). The Norwegian fascination for England and English football have both geographical and cultural historical explanations, especially enhanced by the pan-Nordic introduction of the live television of English league games from the late 1960s. This meant that kids growing up in the 1970s could watch more English than Nordic football on television. However, the historical admiration of English football has much longer traditions in Norway. Regular media coverage of football from England has existed in tandem with the entire history of organised football. It can be traced back to 1902, the year the NFF was founded, with professional British teams regularly playing against many of the newly founded Norwegian teams, with a clear pedagogical intention of "teaching" the Norwegian teams how the game should be played. Newspapers started to cover English football from the early 1920s and pictures of English football stars inside cigarette packages sold in Norway in the 1930s, were evidence of the popularity of the English game (Hognestad, 2003). From 1948 onwards, many familiarised themselves to English football through the football betting when a national, publicly owned lottery was set up to support the spread of sporting facilities through the country (Hjelseth et al., this volume). In 1969, the public Scandinavian broadcasting companies signed an agreement with the English Football Association to start the live broadcast of a game from the English League or FA cup during the winter months, which tremendously enhanced the popularity of English football into the 1970s, especially in Norway. Even if the number of games during a season was only 10–15 during the first years, due to restrictions aimed at protecting the interest for local football and other sports in Norway, many started supporting an English team alongside their local Norwegian team. When restrictions were lifted and live English football became available throughout the season with the introduction of the English Premier League in 1992, along with live football from the other big leagues in Europe, people would regularly have to choose between games from different leagues.

Apart from some honourable exceptions, Norwegian football clubs have never been able to compete at the top European level. Several clubs performed well in Europe in the 1990s as in recent years, but interestingly, this has affected neither attendances at domestic league games nor the strength and spread of supporter cultures in general. Instead, attendances flourished in the years from 2005 to 2009, a period when Norwegian football was stagnating or even declining in sporting terms. During these years, Norwegian top football had twice as high attendances as its Swedish counterpart (Andersson & Hognestad, 2019). Norwegian football became an integral part of popular culture, and the attraction of the supporters was an important part of "the product". Further, new-built stadiums and a new TV deal which massively increased the value of Norwegian football created a lot of attention. In this way, supporter cultures in Norway were in some respects an integral part of the modern, commercialised game, rather than opposing those changes.

From the start, active supporters in Norway drew their inspirations predominantly from their English counterparts. These influences became evident in the ways singing and chanting became a ubiquitous part of the new and more organised styles of support. Often the songs used were translated versions of English chants (or, as already noted, sometimes not even translated). Further, most supporter groups adopted the English ways of singing from the 1970s and 1980s: short chants, often reflecting the course of the game. Songs would often include both humour and self-irony, and not least, they were often spontaneous comments to events on the field. Often, they were celebrating their own team, but at times also intended to insult the opposition or the opposite supporters. The volume of the noise would often vary in accordance with the score, the excitement and the sporting significance of the game. The atmosphere at games would regularly go quiet during less eventful periods.

From the late 1990s, and increasingly from the early 2000s, a schism evolved in many supporter groups between those promoting the English mode of support on the one hand, and those more inspired by Latin and German supporter cultures on the other hand. These cultures differ from the English tradition in many respects. Firstly, these influences became evident in the increasing number of visual manifestations of club identities, including banners, *tifos* and colours.

Secondly, songs were often more enduring in the Latin/German tradition. Chants could sometimes go on for at least 15–20 minutes, creating a monotonous, yet still fascinating, wall of sound. Rather than the spontaneous song to reflect events in the game, the main aim was to keep going throughout the 90 minutes, creating a continuous noisy atmosphere. The Latin-inspired culture also normally included other characteristics that were alien to British styles of support. For example, the use of drums to keep the rhythm of a song and often a *capo* acting as the "director" of the show. The use of a drum was highly controversial in Norway around 2005, as it became a symbol of a totally different approach to supporting a team, and those favouring the English culture were generally strongly opposed to its introduction (Hjelseth, 2006).

The tensions between the two traditions in Norway were, however, never particularly harsh. At least from 2010, it is reasonable to argue that the Latin/German influences dominated in most clubs. New generations emerged with new cultural influences. The introduction of the Premier League was in many ways an attempt to attract spectators with a "consumerist" approach to football (Giulianotti, 2002; King, 2002), and this affected its level of attraction among younger Norwegian supporters seeking to build identities around their support for local clubs. While some supporter groups continue to stick with the English tradition, a gradual generational shift has made the Latin influences more dominant. Cultural influences from Latin stadium traditions are in some respects also more political. The *ultras* movement has for long been an integral part of Latin supporter cultures, and even if ultras took on a slightly different meaning from the start in Norway, a part of its ideological basis has served as a guide for many younger supporters. However, this mix of influences has obviously also produced varying degrees of hybridisation, with elements from both English and Latin styles of support evident, often among supporters of the same football club.

Since 2010, Norwegian football has experienced falling attendances at games, leaving some of the arenas built during the boom years (2005–2010) as half-empty, or even worse at many games. Only 6,551 spectators watched the title-decisive game towards the end of the 2021-season between the top two teams, Molde and Bodø/Glimt. Although this was partly related to COVID-19 (with restrictions lifted shortly before this game), it was a clear sign of the crumbling interest in national league football. Even if the norm of loyalty is at the core of supporter values, anyone watching a game currently will note that the number of active fans has declined significantly compared to 15 years ago. Many supporter groups are still vital, innovative and at times politically relevant, but they struggle to maintain the enthusiasm both from the pioneering period of the early 1990s and from the glory years between 2000 and 2010.

A major challenge for Norwegian supporter groups in recent decades is the popularity of international leagues, and English football in particular. Most top European leagues are available via Norwegian TV channels, and they undoubtedly represent a challenge to Norwegian football, both as arena events and as TV events. This, in turn, has generated local resistance with examples of ridiculing the popularity of and fascination for English football. For instance, when Norwegian club Stabæk hosted Manchester United's reserve team in a friendly match in 2010, the large contingent of Norwegian Manchester United fans stood, unknowingly, in front of a banner put up by Stabæk supporters hours before the game, which carried the message "Anglophile losers" (*"Anglofile tapere"*) (Jansen, 2012). While this example signified a cultural confidence and a creative local response to the allures of the global brand that was Manchester United at the time, the process of creating a local football culture was evident at an earlier stage. A couple of European games between Norwegian and English teams in the late 1990s, arguably played key roles in the development of more creative and locally rooted supporter styles.

The new football ritual

Before 1990, organised support was sporadic and often limited to special occasions. The abolishment of amateurism paved the way also for more professional styles of local support, with more active fans participating in extended match day rituals marked by a privileged male participation that also included travelling to away games. These rituals were fuelled by alcohol and often included singing both before, during and after games (Armstrong & Hognestad, 2006).

The dawn of numerous fanzines from the early 1990s, notably produced by supporters of clubs, such as Brann, Vålerenga and Lillestrøm, gave supporters a voice which had not been heard earlier. Yet supporters of clubs from all over the country started to invent songs, often chanted in their own dialect, which significantly added to the creativity of and belief in "home-made" supporter styles. With the introduction of professional football, Norwegian teams gradually became more able to compete also in European competitions in ways that had been unthinkable just a few years earlier. This was particularly the case with Rosenborg from Trondheim, who regularly competed in the group stages of the Champions League in the second half of the 1990s. But other teams too, notably Brann and Vålerenga, suddenly found themselves able to compete against European opposition. After beating PSV Eindhoven 4-3 on aggregate in the previous round, Brann drew Liverpool in the quarter finals of the Cup Winner's Cup in 1997. This caused a major moral discussion in Bergen, as some fans supporting both Liverpool and Brann faced a schizophrenic dilemma over which team to support (Goksøyr & Hognestad, 1999). Two years later, Vålerenga drew Chelsea, also in the quarter-final of the same tournament, following a memorable match in Istanbul in the previous round, when Vålerenga drew 3-3 with Besiktas after losing 3-0 at half time, to win 4-3 on aggregate. Vålerenga sold out their entire ticket allocation of 4,000 for the away game at Stamford Bridge in London. The co-author of this chapter was present at that game and witnessed a genuinely vibrant away support who performed songs in their own language with an incredible level of noise.

By this time, Vålerenga supporters had developed a hegemonic mythology around their club, built around a peculiar mixture of urban, cosmopolitan and working-class identities. From this position, most other teams were and still are portrayed and addressed as village idiots or "peasants" in songs, fanzines, blogs and other sub-cultural platforms. A major enemy in this respect is their neighbours Lillestrøm, a town in the Romerike district just outside Oslo, an area known for its rich farmland and grain fields. From the rivalry with Lillestrøm SK, Vålerenga supporters forged an identity in which the elements mentioned above were exaggerated, caricatured and thrown into the conflicting "dialogue" between the two. Hence during the 1990s it was common to hear *Klanen*, the independent supporters club of Vålerenga, chant short lines such as "Øl og vold og skamslåtte bønder!" ("Beer and violence and molested peasants!") or simply "For en gjeng med bønder!" ("What a bunch of peasants!"), addressed to Lillestrøm and indeed most other teams not hailing from the capital. Supporter groups such as *Klanen*, *Kanarifansen* ("the Canary fans") of Lillestrøm and *Brann Bataljonen Bergen* ("the Brann Batallion Bergen"), developed a terrace culture with inspirations from abroad but with a principle that all songs and chants should be performed in Norwegian. Hence, when Vålerenga came to play Chelsea in the West End of London on a Thursday night in March 1999, all songs were performed in Norwegian, bouncing up and down towards Fulham Broadway tube stop on the District Line before the game, and inside Stamford Bridge during it. The scenes that developed could best be described as an absurd, carnivalesque theatre, as the home fans were addressed as "peasants" in various derogatory ways, accompanied with gestures mimicking the milking of cows. In a famous match report from the game, titled "Bizarre rituals in the stand", the Independent reporter Steve Tongue focused almost entirely on the behaviours of the away supporters who "outsung and out-performed" the home support, despite Chelsea winning the game 3-0, with the reporter noting that:

> Unlike their fellow Scandinavians from Helsingborg and FC Copenhagen, who had visited the Bridge in previous rounds, they eschewed English lyrics, though the tunes were familiar and Graeme Le Saux was a target of the sort of abuse he normally expects only from British supporters and Liverpool players. (Tongue, 1999)

In many ways this game became an iconic manifestation of the self-styled culture of Norwegian club football around the turn of the millennium, which at the time included an insistence on performing songs with lyrics in their native tongue rather than in English, as was common among some Swedish and, especially, Danish fans, when their clubs played against teams from abroad.

Supporter activism

Supporter cultures may thrive without paying too much attention to the economic or political developments within the game. Internationally, it seems like supporters take on an activist profile if and when changes to the game threaten established rituals and cultural practices. This was very much the case in England when the English Premier League was established, and both researchers and writers paid attention to the possible exclusion not only of categories of spectators, but of whole cultures of support (see, e.g., Wagg, 2004). According to King (2002), the changes in the 1990s can be seen as an attempt to replace the supporter and introduce the *customer* as the most welcome figure at football grounds. This ambition provoked opposition and protest in different ways, often by referring to football as *The People's Game*, a game that was now threatened by commercial interests. Wagg (2004, p. 4) labels this the *Whose-Game-Is-It-Anyway-Tradition*. The football ritual was seen as something that was to some extent *removed* from the groups that had originally produced and enjoyed it.

In Norway, opposition towards commercial strategies followed similar trajectories, but conflicts tended to be less severe. As previously pointed out, the emergence of supporter cultures took place parallel to the professionalisation and commercialisation of the game in Norway. The exclusion of vocal supporters was also less of an option because tickets were usually easily accessible. While English top clubs could sell out games to "consumers" and tourists, most Norwegian clubs welcomed any spectators they could attract and recruit, regardless of their form of support. In turn, ticket prices were therefore also more modest. With the exception of the popular cup final, there was no demand for tickets abandoned by supporters due to higher prices or restrictions on how to express support. This also meant that supporters were entitled to a form of power towards the clubs and the NFF. They were gradually acknowledged as important, both in terms of their numbers and their contribution to an attractive atmosphere.

This was evident in the structure of match events in the men's top division around 2000. By then, many clubs were still testing out ways to recruit more spectators. More often than not, the methods ran counter to what supporters regarded as legitimate forms of atmosphere. For example, many clubs tried to attract new groups to games by downplaying the importance of football itself. This was done by marketing the event as a "total product". Entertainment before the game and during half-time would regularly consist of other things than football, so that even those not interested could have something to look forward to (Hjelseth, 2006). By supporters, these initiatives were regularly ridiculed, and many acted subversively towards them.

In 2003, the NFF themselves initiated a *spectator project* (*publikumsprosjektet*), where a consultant company performed an analysis of how to attract more spectators to top football in Norway. A main conclusion was that clubs should play down all forms of non-football entertainment, and regard supporter groups as attractions in themselves. Supporters should be allowed the opportunity of expressing themselves based on their own values and practices, the report stated (Hjelseth, 2019). The NFF acted on the idea and put more restrictions on how clubs could frame the events. It is likely that these measures contributed to the sudden growth in attendances from 2004 onwards.

Later, supporter groups partly succeeded in restricting the number of top division games that were played outside weekends. In particular, they wanted to get rid of the Monday night games, as they argued that these games were hard to attend for most away fans, in a league with long travel distances. This would hurt the atmosphere at games, which in turn also made the TV experience less attractive. At times, the campaign "football should be played in weekends" has succeeded, and more importantly, supporter organisations are at least consulted when the structure of fixtures is negotiated. However, fans of second tier clubs in the OBOS-league are currently (2022) experiencing a serious backlash with Monday depicted as the main match day for the 2022 season, dictated by the TV company with rights to screen all games in this league, having sparked considerable protests among clubs with notable supporter groups.

An example of how commercial interests may threaten rituals that are important to supporters, was when *Klanen* succeeded in moving the club hymn *Vålerenga Kjerke* (Vålerenga Church) by about ten minutes in 2005, from about 5:40 pm to about 5:50 (kick-off 6 pm). The conflict emerged from the fact that Vålerenga's sponsors wanted to be profiled as close to kick-off as possible, as most spectators had by then arrived. This meant that the hymn – to Vålerenga fans what *You'll Never Walk Alone* is to Liverpool and Celtic fans – had to be played 15–20 minutes before kick-off. Supporters complained, as they found that the ritual aspect of the hymn was severely damaged. Later the same year, the club decided to move the hymn closer to kick-off (Hjelseth, 2006).

These examples illustrate how activism may be efficient if directed towards defending the interests of supporters themselves. When their practices, values and rituals have been threatened by commercial agents or by formal restrictions on behaviour, they have acted as a force that clubs and the NFF have had to pay attention to. Still, activism also occasionally take on a form where supporter groups organise in order to achieve more general aims. In 2021, several supporter groups mobilised to try to get the NFF to boycott the men's World Cup in Qatar 2022, due to the numerous reports about the conditions migrant workers employed to construct the stadiums for the tournament have had to work under, as well as the human rights record of the state of Qatar in general. They did not succeed, but gained significant support and formed alliances with NGOs and various other stakeholders.

At times, activism has been an integral part of what supporters do. It reflects the rejection of the idea of being mere customers. Primarily, supporters care for football and for the right to practice what they conceive as inherited rituals and ways of support. This means that if clubs or the NFF make decisions that run counter to their interests, they are much more likely to use the *voice* option than the *exit* option, to use Hirschman's (1970) terms.

Conclusion and challenges ahead

In sporting terms, Norwegian football is far from its international standing in the 1990s. The men's national team has not qualified for a major tournament since 2000, and the women's national team is also far less dominant than in the 1990s. Currently, there are signs that results are improving, not least at club level. Both Bodø/Glimt and Molde have enjoyed some encouraging results in European tournaments in recent years.

This has, however, not increased attendances. Some might suggest that the main reason for the gradual, but strong drop in attendances at domestic matches in Norway, is that football is no longer attractive to "consumers" or the average spectator, yet supporter cultures have also been on the decline in many clubs. The areas dedicated to "standing and singing" supporters inside stadiums are much less densely populated than 15 years ago (or the areas themselves has been reduced). The culture itself is still vital, but less people are engaged. An important question is whether the popularity and the availability of international football allows room for supporters cherishing their local team. Perspectives on the self in late modern society might suggest that geography is weakening as a source of identity (Giddens, 1991). But even within this theoretical framework, it looks like campaigns such as "support your local team" have some effect. There are signs that some supporters find the atmosphere outside global football more attractive (Dixon, 2013). And curiously, while attendances have declined at Norwegian grounds, they have almost rocketed at stadiums in neighbouring Sweden during the same period, with little or no difference in terms of sporting achievements between Norwegian and Swedish clubs in European competitions (Andersson & Hognestad, 2019).

Even if the revival of the huge supporter crowds that followed Norwegian football between 2005 and 2010 may seem hard to imagine, the dedication of the most ardent supporters may yet again be transferred to larger crowds. Even if the activist fraction of supporters is critical of the way football is run, their love for their clubs will continue to attract attention. Therefore, they can still hope for better times.

Note

1 *Tifo* has an origin from Italian football culture, and is a short form for the Italian word *tifosi*, meaning supporters. Tifo refers to banners and other forms of choreographed visual displays among supporters.

References

Andersson, T., & Hognestad, H. K. (2019). Glocal culture, sporting decline? Globalization and football in Scandinavia. *Sport in Society*, 22(4), 704–716.

Armstrong, G., & Hognestad, H. K. (2006). 'Hitting the bar' – alcohol, football identities and global flows in Norway. In T. Wilson (Ed.), *Food, drink and identity in Europe* (pp. 85–111). Rodopi.
Dixon, K. (2013). *Consuming football in late modern life*. Ashgate.
Football Supporters Association. (2014, December 19). *The birth of the FSA (part 1 Heysel and the early FSA)*. Retrieved September 30, 2022, from https://thefsa.org.uk/news/the-birth-of-the-fsa-part-1-heysel-and-the-early-fsa/
Fossum, L. (2012). Fremvekst og håndtering av alternative supportermiljøer – en studie av norske ultras [The growth and management of alternative supporter groups – a study of Norwegian ultras]. In H. K. Hognestad & A. Hjelseth (Eds.), *Kampen om tribunen – fotball, identitet og makt* [The battle of the stands – football, identity and power] (pp. 169–195). Akademika.
Giddens, A. (1991). *Modernity and self-identity. Self and society in late modern age*. Polity Press.
Giulianotti, R. (1994). Social identity and public order. Political and academic discourses on football violence. In R. Giulianotti, N. Bonney, & M. Hepworth (Eds.), *Football, violence and social identity* (pp. 10–37). Routledge.
Giulianotti, R. (1999). *Football: A sociology of the global game*. Polity Press.
Giulianotti, R. (2002). Supporters, followers, fans, and flaneurs: A taxonomy of spectator identities in football. *Journal of Sport and Social Issues, 26*(1), 25–46.
Giulianotti, R., & Robertson, R. (2004). The globalization of football: A study in the glocalization of the 'serious life'. *The British Journal of Sociology, 55*(4), 545–568.
Giulianotti, R., & Robertson, R. (2009). *Globalization and football*. SAGE Publications.
Goksøyr, M., & Hognestad, H. K. (1999). No longer worlds apart? British influences and Norwegian football. In G. Armstrong & R. Giulianotti (Eds.), *Football cultures and identities* (pp. 201–211). Palgrave.
Goksøyr, M., & Olstad, F. (2002). Fotball! Norges Fotballforbund 100 år [Football! The Norwegian Football Federation 100 years]. Norges Fotballforbund.
Hirschman, A. O. (1970). *Exit, voice and loyalty. Responses to decline in firms, organisations, and states*. Harvard University Press.
Hjelseth, A. (2006). Mellom børs, katedral og karneval. Norske supporteres forhandlinger om kommersialisering av football [Between stock exchange, cathedral and carnival. Norwegian supporters' negotiations about the commercialisation of football]. PhD dissertation, Dept. of Sociology, University of Bergen.
Hjelseth, A. (2019). Publikummet som forsvant. Hva er galt med eliteserien? [The crowd that disappeared. What is wrong with Eliteserien?] (pp. 26–31), *Josimar*, 2/2019.
Hognestad, H. K. (2003). Long-distance football support and liminal identities among Norwegian fans. In E. P. Archetti & N. Dyck (Eds.), *Sport, dance and embodied identities* (pp. 97–113). Berg.
Hognestad, H. K., & Hjelseth, A. (2012). *Kampen om tribunen. Fotball, makt og identitet* [The battle of the stands – football, identity and power]. Akademika.
Jansen, R. (2012). Fotballsupporteren – den krevende kunden [The football supporter – the demanding customer]. In H. K. Hognestad & A. Hjelseth (Eds.), *Kampen om tribunen – Fotball, identitet og makt* [The battle of the stands – football, identity and power] (pp. 221–228). Akademika.
King, A. (2002). *The end of the terraces. The transformation of English football in the 1990s*. Revised Edition. Leicester University Press.

Reim, N. (2012). 'Det er oss som bestemmer på Vestbredden og Gaza!' – Et innspill rundt temaet supporterkulturell autonomi ['We decide at the West Bank and Gaza!' – An input on the topic of autonomy among supporters]. In H. K. Hognestad & A. Hjelseth (Eds.), *Kampen om tribunen* – Fotball, identitet og makt [The battle of the stands – Football, identity and power] (pp. 197–219). Akademika.

Sandvoss, C. (2003). *A game of two halves. Football, television and globalization*. Routledge.

Tongue, S. (1999, March 5). Bizarre rituals in the stand. *Independent*. Retrieved May 13, 2022, https://independent.co.uk/sport/football-bizarre-rituals-in-the-stand-1078532

Wagg, S. (2004). Fat city? British football and the politics of social exclusion at the turn of the twenty-first century. In S. Wagg (Ed.), *British football and social exclusion* (pp. 1–25). Routledge.

Chapter 15

Nordic Spectator Studies
The Literature on Attendance and Satisfaction at Professional Football Matches

Morten Kringstad, Tor Georg Jakobsen, and Rasmus K. Storm

Introduction

This chapter reviews Nordic spectator studies dealing with attendance and satisfaction at men's football matches. This is a relatively new and not very extensive field in the Nordic countries. Football is the largest – and most popular – spectator sport globally, and the same is true for the Nordic countries except for Finland, where it is second only to ice hockey (Storm & Nielsen, 2022). Many people choose to attend matches in the six Nordic leagues (the name of the top tier in the league system are in brackets), which include Sweden (*Allsvenskan*), Denmark (*Superligaen*), Norway (*Eliteserien*), Finland (*Veikkausliiga/Tipsligan*), Iceland (*Úrvalsdeild*) and the Faroe Islands (*Betrideildin*). Gammelsæter and Senaux (2011) claim there is more "self-government" among national football authorities in Northern than Southern Europe. Further, they emphasise, on the basis of Gammelsæter et al. (2011, p. 279), that in Scandinavia, "governments seem to be absent from the governance of top football". In Scandinavia, football clubs started as voluntary non-profit organisations, whereas, for example, in Norway first, as late as 1991, accepted full professionalism (Gammelsæter, 2009). Both Norway and Sweden introduced financial licensing systems during the 1990s. Telseth and Halldorsson (2019) use characteristics such as voluntary sport organisations and amateur ideology in relation to Nordic football. From the increased professionalism and commercialism commencing at the start of the 1990s, Scandinavian football has been a mix of voluntarism and commercialism on the basis of a welfare state system (Andersson & Carlsson, 2009).

This chapter provides an overview of research on why attendance and satisfaction with the product vary due to the impact of different factors in these Nordic leagues. In general, the consumption of goods and services – a football match can be seen as such a product – is influenced by price and income. However, regarding consumers, other factors can play a part, including team performance, uncertainty of outcome, competition from televised games, sociological factors, match scheduling, weather conditions, the rivalry of teams, the size of the league and others.

DOI: 10.4324/9781003280729-21

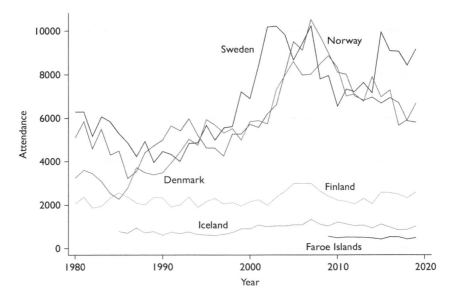

Figure 15.1 Average attendance in the Nordic leagues, 1980–2019.

Historically, attendance was higher in the Nordic leagues back in the 1960s, when the social connection to a team was more substantial, and the overall competition from other leisure activities and products were less (Andersson & Carlsson, 2011). Figure 15.1 shows average match-day attendance development among the six Union of European Football Associations (UEFA) recognised Nordic leagues[1] in the 1980–2019 period (pre-COVID-19 period). The three biggest leagues (Norway, Sweden and Denmark) moved in tandem, experiencing an increase in the 1990s and the 2000s. However, there was a declining trend for Norway and Denmark from 2009 and onwards, while Sweden had a comeback in the middle of the 2010s, becoming the most attended Nordic league. The other leagues were more stable in this period. This chapter aims to show what the drivers of these numbers are.

The development of the Nordic leagues

The Swedish *Allsvenskan* traces its roots back to *Storserien* in 1924 and became genuinely national (with the inclusion of a northern Swedish team) in 1965, following the qualification of GIF Sundsval. In recent years, *Allsvenskan* included 14 teams in the 1994–2007 period and 16 teams in the 2008–2021 period. The Danish *Superligaen* is built on the older Danish first division, a predecessor to *Landsfodboldturneringen*, which saw its beginning in the 1912/1913 season. At that time, the tournament only included teams from the Copenhagen region, who met the winner of a knockout tournament in a final, including the provincial teams. The first genuine national series was the *Mesterskabsserien* in 1929/1930. The *Superligaen* has seen several structural changes in later years, including different playoff formats.

The Norwegian *Eliteserien* has its roots in the formation of *Norgesserien* in 1937/1938, which included eight regional series followed by a post-seasonal playoff. This system transformed into *Hovedserien* in 1948/1949, including only two regional series followed by a post-seasonal final. It was not until 1961/1962 that the format included only one top-level series (*First division* from 1963). However, in 1972 the league became truly national and allowed the inclusion of teams from northern Norway. *Eliteserien* included 14 teams from 1994 to 2008 before expanding to 16 teams in recent years.

The Finnish league started under the name *Mestaruussarja/Mästerskapsserien* in 1930 and was nationwide from the start-up. In later years, the structure of the *Veikkausliiga/Tipsligan* has varied with regard to the number of teams and whether post-seasonal playoffs are included. The Icelandic *Úrvalsdeild* started in 1912 with only three teams and has gradually expanded over the years; today, it consists of 12 teams.

In the Faroe Islands, the history of *Betrideildin* goes back to *Meistaradeildin*, which started as a knockout tournament in 1942 and progressed to a single league in 1947. The football association became a UEFA member in 1990, while the football associations for the other Nordic leagues were among the founding members in 1954.

The driving forces behind attendance and match-day satisfaction

We performed systematic searches of previously published research studies on attendance and satisfaction at football matches in Norway, Denmark, Sweden, Finland and Iceland. We aimed to identify patterns in the present literature as well as provide an overview for researchers and students interested in football studies in Nordic countries. As this is not a very extensive field, our review also includes (in addition to the present peer-reviewed articles on this topic) the most relevant student works (including both master's and bachelor's theses). In sum, we reviewed 31 Nordic studies, 15 peer-reviewed journal articles and 16 student works. The lion's share of the literature deals with the Norwegian league (18 studies), followed by the Danish (seven studies), Swedish (three studies) and Finnish (two studies) as well as one study focusing on the three Scandinavian countries.

About two-thirds of the Norwegian studies were from Molde University College and the Norwegian University of Science and Technology (NTNU). An interesting observation is that these studies were from either the business schools (Molde and NTNU) or sport sociology (NTNU). Almost all studies from Denmark had the involvement of the Danish Institute for Sports Studies

(*Idrættens Analyseinstitut*). In other words, the main production of studies was from only three research institutions. This means that research groups focusing on sport management, business, economics and sociology are an important driver for this research. It may be more of a coincidence that these groups are in Norway and Denmark.

The importance of spectator demand studies in professional team sports is described by Peel and Thomas (1988), claiming that: "The nature of the demand function in any professional team sport is important for the analysis of club and league behaviour and decision making" (p. 242). The seminal paper on the economics of professional team sports by Rottenberg (1956) concerned attendance, and from here, we have the well-known uncertainty of outcome hypothesis. In general, demand studies for professional team sports have been popular in the economics of professional team sports. Cairns et al. (1986) provide an overview of early studies related to this topic. Later, similar reviews provided helpful overviews of the research frontier, such as Borland and Macdonald (2003), Downward and Dawson (2000), Dobson and Goddard (2001) and García and Rodríguez (2009), to mention a few. These reviews are typically organised into different categories of (independent) variables, but how these are structured differs across studies. In contrast, a more recent study by Schreyer and Ansari (2021) used a scoping approach.

In this chapter, we follow Borland and Macdonald (2003), dividing demand variables into consumer preferences, economic variables, quality of viewing and characteristics of the sporting contest. This is in correspondence with recent studies such as Caruso et al. (2019) and Bond and Addesa (2020), who also applied Borland and Macdonald's work as a starting point. Note that Borland and Macdonald included supply capacity among the demand categories. We follow Dobson and Goddard (2011) and disregard this category based on the argument that supply capacity should not be regarded as a demand variable.

Further, we follow the arguments of Kringstad et al. (2021) about using the framework developed by Borland and Macdonald (2003) and their statement that:

> Sports marketing and management scholars have also developed typologies to identify different sources of demand. These typologies build on research that explains the structural relationship between fan interest or "fandom" and various psychological and sociological factors. The broad conclusions from this research correlate with the approach of the economic literature. (p. 480)

This fits with Clemes et al. (2011), who claimed that: "Managers increasingly recognise the importance of service quality and customer satisfaction to consistently attract profitable attendance at sporting events" (p. 370). Below, we present the different groups of variables.

Studies on consumer preferences

Borland and Macdonald (2003) used habit, conspicuous consumption and bandwagon effects as possible drivers for consumer preferences regarding the demand for sporting events, such as football matches. Their review found the first to be a typically positive driver for attendance, while they claimed the two others not to "have received attention" (p. 490).

Mehus and Osborn (2010) conducted a survey-based case study of *Rosenborg BK* (Trondheim) in the Norwegian league, finding that women and families (who consume less football) scored higher on social motives for attending a game than more traditional fans. All types of fans were motivated by team identification and excitement motives. Earlier, Mehus (2005) juxtaposed spectators of ski-jumping and football in Trondheim, showing that excitement motives were more important for football spectators than social motives. Ski-jumping spectators were shown to have a higher educational background than the average football spectators.

Studies on economic variables

In a demand study, economic variables are essential for the potential spectators' budget constraints and for factors that affect their attendance costs. The expectation is that an increased budget for the individual and lower costs increase demand. Income level and unemployment rate are examples of variables representing the budget constraints for individual fans (measured at the macro-economic level). The cost side is related to ticket price and opportunity costs such as travelling costs, parking costs, time costs, etc. Further, Borland and Macdonald (2003) put the geographical variable regarding the size of the population in the area in question into this category.

Based on García and Rodríguez (2009), most studies find a negative relationship between price and demand, while it is more difficult to find a clear relationship between income and demand. Some studies find evidence to support football being a normal good, while others suggest it is an inferior good. As expected, population is typically a significant driver for attendance.

In an early study using data from Denmark, Norway and Sweden, Thrane (2001) found household income to be positively associated with sports' spectatorship in general. However, he did not analyse football specifically. According to Framås (2015), recessions (in Norway) and higher levels of unemployment are positively correlated with attendance. He presented that increased spare time and a sense of belonging to the working class outweighed the direct decrease in purchasing power. Jennett (1984) found the opposite in the Scottish top division during the 1975–1981 period.

In Sweden, the case study of one club (AIK) showed that more people would purchase tickets in periods of economic growth (Holmlund, 2016). In Finland, Dick and Kernick (2016) found that free time and financial constraints were the only factors preventing the most engaged fans from watching matches in a stadium.

Regarding the least active football followers, the main reason preventing their attendance is a firm lack of interest in the league. In another study of the Finnish League, Iho and Heikkilä (2010) investigated the effect of advance ticket sales, which had an isolated positive impact on attendance for the teams in the league. From a study on a single Norwegian club (*IK Start*) in the period 2000–2014, Gjestvang and Reinhardsen (2015) found a short-term effect of more affordable tickets. Ticket price had also earlier been found to have a significant impact by Mæle (2014), who studied a selection of teams (Rosenborg, Brann, Lillestrøm, Viking and Molde) in *Eliteserien* in the 2002–2013 period.

Kringstad et al. (2018) found population to be a significant positive attendance driver for Norwegian football in their multi-level models, a finding that was confirmed in the "all data" sample studies by Ermakov (2020) and Ermakov and Krumer (2022). However, they found the significance level to be weak.

Another aspect regarding economic variables is substitution effects. Borland and Macdonald (2003) distinguished between direct substitutes (i.e., the possibility to watch the broadcast game in the same league or in another league) and indirect substitutes (i.e., other events, contests and entertainment arrangements). Live broadcasts can be seen as both complementary and as a substitute. The first is related to the positive marketing effect, while the second is that potential stadium spectators may watch the game from outside the stadium. From a sports management point of view, this variable is even more complex because, as described in Baimbridge et al. (1996) for their analysis of the 1993–1994 season in the English Premier League, a significant decline in attendance because of live broadcasted Monday matches was financially overcompensated by the broadcast fee to the league.

An interesting study regarding the effects on stadium attendance from broadcasts is from Spanish football by García and Rodríguez (2002). This study divided matches on free-to-air public channels and subscription private channels. Both categories substituted stadium spectators, but this effect was more significant when games were accessible on public channels.

Jordhøy (2012) pointed out that competition regarding consumer preferences increased for teams in the Norwegian league from 2007 to 2011. The result was that attendance dropped while media availability became greater. It was also important which teams did well in the period, as the four largest clubs drove the downturn to a large degree. In an early study, Sjuls (2008) used data from *Eliteserien* in 2006 and 2007 and found no evidence that public broadcasting of games reduced attendance significantly. Rather, Kringstad et al. (2018), Ermakov (2020) and Ermakov and Krumer (2022) found matches on free or public television to be a significant, strong positive attendance driver.

Skjæveland (2011) also found that games televised live on public channels were positively correlated with attendance, while pay-to-view channels reduced attendance. On the other hand, Solberg and Mehus (2014) found that fans of clubs most often shown on public television channels attended fewer matches than other fans. Johansen (2020) studied the fall in spectator attendance in the Norwegian league between 2009 and 2019 (see Figure 15.1). According to his respondents, the rationale was that it was easier to watch a game on television than actually going to the stadium. There was an increase in the number of matches shown on television in this period.

For the Norwegian club *IK Start* in the period 2000–2014, Gjestvang and Reinhardsen (2015) found a significant negative effect on attendance if one of the top-three most popular Premier League teams (Liverpool, Arsenal, Manchester United) played a televised match at the same time. Kringstad et al. (2018) performed fixed effects regression on attendance in *Eliteserien* 2005–2011 and confirmed the finding mentioned above. They found that colliding with matches from the big-five European leagues (England, Spain, Italy, Germany, France) hurt attendance.

In a study of the Danish first-tier (Superligaen) from 2010/11–2015/16, Nielsen et al. (2019) produced a non-finding: Matches clashing with broadcasts of major English Premier League games did not suffer in attendance. In the Norwegian league, the tendency was rather negative effects from English Premier League (EPL) matches on television, though weak or insignificant in Ermakov (2020) and Ermakov and Krumer (2022).

Studies on quality of viewing

In general, Borland and Macdonald (2003) emphasise that "Attendance is higher at newer stadiums, and is responsive to weather and match timing" (p. 492). They divided this category into stadium facilities and the time aspect of the match. The first involves not only the quality of seats and the stadium facilities but also weather conditions. Time is related to match day and kick-off time. The age of the stadium is one measure that has been used to proxy stadium-quality in Major League Baseball, according to Borland and Macdonald (2003), and results show a negative effect on attendance. A positive effect was also demonstrated when looking at the impacts of new stadiums in the review by García and Rodríguez (2009).

In his study of the Norwegian league, Framås (2015) found that stadium development and improvement increased attendance. However, this positive effect seemed to decrease over time, consistent with Ermakov (2020) and Ermakov and Krumer (2022) for the Norwegian *Eliteserien*. There was also significant variation from club to club in the Norwegian series. For example, Haugen (2002) found positive effects when analysing effects on attendance of a new stadium for a single club, Molde FK. Frøysa and Rødal (2012) and Kringstad et al. (2018) used a dummy variable for the first five years after building or rebuilding stadiums and find this to have a significant positive effect on attendance in Norway. According to Haugen et al. (2014), a five-year period is when the stadium effect is at its peak in Norwegian football.

Weather conditions in spectator demand studies have concerned precipitation, temperature and season. Results are, according to the review by García and Rodríguez (2009), variable. Still, Borland and Macdonald (2003), in their review, claimed that "types of weather conditions that are known to disrupt play in a sporting contest will have a negative effect on attendance" (p. 488).

Temperature has also influenced attendance in *Eliteserien* (Mæle, 2014). However, Ermakow (2020) and Ermakow and Krumer (2022) found the effect to be curvilinear. In their study of the Danish *Superligaen*, Nielsen et al. (2019) found that weather was an important driver of demand. Bad weather (in the form of precipitation) had a significant negative effect on attendance demand, while the temperature variable showed a positive curvilinear effect maximised at 17.3 degrees Celsius. In Sweden, Holmlund (2016) found that rain implied a decrease of 1,694 spectators on average at AIK's home games. Stolt and Waldenor (2010) found that high temperatures positively influenced attendance for the Swedish league. In their case study of the Norwegian football club *IK Start* (from Kristiansand), Gjestvang and Reinhardsen (2015) found that attendance dropped by 633 spectators if it rained.

Scheduling of matches usually affects attendance. In their review, Borland and Macdonald (2003) found that games played on public holidays had higher attendance, *ceteris paribus*, while García and Rodríguez (2009) also found that Sunday matches had the same tendency. Based on several studies, they further found that the game's kick-off time seemed not to be a significant driver.

In the Norwegian league, Bakken and Strømsnes (2011) performed a statistical study of a single club, Tromsø IL. They followed the club for over 20 years (1991–2010) and found that the first match of the season and matches played on 16 May[2] positively affected attendance. These results were confirmed (for the Norwegian league) by Mæle (2014). The positive 16 May effect in Norway was also confirmed by Ermakov (2020); Ermakov and Krumer (2022) and Kringstad et al. (2018). Frøysa and Rødal (2012) pointed out that matches played on Saturday or Sunday achieved better attendance than regular weekdays, consistent with Kringstad et al. (2018). This finding was confirmed by Gjestvang and Reinhardsen (2015) in their case study of *IK Start*, as well as by Ermakov (2020) and Ermakov and Krumer (2022) concerning Saturdays.

Studies on characteristics of the sporting contest

This category of the sporting contest looks at both absolute and relative quality. Absolute quality is related to the sporting quality of the teams (can be for both the home and the away team), for example, related to sporting success, such as league standing, goals scored and points achieved during recent games. According to the review in Borland and Macdonald (2003), empirical results showed that sporting success for the home team was a significant driver for attendance, while the results were either non-significant or significantly positive for the away team.

In a study of the Norwegian club Tromsø IL, current season home team performance was important for attendance (Bakken & Strømsnes, 2011). This is consistent with the recent performance for AIK in Sweden, but for AIK, the league standing prior to the match was a more unclear driver (Holmlund, 2016). Framås (2015) investigated the Norwegian league in the period 1995–2014. He found a solid international (European cup) performance by the home side to be positively correlated with attendance, supported by Ermakov (2020) and Ermakov and Krumer (2022) when it comes to the game before a European cup game. However, success for the national side had no effect on the league as a whole, consistent with the findings of Haugen et al. (2014). The study of IK Start in Norway found that matches against high-ranked opposition had a positive effect (Gjestvang & Reinhardsen, 2015). This was similar to the findings in the AIK study from Sweden (Holmlund, 2016) and consistent with regard to *Allsvenskan* as a whole by Stolt and Waldenor (2010). For the Norwegian league, Kringstad et al. (2018) found that the rank of both the home and away teams were positive attendance drivers. This was also the case when a historical team (Rosenborg BK) was the away team. Ermakov confirmed the latter (2020), and as did Ermakov and Krumer (2022), as well as the positive quality effects for the home team. On the other hand, they found that the quality effect on the away team was a less clear attendance driver.

Relative quality is related to the quality differences among the teams, i.e., competitive balance (see, e.g., Gerrard & Kringstad, 2021 for conceptual discussions). In demand studies on match level, this is further related to the concept of uncertainty of outcome. Rottenberg's uncertainty of outcome hypothesis suggests a positive relationship between improved uncertainty of outcome and attendance. Uncertainty of outcome as a concept is complex, as it relates to different aspects, divided between match uncertainty, match significance, seasonal uncertainty and long-run uncertainty (e.g., Cairns et al., 1986).

For match uncertainty, Borland and Macdonald (2003) claimed that the review showed that the effect on attendance was "relatively weak" (p. 486). At the seasonal level, match significance is typically a significant driver of attendance (Borland & Macdonald, 2003; Jennett, 1984). In their review, Borland and Macdonald (2003) also claimed that: "A relatively consistent finding from these studies [are] that higher intra-season unevenness – with dispersion being represented by games behind league – in a competition will lower attendance" (p. 486).

For the Norwegian football league, match uncertainty was not significant in Kringstad et al. (2018). Johansson and Hallén (2018) analysed effects from uncertainty of outcome on attendance in the Swedish *Allsvenskan* from 2014 to 2016. They found support for match uncertainty as a positive attendance driver by using betting odds to calculate the probability of wins for the home team. For the Norwegian *Eliteserien*, Ermakov (2020) and Ermakov and Krumer (2022) measured what Jennett (1984) called the "glory factor" and "despair factor" (p. 186), referring to matches for the team that has already won the championship and for teams that are already relegated and found these to be significant for the home teams, consistent with Jennett (1984), but not for the away team, opposite of Jennett (1984).

Another part of this category is the presence of star players, which is suggested to increase the attractiveness of the contests. Further, a relevant variable is derby (or rivalry) matches, which may be both locally and historically related (García & Rodríguez, 2009). The review from Borland and Macdonald (2003) suggested that star players either contributed significantly positively or, as most studies found, there was no significant effect. For derby (rivalry) matches, for example, García and Rodríguez (2002) found that this variable was a significant attendance driver.

In a study of 15 Danish national men's A-team matches 2013–2017, Jakobsen et al. (2021) found that players' contributions on the pitch, atmosphere and the spectators' impression of the match stewards were the most critical factors contributing to driving word-of-mouth to friends and colleagues in a positive direction.

Derbies had a positive effect on attendance for the Norwegian club IK Start (Gjestvang & Reinhardsen, 2015), for the Swedish club AIK (Holmlund, 2016), for the *Allsvenskan* in general (Stolt & Waldenor, 2010) and the Norwegian league as a whole (Ermakov, 2020; Ermakov & Krumer, 2022; Kringstad et al., 2018). Positive effects of derbies were also confirmed by Mæle (2014). Johansson and Hallén (2018) found that geographical rivalry was a positive significant attendance driver in Sweden.

Skjetne (2013) looked at the effect of expanding the Norwegian league by adding two teams. He found no significant impact, neither positive nor negative. The expansion implied some changes that would, in theory, reduce attendance (like more matches with greater points' difference between the teams and more matches of less importance, more matches with cold weather, and the inclusion of teams from smaller towns). However, it also meant more local derbies, which had a positive effect. On the other hand, Framås (2015) found that expansion in the Norwegian top division from 14 to 16 teams compromised attendance.

Discussion, conclusion and future research perspectives

Based on only a few case studies on consumer preferences, we found indications of the importance of team identification and excitement motives. Except for increased attendance when there was a higher unemployment rate in Norway, the studies from Scandinavia and Finland followed the expected relationship between economic factors and attendance related to budget constraints and costs. Population size seems to be a positive driver based on research in the Norwegian league.

Broadcasted games on free or public television were positive drivers for attendance in Norway, suggesting complementary though positive marketing factors. However, we cannot exclude that these broadcasted games included selection bias, as they may have included a large share of the most interesting games. On the other hand, matches on television from the EPL or the biggest European football leagues seemed to be a substitute for attending matches in Norway, while no effect was found in Denmark.

When it comes to quality of viewing, stadium development is a positive attendance driver, at least in the first seasons, among Norwegian teams. In Norway, studies that included match schedules found this relevant for attendance. Weather is another relevant factor, and this was found to have an impact in studies among all three Scandinavian countries.

Sporting success by the home team is a significant demand driver. The opponent's sporting success is mostly a positive driver. Uncertainty of outcome is nearly not studied among the Nordic leagues. One study found no effect on match uncertainty in Norway, while another suggested that there was such an effect in Sweden. The "glory factor" and "despair factor" seem to exist in Norway for the home team, referring to increased attendance for the first effect and the opposite for the latter. Studies in Norway and Sweden confirmed that derbies and matches against rival teams were positive for match attendance. Two studies on league expansions in Norway found no effect on attendance or a negative impact.

In general, spectator demand studies on Nordic football leagues remain an underdeveloped research area, with the number of studies on women's football being especially low. For Iceland and the Faroe Islands, we did not find any relevant studies, while in Finland, the number of studies was very small. Here, we, therefore, have topics of great interest for future research, as well as for national team matches, that have mainly been addressed to Denmark.

Norway is the league where we collected most demand studies. We also found that there was a larger number of econometric demand studies compared to studies related to consumer preferences. It must be pointed out that the focus in this chapter has been on drivers of stadium attendance. This means that, for example, studies focusing on demand for broadcasted matches, such as Johnsen and Solvoll (2007) for Norway and Denmark, were not included. Still, future research on broadcasted games in the middle- to small-sized markets, such as the Nordic countries, should be of considerable interest.

Notes

1 The numbers are gathered from www.worldfootball.net, www.european-football-statistics.co.uk and other country specific sources. Note that the Danish league covers two calendar years. The number in the figure represents the year the Danish league finished.

2 The matches played on 16 May (the day before the national day) in Norway are considered an event of their own, due to tradition. Attendances are usually high, and these are often played between local rivals.

References

Andersson, T., & Carlsson, B. (2009). Football in Scandinavia: A fusion of welfare policy and the market. *Soccer & Society, 10*(3–4), 299–304. 10.1080/14660970902771365

Andersson, T., & Carlsson, B. (2011). A diagnosis of the commercial immaturity of Swedish club football. *Soccer & Society, 12*(6), 754–773.

Bakken, C., & Strømsnes, T. (2011). *Etterspørselen etter fotball: En empirisk studie av tilskuertall på Alfheim* [Master's thesis, University of Tromsø]. UiT Munin.

Baimbridge, M., Cameron, S., & Dawson, P. (1996). Satellite television and the demand for football: A whole new ball game? *Scottish Journal of Political Economy, 43*(3), 317–333.

Bond, A. J., & Addesa, F. (2020). Competitive intensity, fans' expectations and match-day tickets sold in the Italian football Serie A, 2012–2015. *Journal of Sports Economics, 20*(1), 20–43.

Borland, J., & Macdonald, R. D. (2003). Demand for sport. *Oxford Review of Economic Policy, 19*(4), 478–502.

Cairns, J., Jennett, N., & Sloane, P. J. (1986). The economics of professional team sports: A survey of theory and evidence. *Journal of Economic Studies, 13*(1), 3–80.

Caruso, R., Addessa, F., & Di Domizio, M. (2019). The determinants of the TV demand for soccer: Empirical evidence on Italian Serie A for the period 2008–2015. *Journal of Sport Economics, 20*(1), 25–49.

Clemes, M. D., Brush, G. J., & Collins, M. J. (2011). Analyzing the professional sport experience: A hierarchical approach. *Sport Management Review, 14*(4), 370–388.

Dick, M., & Kernick, P. (2016). *The motivational factors affecting football fan attendance in Finland: A study and segmentation* [Bachelor's Thesis, Haaga-Helia University of Applied Sciences, Finland].

Dobson, S. M., & Goddard, J. A. (2001). *The economics of football*. Cambridge University Press.

Dobson, S. M., & Goddard, J. A. (2011). *The economics of football. 2nd Edition*. Cambridge University Press.

Downward, P., & Dawson, A. (2000). *The economics of professional team sports*. Routledge.

Ermakov, S. (2020). *The effect of Saturday matches on stadium attendance in Norwegian Eliteserien* [Master's thesis, Molde University College]. Molde University College.

Ermakov, S., & Krumer, A. (2022). Saturday in the stadium: On higher attendance on Saturdays in Norwegian Elitserien soccer league. *European Sport Management Quarterly*. Advance online publication. 10.1080/16184742.2022.2067208

Framås, M. H. (2015). *Etterspørselsanalyse av tilskuertallet i Tippeligaen: En empirisk analyse av tilskuertallet mellom 1995–2014* [Master's thesis, Norwegian University of Science and Technology]. NTNU Open.

Frøysa, P. S., & Rødal, E. N. (2012). *Etterspørsel etter stadionfotball i norsk Tippeliga* [Master's thesis, Trondheim Business School, Norway].

Gammelsæter, H. (2009). The organization of professional football in Scandinavia. *Soccer & Society, 10*(3–4), 305–323. 10.1080/14660970902771373

Gammelsæter, H., & Senaux, B. (2011). Understanding the governance of football across Europe. In H. Gammelsæter & B. Senaux (Eds.), *The organisation and governance of top football across Europe: An institutional perspective* (pp. 268–291). Routledge.

Gammelsæter, H., Storm, R. K., & Söderman, S. (2011). Diverging Scandinavian approaches to professional football. In H. Gammelsæter & B. Senaux (Eds.), *The organisation and governance of top football across Europe: An institutional perspective* (pp. 77–92). Routledge.

García, J., & Rodríguez, P. (2002). The determinants of football match attendance revisited: Empirical evidence from the Spanish Football League. *Journal of Sports Economics, 3*(1), 18–38. 10.1177/152700250200300103

García, J., & Rodríguez, P. (2009). Sport attendance: A survey of the literature, 1973–2007. *Rivista di Diritto ed Economia dello Sport, 5*(2), 111–151.

Gerrard, B., & Kringstad, M. (2021). The multi-dimensionality of competitive balance: Evidence from European football. *Sport, Business and Management.* Advance online publication. 10.1108/SBM-04-2021-0054

Gjestvang, K., & Reinhardsen, J. O. (2015). *Hva påvirker etterspørselen etter fotballbilletter for IK Start?* [Master's thesis, University of Agder] University of Agder AURA.

Haugen, K. K. (2002). *Samfunnsøkonomiske konsekvenser av anleggsinvesteringer i fotballnæringen* [Socio-economic consequences of stadium investments in the football industry]. Lecture at the Top-football seminar, Gardermoen, Oslo.

Haugen, K. K., Hervik, A., & Gammelsæter, H. (2014). A regression that probably never should have been performed – The case of Norwegian top-league football attendance. *European Journal of Sport Studies, 2*(2), 61–71.

Holmlund, R. (2016). *En publiksiffra, multipla förklaringar: En Statistisk analys av publikantalet på AIK fotbolls hemmamatcher* [A statistical analysis of the crowd at AIK football's home matches] [Bachelor thesis, Stockholm University]. Stockholm University.

Iho, A., & Heikkilä, J. (2010). Impact of advance ticket sales on attendance in the Finnish Football League. *Journal of Sports Economics, 11*(2), 214–226.

Jakobsen, T. G., Storm, R. K., & Schelde, N. (2021). Stadium experience and word-of-mouth: A panel data analysis of national A-team men's football matches in Denmark, 2013–17. *Managing Sport and Leisure, 26*(6), 508–523.

Jennett, N. (1984). Attendances, uncertainty of outcome and policy in Scottish League Football. *Scottish Journal of Political Economy, 31*(2), 176–198.

Johansen, A. Ø. (2020). *En kvantitativ studie som definerer faktorer bak de dalende tilskuertallene i Eliteserien* (Bachelor thesis, Molde University College). Molde University College.

Johansson, G., & Hallén, G. (2018). *Reference-dependent preferences in the case of Allsvenskan. Outcome uncertainty and live-game attendance* (Bachelor thesis, Lund University). Lund University Libraries.

Johnsen, H., & Solvoll, M. (2007). The demand for televised football. *European Sport Management Quarterly, 7*(4), 3113–3135.

Jordhøy, K. (2012). *Hva forklarer reduksjonen i tilskuertallene i Tippeligaen i perioden 2007–11* [Bachelor thesis, Molde University College]. Molde University College.

Kringstad, M., Olsen, T. E., Jakobsen, T. G., Storm, R. K., & Schelde, N. (2021). Match experience at the Danish women's soccer national A-team matches: An explorative study. *Sustainability, 13*(5), 1–20.

Kringstad, M., Solberg, H. A., & Jakobsen, T. G. (2018). Does live broadcasting reduce stadium attendance? The case of Norwegian football. *Sport, Business and Management: An International Journal*, 8(1), 67–81.

Mæle, T. T. (2014). *Hva påvirker etterspørselen etter stadionfotball i tippeligaen?* (Master's thesis, University of Stavanger). University of Stavanger.

Mehus, I. (2005). Sociability and excitement motives of spectators attending entertainment sport events: Spectators of soccer and ski-jumping. *Journal of Sport Behavior*, 28(4), 333–350.

Mehus, I., & Osborn, G. (2010). Consuming football: The Norwegian experience, the English impact, and the possibilities of interdisciplinary research. *Scandinavian Sport Studies Forum*, 1(1), 89–113.

Nielsen, C. G., Storm, R. K., & Jakobsen, T. G. (2019). The impact of English Premier League broadcasts on Danish spectator demand: A small league perspective. *Journal of Business Economics*, 89(6), 633–653.

Peel, D., & Thomas, D. (1988). Outcome uncertainty and the demand for football: An analysis of match attendances in the English football league. *Scottish Journal of Political Economy*, 35(3), 242–249.

Rottenberg, S. (1956). The baseball players' labor market. *Journal of Political Economy*, 64(3), 242–258.

Schreyer, D., & Ansari, P. (2021). Stadium attendance demand research: A scoping review. *Journal of Sports Economics*, 23(6), (749–788). 10.1177/15270025211000404

Sjuls, M. (2008). *Demand for Norwegian premiership football: The impact of public broadcasting of games* [Master's thesis, University of Oslo].

Skjetne, S. B. (2013). *Effekten av en utvidelse av Tippeligaen fra 14 til 16 lag: En empirisk analyse av tilskuertallet i norsk football* [The effect of the expansion of the Tippeligaen from 14 to 16 teams: An empirical analysis of the number of spectators in Norwegian football] [Master's thesis, Norwegian University of Science and Technology]. NTNU Open, Trondheim.

Skjæveland, K. (2011). *Spectator analysis in Norway: The impact of live football broadcasting on stadium attendance* [Master's thesis, University of Stavanger].

Solberg, H. A., & Mehus, I. (2014). The challenge of attracting football fans to stadia? *International Journal of Sport Finance*, 9(1), 3–19.

Stolt, M., & Waldenor, C. (2010). *The demand for football attendances in Sweden* [Bachelor's thesis, Stockholm School of Economics, Sweden].

Storm, R. K., & Nielsen, K. (2022). *Elite sports in Finland. External international evaluation.* Danish Institute for Sports Studies. https://www.idan.dk/media/cpnbe0n0/report-on-finnish-elite-sport-2022.pdf

Telseth, F., & Halldorsson, V. (2019). The success culture of Nordic football: The cases of the national men's teams of Norway in the 1990s and Iceland in the 2010s. *Sport in Society*, 22(4), 689–703. 10.1080/17430437.2017.1390928

Thrane, C. (2001). Sport spectatorship in Scandinavia: A class phenomenon? *International Review for the Sociology of Sport*, 36(2), 149–163.

Chapter 16

Ethnicity and Aesthetics in Swedish Football

Playing Like a Swede, Fighting Like a Kurd

Tiago Duarte Dias

Introduction: The beautiful game in between Kurdishness and Swedishness

During my early days of fieldwork with Dalkurd FF, I went with Cihan, who worked as Dalkurd FF's head of communication, around the city, helping him affix posters for the game against Degerfors IP at Studenternas, for the last round of the 2019 *Superettan*, the second tier of Swedish male professional football. In the car, we talked about the team and their short yet rich history. On our drive around the city, in between talking about my beloved Flamengo and his beloved Parma, we ended up talking about how Dalkurd FF often played, in terms of tactics and strategy.

Dalkurd FF was founded in 2004 and had climbed the lower leagues of Swedish football, having even reached the country's top division, *Allsvenskan*, in 2018. Currently, in 2022, they play in the Superettan after being promoted. Diaspora Kurds in Sweden were, as of 2014, around 60,000–70,000, as Khayati and Dahlstedt mention (2014, p. 58). Important politicians and artists of Kurdish origin are a part of the constellation of public figures in the country. Furthermore, the Kurdish diaspora in the country have played an important role in the diffusion and maintenance of Kurdish literature, due to the support of the Swedish state from the 1970s onwards (Khayati & Dahlstedt, 2014, p. 57).

This chapter draws from the ethnographic material I gathered in order to write my doctoral dissertation. In the course of around 18 months, I conducted fieldwork with Dalkurd FF fans, members and employees. The data comes from formal and informal interviews, by attending matches (while it was possible, due to the pandemic), watching games at bars and pubs with fans, personal conversations, several visits to the club. My informants were fairly varied in age, gender, class and relation to the club. Some were employed by Dalkurd FF, while others were more casual fans; some dedicated a significant amount of time to supporting them. Some were Dalkurd FF fans from the club's infancy, while others have begun supporting Dalkurd FF later in their lives.

DOI: 10.4324/9781003280729-22

Through the course of my data collection and its subsequent analysis, I could identify some key aspects of Dalkurd FF from the perspective of the people who made it a relevant institution. An important aspect is the one being analysed in this chapter, namely, how the aesthetics of the game would contribute to the building of a football identity that related to its ethnic belonging, and how it serves as a tool for differentiation. As per Bromberger et al. (1995), football can be an effective tool in affirming an imaginary identity through a conceptualisation of how one's favourite team plays (pp. 121–153). This would lead to local ethnic identities being affirmed through football, within a framework of a larger national identity in France and Italy.

Cihan asked if I had watched any Dalkurd FF matches before the one where we first met in Stockholm in the previous weekend. I told him that in fact, I had not, watching only highlights at YouTube. He then told me about how Dalkurd FF would play:

> Dalkurd FF has a very different style of playing football than what you probably know and expect from Swedish football. We often play with three players upfront and we were the first team in the country to also use a backline of three. We play a brand of very offensive football, and we value having the ball, and passing it around, instead of just relying on strength or on defensive tactics. Swedish football is more like 4-4-2 with two big strikes up front, and a lot of long balls to those players, or at least it used to be like that a lot. We are more into 3-4-3 or 4-3-3. We play football that is more modern.

He would not be the only one to mention how Dalkurd FF would play football; or how they would perform. As my fieldwork progressed, my conversations with everyone surrounding the club would often circle back to how the game was played. According to them, this would make Dalkurd FF interesting and appealing to their fans. There would clearly exist an idealised version of football that Dalkurd FF would often be measured against. Dalkurd FF either would or should play in this specific manner, as this would be their identity.

Dalkurd FF was not only expected to represent Kurdishness while being on a football pitch in Sweden through Kurdish symbols and colours, but also to fully embody Kurdish values and to display Kurdishness. They would be expected to do so in ways that were seen as both entertaining to people who would admire football as an aesthetic endeavour, and also as a way of differentiating themselves from other forms of Swedishness they would play against. Having Kurdish symbols or being an articulation of Kurdishness and Swedishness is not enough to explain what makes Dalkurd FF a relevant social institution. The way they would be constructed and idealised as a football team on the pitch would be intrinsic to their success. Their history as a football club, climbing the steps of the Swedish football pyramid would often be conceptualised as a deviation of local and established footballing practices in the country, only possible, according to the fanbase, due to its Kurdishness.

Dalkurd FF could offer something new, more interesting and more aesthetically pleasing. They would play better than what my informants would disparagingly describe as "farmers football" in reference to the clubs that Dalkurd FF played against, and which would supposedly represent a traditional way of playing football in Sweden. The aesthetic advantage of Dalkurd FF, one that would be in consonance with their perception of Swedishness and of Kurdishness, would lay in their ability to produce a footballing performance more in touch with a more cosmopolitan view of the game. Therefore, this chapter discusses how topics related to identity are understood through an aesthetic understanding of football.

"We don't play like those farmers": Aesthetic appreciation and ethnicity

Hume (1757) proposes that aesthetic appreciation relates to a capacity for enjoyment of an object, more than the ability to fully understand the pieces that compose it. The enjoyment from anything would not necessarily be an objective standard; nevertheless, the accumulation of experience can lead to a higher sensitivity to beauty. Thus, I propose that the perception of Dalkurd FF's footballing practices would come from a knowledge of both Swedishness and Kurdishness, how those two sets of traditions play out in the pitch and is interpreted from it.

What happens on the pitch creates a symbolic dialogue between what Kurdishness is, and what it ought to be. There is a universe of characteristics that my informants would associate with Kurdishness, with Swedishness and with being a Kurd in Sweden. They influence how they interpret the game of football in general. Thus, the performance of the game, and how that said performance is interpreted through a perspective that centres around Dalkurd FF and the lived experiences of my informants, ends up shaping the importance of the club to them. The concept of performance in this work is one akin to what Victor Turner (1987) defined. He writes that "man is a self-performing animal – his performances are, in a way, reflexive, in performing he reveals himself to himself" (Turner, 1987, p. 81). Turner, in his turn, by evoking Goffman's work (1956) would affirm that "the basic stuff of social life is performance", and that one's self would be "presented through the performance of roles" (Turner, 1987, p. 81).

To my informants, several aspects of their identity are at play, with the club being a catalyst of Kurdishness in a ritualistic dispute with other identities in Sweden. The competitive performance (as in, the act of giving form or accomplishing something) of the team defines the performance (in the Turnerian sense) of Dalkurd FF as an institution formed by its fans and members. The performing aspect of the self comes from what is presented and what happens in the matches (but not only), as the social life that is generated around the club around the games and their results. As Goffman (1956) puts, social interaction would be similar to theatre insomuch so as individuals are performers in a stage, while an audience could follow the social interaction, and with the existence of a backstage, where the actors can prepare themselves or develop the usage of props. As it concerns Dalkurd FF, the audience of a game, that is the fans, become the actors themselves, and the action played out in the football pitch is the interaction that they have to improvise with while weaving a narrative about the club around the results and how they came to be.

Christopher Pinney's concept of "corpothetics" can be useful in understanding how the performative aspect of football on the pitch can help understand football as an important media for Kurdishness in Sweden. Corpothetics would mobilise "both eyes and body" (Pinney, 2001, pp. 161–162) in order to really apprehend an image. In much the same manner, Dalkurd FF fans perform their support in the stands (or in front of a TV), while the players embody values of Kurdishness on the pitch. Thus, it would be expected from the players to fully incorporate Kurdishness in the pitch, as an opposition to a Swedishness conceptualised as "boring".

Most of my informants would conceptualise Dalkurd FF in an opposition to a "real Swedishness", and as a large part of their history, which occurred in the lower divisions, where they would often be playing "Swedish farmers". In the years in which they had ascended through the lower leagues, their victorious sequence would be conceptualised as a triumph of a more exciting way of playing football, more attuned with the current cosmopolitan reality of the country. Their opposition would be "a bunch of old school farmers", of which, in IK Brage, their rivals from their former hometown of Borlänge, would be seen as a clear representation. As mentioned by one of my informants in a casual conversation:

> We played different than most of those Swedish farmers. We played the ball around; we scored a lot of goals. I know it was only the lower leagues in Sweden, but we played football in a nice way, much nicer than the other teams played. I think we still have the record of most goals scored on Division 1.

The reference to Swedish farmers would often be made by several Dalkurd FF supporters. The construction around the category of "farmer" would refer to a negatively idealised, agrarian Sweden. An emic category that my informants would use to describe aspects of Swedishness that would be nostalgic to a romanticised period in Swedish history in which Kurdish (along with other ethnicities) were not a part of Swedish society. Farmer can, thus, in this context be understood as backwards looking, simple, unsophisticated and, often, racist.

From the lower leagues to the national arena

As the lower leagues are progressively less professional, less wealthy and also more localised, they would often be a part of weekend activities by men with other professions and who would participate in matches and training sessions on their spare time. This was known informally as *korpen,* meaning corporation, as it would have its roots into sports being practiced and organised around companies in the country. The term would, in this context, be expanded to mean organised, amateur football, within the national pyramid, but almost always within local spheres. The years in which Dalkurd FF had spent playing in between Division 6 and Division 2 (and perhaps also on Division 1) were spent on competing against a multitude of local amateur sides, very often representing small villages or small cities, or else being the smaller, and less successful team in bigger communities.

My informants also perceived the most famous and larger teams in Sweden, from the affluent and larger cities had been already, in way or the other, co-opted into a transnational dynamic of the sport, as their economic structure would be fully dependent on globalisation and its financial aspects (Andersson & Carlsson, 2011). If Dalkurd FF would have built its identity amongst local clubs in Dalarna, it would be in the national arena, however, that they would become a more relevant institution, with a national profile. On this level of competition, Dalkurd FF would identify the larger clubs as being uncoupled from its fanbase precisely due to the capitalistic influence on them, even if they would recognise Sweden as less affected by that than other countries, while still, however, aesthetically attached to a "Swedish way of playing", as those teams would be seen as, with exceptions, not playing with a fighting spirit or in an entertaining manner.

My informants would conceptualise this traditionalistic approach to football from the lower leagues as "boring and predictable", both in the aesthetics of the play element and of the performance. Dalkurd FF would present a more competitive, more cosmopolitan interpretation of football, one in which would also be more aesthetically pleasing to my informants, as an 18-year-old member of their supporters association would tell me:

> I personally like how we play football. I like how we think about the game. How we value possession, how we always try to pass the ball around. It's a more beautiful version of the game, and it's something everyone else is doing in the world.

Hence, fans would be interested in the aesthetics of the game, as Kurdishness is played out on a backdrop of Swedish traditions and institutions. The Kurdishness would be expressed through playing football in ways perceived to be more creative and resourceful. Swedish football would be perceived as more collective and less technical, while Dalkurd FF's Kurdishness could provide

Swedish football to an inspiration more attuned to the international influences on the sport.

Russell Sharman (1997, pp. 177–178) defines aesthetics as "attachment of values to experience" and aesthetic perception as the "re-creation of experience through which those values are reconstituted and/or transformed", in a dialogue with Kant's view of aesthetics as "disinterested appreciation". My informants would, therefore, build a series of values around the performance in and around the game, and appreciate it without any desire to attain any material gains from it. The experience of watching the game actively creates a situation in which their identity as Kurds within Swedish society is at play. The manner which Dalkurd FF plays, thus, need to reflect Kurdish values on a positive light, while affirming a belonging to a Swedishness.

Football in this case offers a "social semantics" (Geertz, 1973, pp. 36–38) of the projected value and role of Kurdishness as a minority identity within Sweden. As Kurdish colours, symbols, songs, values, fans are, therefore, expected to be metonymical devises for Kurdishness, those values would be embodied by the players on the pitch. Play, as a whole, becomes a way of "waging war" through other means (Aubin-Boltanski, 2021, pp. 354–355). The athletes on the pitch, more than winning and losing, are expected to always maintain a connection to the values of Kurdishness. Their bodies and their performances become a conduit to being Kurdish.

It is essential to understand what would create the symbolic references that my informants would consider as inherently "positive", "beautiful", "good" or "desirable" in the context of Dalkurd FF, and the matches they play. Those conceptualisations are the framework in which Dalkurd FF is analysed by their fans. Although Swedish football, especially in its second and third tiers, is hardly the place to find state-of-the-art football, a fact my informants are well-aware of, it is also the locus where they choose to express themselves. Dalkurd FF creates a contextual interpretation of how football should be played in an aesthetically pleasing way in a way as reflection of their identities as football fans. Understanding what constitutes this symbolic framework, therefore, becomes a key aspect in understanding the club and their fans.

Kurds never give up: Conceptualising defeat and ethnicity

The way that Dalkurd FF's way of playing football was ideally conceptualised by my informants, which would suggest an inherent superiority of the Kurdish interpretation of Swedish football over the other local identities present in the country. However, the season in which I followed Dalkurd FF as a part of my ethnographic fieldwork was a season that ended up in relegation from the Superettan. This was a season in which Dalkurd FF lost more than they won. Thus, one must ask, how Dalkurd FF's fandom conceptualises bad performances, in light of their ethnic interpretation of the sport and how it reacts to defeat in relation to their ethnicity.

A common narrative thread that would run through Dalkurd FF, from fans to board members, and employees, was that Kurds, and thus Dalkurd FF, would have a fighting spirit not only reflected on how they played, but also a metaphor for Kurdishness and its history of surviving oppression. As Kurds have faced geopolitical struggles that have robbed them of the possibility of self-determination through a national state (McDowall, 2003, pp. 89–96), leading to a situation that my informants would define as Kurdistan being occupied by foreign forces. This occupation has led to Kurds not being able to express themselves fully as Kurds, but nevertheless, Kurds would never give up on their dream and desire for freedom to be Kurdish. The idealisation of always fighting would turn the football pitch into an arena where the players would ideally embrace the values Kurdishness resisting in the face of stronger foes. This fighting spirit would be intertwined with the aesthetic and performance aspect of football.

For example, Dalkurd FF played Djurgården, then reigning champions of Sweden, for the Swedish Cup. After a disappointing beginning, in which they conceded three goals in the first half, Dalkurd FF managed to score two goals in the second half while pressuring the opponents at their own arena in Stockholm. There were around 100 fans in the away area who chanted and cheered, and saluted the players after the game was over. I spoke to many fans after the match. They were satisfied with the match. They had faced a stronger foe and, in spite of losing, they had, according to them, fought until the last second. They had not given up and this in itself was commendable. The fans, themselves, were satisfied with their performance, as well. According to one of them, they "had silenced Djurgården's fans at some moments". They, the fans, had also not given up. Kurdish symbols would be strong enough to provide Dalkurd FF with an edge that could be activated if the team were to have players that understood this meaning. The embodiment by the players of Kurdish values was supposed to bring a fighting spirit and competitiveness expressed in the pitch, and activated by the fans themselves.

The 2020 season was quite disappointing for most Dalkurd FF fans. Oftentimes bad results would be interpreted through a lack of characteristics within the squad associated with Kurdishness, in opposition to Swedishness. Swedishness was seen as peaceful and avert to conflict and ambitious pursuits, as the country's national identity comes without an opposition to a foreign enemy, unlike its neighbours (Löfgren, 1991, p. 106). Sweden would be, per one of my informants, a country where "everything is easy". This idyllic version of a nation not involved on any wars since the early 19th century, was opposed to a view of Kurdishness, constantly fighting for survival. This difference would reflect on the pitch.

Dalkurd FF fans would create a narrative in which their players, in an idealised situation, would (or should) never give up, due to the Kurdishness imbedded in the club. If Kurds cannot afford to give up, to be soft, to open up their guards while in a war, in the same transitive way, neither can Dalkurd FF fans nor its players. Kurdishness would be activated as an aesthetic evaluation whenever tough games would be won, or at the very least, played with a perceived sense of selflessness. The evaluation throughout the season had been that Dalkurd FF did not have players "good enough" (though that did play a part), but also, that most players did not possess an edge that would lead them to fully give everything they had on the pitch. They were merely "employees", instead of truly embracing Kurdishness.

Thus, all games are analysed as whether they had been able to portray a Kurdish spirit or not. The result mattered less than the performance itself. A tie against a highly ranked team, such as Halmstad, or a loss against a top-tier team as Djurgården could be interpreted as a beautiful, selfless, prestation from the players. Ties such as the one against Akropolis with virtually no shots on goal from any team, however, were seen as lacking not only technically but also in Kurdish values.

Kurdish DNA and the fighting spirit

Sometimes players play well, and sometimes they play badly, as an informant would tell me. How they were played, however, differed. Failing on a run, on a cross, on a tackle, a pass or a shot was better than not working oneself to be in that position to try. A truly aesthetic appreciation, would come from a relentlessness, demonstrated on and off the pitch. My informants perceived the lack of a fighting spirit within the squad as the main cause for relegation. As the margins between relegation and clinging to the Superettan were seen as quite small, the club would have lost, not for being objectively worse, but rather for not fighting as much or as hard. In the days after Dalkurd FF's relegation from the Superettan, Dalkurd FF's Instagram and Facebook pages posted the following:

> It's hard for all of us today. But the story of Dalkurd doesn't stop here. We always come back! During our only 16-year history, we have encountered more challenges and obstacles than 100-year-old associations have done. (…) Because it's in our DNA and in our identity. Giving up is NOT. Since when, have we Kurds laid down and just given up?! (…) Now it's time for everyone to come together. All who have given their souls and lives to Dalkurd. Everyone who supports and cheers for Dalkurd FF and everyone who claims to do so, must come together and give our club the support they deserve and need. A chain's as strong as its weakest link, and it was when we were united that we were our strongest and unbeatable. This isn't a tired cliché, but a fact![1] (Dalkurd FF [@dalkurdff], 2020)

A member of Dalkurd FF's fan group told me that "if in the mountains (paraphrasing a common Kurdish expression that Kurds have no friends, but the mountains), Kurds don't give up, they had no reason to do so in the football pitches of Sweden". Kurdish DNA is supposed to show how to give up would be inherently incompatible with being a Kurd, as no Kurd would possibly inherit this characteristic. One would be defined by one's DNA[2]; to come back, to fight, would be intrinsically connected to being a Kurd. It would be, in itself, Kurdishness. To fight back against adversity was a path that Kurds would be bounded to follow from birth. The usage of DNA to exemplify this call to arms from the organisation to its members, employees and fans is one which defines Kurdishness as never giving up. If they were to give up, either they would no longer be able to call themselves real Kurds, or the club in itself could not see itself as being fully Kurdish any longer. By using both DNA and identity, the post both riles up everyone around the club, but also points to the inevitability of the struggle, of the act of fighting back and the act of suffering from adversity in itself as a formative element in Kurdishness.

Many fans would mention the need, or their desire, of having a Kurdish player in the squad. This idea of "spirit" or "soul" would transcend having a Kurd in the squad, as it would be a characteristic intrinsically connected to the club and its symbols, yet one that had to be activated by the players and fans themselves. In some cases, some players would never be able to have it, as others would only have it, in case they were provoked to do so. An active fandom, therefore, would incite the players, through their own performance, to perform aesthetically well through a Kurdish perspective. In a practical sense, this Kurdish spirit could manifest itself in the pitch with players giving everything on every single play. It would mean a total dedication to winning, and an impossibility of accepting defeat and giving up, no matter the scoreboard. This spirit of fight would be the edge that only Dalkurd FF would possess in Swedish football, and it would be the reason why they would have the appeal that they would have amongst their fans.

Thus, it would not only be the tactical acumen and the tactical innovations that would make Dalkurd FF win, as all of this would be rather empty and lifeless without a "spirit". This spirit would live up the players and make the spectacle truly appreciable. They would make the game not only fun, but truly something beautiful and exciting to my informants, as this spirit would be a "part of their DNA", and therefore, being instantly recognisable by the club's fanbase. The possibility of displaying Kurdishness on Swedish pitches renders the club affectively relevant to its fanbase, privy to Kurdishness manifested in a Swedish context.

Conclusion

In the course of 90 minutes, one can see how Roger Caillois's (2001, pp. 22–29) distinction of four types of play: competition, chance, mimesis and vertigo could be found in a football game. It offers the agonistic or competitive aspect, as both players and fans compete to see who emerges victorious after 90 minutes. It offers also the idea of chance as much as it offers the idea of being a game of skill. Oftentimes the team who is perceived as the best one not be able to win; upsets occur and they tend to leave an imprint on those who witness them. Moreover, many games are decided on a matter of details could have had a different story, had things been ever so slightly different. It is mimicry as fans become a part of the spectacle and roleplay with their identity and make it so that they perceive themselves as being as responsible for what occurs in the pitch than the players inside of it. And it offers the vertigo of the multitude of emotions and the altered perceptions within it, whether positive or negative. Those emotions help strengthen the bond between the teams and the fans.

Within those aspects of play, however, there would be a system of aesthetical appreciation, based on values extrinsic from the game, but interpreted through what would take place in the game in itself. The match was to offer the raw material in which the fans would construct an aesthetic appreciation of it. As the season had ended on the worst possible note for Dalkurd FF, everyone at the club were left to reminisce about what had gone wrong through the course of a very atypical year. In conversations with fans, there was the conclusion that both the squad lacked quality, the board lacked leadership and that the staff and the coaches had made several mistakes; but they also would fully agree on the idea of a Kurdish spirit being absent this year.

There exists an idealised view of how Dalkurd FF practiced the game, it would equate Kurdishness into an act of resistance; as Kurdishness surviving in spite of being denied free expression in Kurdistan, it was a history of how Kurds, when given fair conditions, would thrive and achieve success. The "Kurdish DNA" that they wrote on the post and the Kurdish identity in the club that was alluded to when talking about the club would be the main thread running through the tactical innovations, the integration of other ethnicities, the fighting spirit and their ambition.

This set of relationships between club, fans, Kurdish diaspora, football, integration and tactics was the many threads that lead to Dalkurd FF acquiring meaning to its fans. All those threads, the one that pervaded all of them present was a self-idealised view of Kurdishness that would come to life and would be able to be observed on a football pitch, competing equally with other identities within a Swedish context. It would also show that Kurds could compete equally with anyone. And it would be around football matches, that this connection between fans and the elements that make the club, would take place a Durkheimian context of collective effervescence, an event that would give this social group a lived experience of their social bonds and social shared elements (Durkheim, 1968).

During Dalkurd FF games, Kurdishness would be a lived experience shared by people watching the game simultaneously, but also to those who would watch it by themselves at home (the large majority due to the pandemic), and it would be after the games, that fans would talk about the game, that the memory of the many events of this collective effervescence would slowly build into a narrative of past matches becoming relevant in the present and the future. This multisited aspect of football appreciation an aspect not only circumscribed to the Nordic countries, but rather a global phenomenon.

The idea of Kurdishness, as mentioned before, could not be taken for granted, as it could increase, decrease or even cease to exist. For the Kurdishness in Dalkurd FF to persist, burning, it needed the fuel from the stands, from the staff and the players. The fighting spirit, the overcoming of difficult situations, the entertaining approach to football, all of this was supposed to be enacted through the force of the people who would make the club, and for whom the club would matter the most. If, on the one hand, the club was founded on an idealised interpretation of Kurdishness from Kurds themselves, in another, this idealised version of Kurdishness and Kurdish values was always on the risk of becoming merely colours and a crest, instead of a lived experience.

In order for the club to continue to become a symbol of Kurdishness, thus, it had to be performed, it had to acquire a living aspect, it had to always become Kurdish for it could not simply just be Kurdish. Dalkurd FF connects to an experience of football shared by sports fans all over the planet. It is place where identities are shaped and reconstructed, and where sociability occurs. As the club is a direct result of historical aspects of both Sweden and Kurdistan, as a transnational combination of both, being particular in this sense, it also shares similarities with professional sports in other countries, as football identities are never circumscribed to a single locality, but are a rather fluid and interconnected experience (Hannerz, 2002).

Therefore, by articulating both local and transnational aspects of Kurdish identity, Dalkurd FF creates an identity for its fans, based on a belonging to both Sweden and Kurdistan by the part of the club. This belonging takes place by a series of articulations based on the aesthetic element of the sport, which provides them the possibility to interpret both their sport and their place within the footballing structures of Sweden through centring their own identity as Kurds, as Swedish, and as fans of Dalkurd FF.

Notes

1 Translated by the author from Swedish.
2 Here we see an interesting use of a scientific term as a metaphor for a topic that is inherently social. This type of hybridisation is a relevant part of how Western societies, such as Sweden, create metaphors using nature, which are socially accepted and understood, while showing how nature and culture are never far from each other (Latour, 1993). This usage of DNA-as-metaphor can show how integrated they (as Kurds and as football fans) are into the mythological framework of Sweden.

References

Andersson, T., & Carlsson, B. (2011). A diagnosis of the commercial immaturity of Swedish club football. *Soccer & Society, 12*(6), 754–773. 10.1080/14660970.2011.609678

Aubin-Boltanski, E. (2021). A life with birds: The ethnography of a passion for racing pigeons (Lebanon). *Ethnologie française, 51*, 347–361. 10.3917/ethn.212.0347

Bromberger, C., Hayot, A., & Mariottini, J. (1995). *Le match de football* [The game of football]. Maison des Sciences de l'Homme.

Caillois, R. (2001). *Man, play and games*. University of Chicago Press.

Durkheim, E. (1968). *The elementary forms of the religious life*. Free Press.

Dalkurd FF [@dalkurdff]. (2020, December 14) *Det är tungt för oss alla idag. Men historien om Dalkurd stannar inte här. Vi kommer alltid tillbaka!* [It is tough for all of us today. But Dalkurd's history does not stop here. We always come back!] *as a* [Post]. Instagram. https://www.instagram.com/p/CIyD3ihoNSy/

Geertz, C. (1973). *The interpretation of cultures*. Basic Books.

Goffman, E. (1956). *The presentation of self in everyday life*. Double Day.

Hannerz, U. (2002). *Transnational connections*. Taylor and Francis.

Hume, D. (1757). *Four dissertations*. A. Millar.

Khayati, K., & Dahlstedt, M. (2014). Diaspora formation among Kurds in Sweden: Transborder citizenship and politics of belonging. *Nordic Journal of Migration Research, 4*(2), 57–64. 10.2478/njmr-2014-0010

Latour, B. (1993). *We have never been modern*. Harvard University Press.

Löfgren, O. (1991). The nationalization of culture: Constructing Swedishness. *Studia Ethnologica, 3*, 101–116.

McDowall, D. (2003). *A modern history of the Kurds*. Bloomsbury.

Pinney, C. (2001). Piercing the skin of the idol. In C. Pinney & N. Thomas (Eds.), *Beyond aesthetics: Art and the technologies of enchantment* (pp. 157–181). Routledge.

Sharman, R. (1997). The anthropology of aesthetics: A cross-cultural approach. *JASO, 28*(2), 177–192.

Turner, V. (1987). *The anthropology of performance*. PAJ Publications.

Conclusion

Similarities, Differences and Future Research in Football in the Nordic Countries

Hannu Itkonen, Mihaly Szerovay, and Arto Nevala

An abundance of similarities

The historical overviews in Part I and the thematic sections in Part II set the scene for an evaluation of football cultures in the Nordic countries. In the following, we offer some critical reflections to highlight key similarities and differences across Denmark, Finland, Iceland, Norway and Sweden. We then position the Nordic countries within the global football context while sketching potential future pathways for football and suggest research avenues.

The emergence of the Nordic welfare states laid the foundations for the development of football cultures, as the steering policies of the public sector have extended into the domain of sport. The norms dictated by the state and municipalities have exerted their impact in multifaceted ways. One example is the expectation that football organisations and practitioners should embrace and promote equality, equal opportunities and accessibility. Those involved in football should also consider ecological and social sustainability in all activities. Simultaneously, engaging with the norms set by the public sector has provided Nordic football organisations an evident opportunity to be an active agent in shaping the welfare society, which is based on civic activity and highlights inclusion, equality and tolerance. As Rafnsson and Kristjánsdóttir (2023, this volume) point out, change in Icelandic women's football is, instead of being triggered top-down by institutions, being initiated by the decisions of ordinary people in the third sector. The Nordic football contexts have also paved the way for the emergence of activities besides traditional football, such as futsal and recreational as well as walking football, which have broadened the pool of potential participants and benefits.

In postmodern societies, sport organisations must constantly renew and negotiate their partnerships and networks. The changing field of sport clubs in the Nordic countries is characterised by the increasing involvement in public service provision, the businessification of club activities and growing collaboration with the private sector (Huhtanen & Itkonen, 2022). Even though the public sector has traditionally taken charge of training and competition facilities by building and maintaining them (Itkonen & Salmikangas, 2015), the private commercial sector has participated in providing and running facilities to a growing extent (Laine & Vehmas, 2017; Szerovay, 2022). Those participating in football in various roles and segments have to navigate these hybrid practices.

Due to the strong civic tradition in the sporting culture of Nordic countries, a wide range of sports have emerged and developed, with their basis in the culture of voluntary-based sport and physical activity. From a historical perspective, all of the Nordic countries have seen continuous growth in the number of sports that are played, as new formats and competitions have continued to evolve. This means that football has had to compete for participants and popularity with other sports. Climate has also shaped the emergence of different sports and the power relationship between them, and football in the Nordic region has been no exception. The long winters and darkness have required the construction of facilities that allow the season to be lengthened. The case of Iceland is instructive here. With the country's first indoor football pitch constructed in 2000, further investments in facilities including football turf and mini-football pitches as well as floodlights transformed Icelandic football from a summer sport to a year-round activity where participants of all ages could play the game despite harsh winter weather (Halldorsson & Johannsson, 2023, this volume). At the same time, playing football indoors and under artificial lights has sparked critical discussions about whether the game is an ecological and environmental burden in the Nordic countries.

The Nordic countries have also shared specific phases in their development in football. The initial phases were often defined by leisure activities, but then sport clubs dedicated to football started to emerge or football was added to the programme of existing clubs. As a next step, national competitions began to be arranged, heeding the expectations of clubs and supporters. Later, clubs based on voluntary activities have slowly shifted towards professionalism, which has meant that player pathways could extend as far as being a full professional player. This has allowed players to seek employment all over the world and further connected the Nordic countries – which have experienced relatively late professionalisation when compared to their leading European counterparts – to the global labour market. For a long time, leadership and management were solely based on volunteer work, but nowadays professional knowledge is imperative, especially on the elite level. Clubs in the highest divisions are well-developed products for entertainment, operating based on market principles and run by professionals. With these developments the traditional model of sport has been challenged and power relations have shifted as leading football clubs have started to operate – particularly in male football – as corporations, while there is a growing tendency to do the same in women's football as well (Horgby & Ericsson, 2020). Although the phases in Nordic countries have been similar – as explored in Part I of this book – there is variety in their timing, shaped by, among other factors, the wealth of the country and its connectedness to the international football system.

Although women's football has exhibited similar development phases, the changes have taken place considerably later than they did for men's football. In each Nordic country women's football started to gain popularity in the 1970s, with the first national divisions being launched that decade. The developments have run parallel to wider societal changes and, in football, with FIFA and UEFA setting up several international competitions during the 2000s (Skogvang, 2019). Nevertheless, achieving full professional practices in sport clubs still has a long way to go. In Finland's premier division (*Kansallinen Liiga*), for example, there is only one club where most of the players are regarded as professionals and who can focus fully on football. In this sense, equality has not been achieved.

Nordic football associations have been active internationally for decades, playing a prominent role in football organisations since World War II. The strong position of the Nordic countries has been based not only on success on the pitch and the Eurocentricity of the football world, but also on their typically neutral political position between East and West. The best example of this is the 1958 World Cup finals, which was awarded to Sweden despite Argentina, Chile and Mexico had also applied to host the tournament. The most influential Nordic football leader, Swedish Lennart Johansson, was the president of UEFA for almost 20 years (1990–2007) and also vice-president of FIFA. Johansson's long career and crucial position also paved the way for other Nordic actors in the UEFA and FIFA organisations.

In the 2000s the role of the Nordic countries in the international football community has assumed new forms. The Nordic countries can be seen more and more as the "conscience" of the football world. They have criticised practices in football related to gender equality, parity, distribution of money and especially the arranging of the World Cup 2022 in Qatar. Lisa Klaveness, president of the Norwegian Football Federation, has been publicly highly critical of the Qatar World Cup, and the poor human rights situation in the country has also been highlighted by, among others, Tim Sparv, the former captain of the Finnish men's national team. For FIFA and Qatar, the criticism is embarrassing. However, it can be interpreted as indicating a clash of values: Klaveness and Sparv have only been defending values traditionally important in the Nordic societies, such as equality, freedom of speech and non-discrimination. However, these values are not necessarily shared by all member countries, and the decisions taken by FIFA, despite their fine language, are not always based on them either.

A wealth of differences

It should be noted that the Nordic model – the basic tenets of which are outlined in more detail in the introduction of the book – is not homogenous, and there are significant differences both between and within countries (Andersen & Ronglan, 2012; de la Porte et al., 2022; Green et al., 2020; Tin et al., 2020).

This is reflected in the football cultures as well. Out of the numerous potential differences, we have chosen to highlight five here – primarily selected based on the texts in the book.

First, when taking a look at the popularity and status of football compared to other sports within each country's sporting culture, we can observe variations. In Denmark, Iceland, Norway and Sweden, football can be seen as the most popular sport in both participation and viewership. The role of football in these countries has been relevant in the formation of national as well as local identity, especially in cities. This has led to the emergence of fierce rivalries, such as those in Sweden involving Gothenburg, Stockholm and in the county of Scania, as introduced in Part II. In Norway, football became a source of regional and national pride as early as the 1920s, and the playing style of a team could indicate the expression of local football identities (Goksøyr & Olstad, 2002).

The status and popularity of football have been challenged by other sports in various ways. In Finland, ice hockey has been ahead of football in many respects, including in business turnover and viewership. While football has seen limited international success in qualifications for major tournaments when taking both women's and men's football into account, men's ice hockey has been a modern indoor sport since the 1960s, with state-of-the-art facilities that allowed a shift towards professionalism much earlier than in football. As a result, since the 1990s, Finland has been competitive internationally and won numerous medals at the Ice Hockey World Championships and Olympic Winter Games (Isotalo et al., 2020). Sweden is also a powerful ice hockey country, in contrast to Denmark, Iceland and Norway, yet premier division clubs in Sweden typically come from smaller cities than high-level football teams do. In Finland, most teams from the highest divisions in both ice hockey and football are concentrated in larger cities, with the result that the two sports often compete for participants, spectators and sponsors (Backman, 2018; Isotalo et al., 2020).

In Iceland, despite football's position as the most popular sport, the status of national sport belongs to handball due to the country's long-standing international success in it (Thorlindsson & Halldorsson, 2019). In Norway, even though the major ski and speed skating competitions bring in large audiences, football – due to its weekly matches – emerged as the major spectator sport in the post-war decades and is today clearly the most popular sport by participation as well (see Hjelseth et al., 2023, this volume). In Denmark, where football is the clear the number one sport, Team Denmark, an organisation which focuses on promoting elite sport, shifted from a "public service" to a "targeted approach" regarding the funding of elite sports in the 2000s, prioritising a limited number of strategic sports – including football – according to their potential to bring home success internationally (Storm, 2012). In Sweden, the dominant position of football has been supported by commercial interests, increased professionalisation and media attention, which has sparked conflicts because the football association's interests do not always correspond to those of other sport federations (Ljunggren, 2020). Finland has a distinctive situation, where the traditional national sport of Finnish baseball (*pesäpallo*) has challenged the status of football as a summer sport. The status of Finnish baseball, however, has weakened due to urbanisation and modernisation, among other factors, with the result that Finnish baseball is today played on the highest level mostly in smaller towns.

The second perspective of differences looks at the development of women's football. The process of professionalisation, for example, has occurred with considerably different timing in each country, which can be highlighted when studying player migration. Players from Finland and Iceland have often moved to play in other Nordic countries, especially in Sweden, as a first step, after some of the best players moved on to other European clubs. The migration of players from other Nordic countries often led directly to top leagues in Europe and the United States. In contrast, the migration patterns of female football players seem to be different than those in of men's football (Agergaard & Botelho, 2014; Skogvang, 2019; Taylor, 2006). The Swedish premier division (*Damallsvenskan*) in the late 1990s and early 2000s was arguably the leading women's league in Europe. Norway was also a dominant nation in international football in the 1990s, winning gold at the 1995 World Cup and at the Olympic Games in 2000.

As a third difference, we have identified levels of participation in football. Population and demographic variables shape the number of participants as well as the possibilities to recruit participants. As shown in Table 1, football is the most popular team sport in all the Nordic countries in terms of the number of registered players, but in Finland ice hockey is a more popular spectator sport than football is. The most interesting differences between the Nordic countries are in the number of registered players in proportion to the population and in the number and proportion of girl and female players. There are a couple of caveats regarding the numbers. It should be noted that the practices of counting and registering players may vary slightly across countries. Also, there may be considerable differences in the number of adult recreational players, which is reflected in the total number of registered players in each country. According to the table, the "real" football countries are Iceland and Norway, where the percentage of players in the population is the highest. Girl and female players also account for a large proportion of registered players in Iceland and Norway, about a third. In Sweden, girl and female players account for an equal share of registered players, and in Finland slightly less, about a quarter, but in Denmark only about 17%. Despite this, throughout the 2000s, all of the Nordic countries were ranked very high in the FIFA women rankings, unlike in the men's side, where Denmark and Sweden were traditionally ranked high and Norway in the "middle class", while the ranking of Finland and Iceland did not rise until the 2010s. The Nordic countries, it seems, have had somewhat different starting points as a football country. Some diversity can also be found when looking at the pace of change and the situation today. However, the differences have clearly narrowed in the 2000s, as Finland and Iceland have started to close the gap with other Nordic countries.

Table 1 Popularity, participation and international ranking of football in the Nordic countries

	Denmark	Finland	Iceland	Norway	Sweden
Most popular team sport by participation	Football	Football	Football	Football	Football
Most popular spectator sport	Football	Ice hockey	Football	Football	Football
Other popular participation sports today	Gymnastics, swimming, golf	Floorball, athletics, golf	Handball, basketball, gymnastics	Cross country skiing, handball, golf	Ice hockey, golf, gymnastics
Population (2021)	5.85 million	5.5 million	376,000	5.47 million	10.5 million
No. of total registered players (2021)	345,000	140,000	28,000	372,000	343,000
Proportion of registered players in population	5.9%	2.5%	7.4%	6.8%	3.3%
No. of female/girl players (2021)	70,000	37,000	9,000	109,000	93,000
FIFA ranking men (average since 1993)	19	58	64	33	25
FIFA ranking women (average since 2003)	12	22	18	9	2

Fourth, support by commercial actors and the private sector varies considerably across Nordic countries, which is affected by the popularity of football as well as by football's status compared to other sports. Today, sponsors no longer operate as philanthropists, even though many clubs have a financially strong owner behind them – and they expect value for their money. Given the differences in spectators in the top tiers, the variation in the interest of sponsors is understandable (for more details see UEFA, 2021), and the number of spectators affects the clubs economically. Commercialisation has sparked tensions as well. For example, supporter groups have often protested against unpredictable fixtures stemming from broadcasting demands, and have opposed sponsor logos that did not with the team's jersey (see Hjelseth et al., 2023, this volume). Relatedly, the timing of professionalisation – now looking at men's football – has varied considerably, in which the aforementioned commercial opportunities played a considerable role. In Sweden, amateur regulations were overturned in 1967, professional football was introduced in Denmark in 1978, and non-amateur regulations came into force in Norway in 1984. Finland and Iceland have lagged behind in this respect. Even though amateur regulations were removed from the competition rules in 1978 and the league system was established in 1989 in Finland, today the highest division remains mainly characterised by various levels of semi-professionalism. Iceland's premier division is also still clearly semi-professional.

Fifth, this edited collection sheds light on the scope of football research currently being conducted in the Nordic countries. Football is arguably the most researched sport, with academic journals and various international conferences dedicated to the sport. In Denmark, Norway and Sweden, football has clearly been a topic of interest for social scientists while far fewer academic texts deal with the Icelandic and Finnish football contexts. In addition, as shown in this book, in Norway, the exploitation of scientific research played an important role in the country's international success in the 1990s. On the other hand, in Finland, for example, research data have only been produced and used for a short time as part of the development of football. In the emerging research area of spectator studies, Norway and Denmark have seen the most studies, as this collection shows. Variations can be observed regarding scientific fields and themes, too. Analysing these more in depth would indeed be a fruitful future research avenue.

In the 2000s, all the Nordic countries are more football countries than ever before. However, they have followed slightly different routes and moved at a different pace. The differing status of football reflects the economic, social and cultural background of each Nordic country. Relative economic wealth, modernisation, demographic and regional factors as well as the position of football compared to other sports have shaped the popularity of football in its different development phases. To illustrate three cases, Finland's participation in World War II and its recovery based on the small farms' policy slowed urbanisation and strongly affected the whole society as well as sport and the resources available

Table 2 Key similarities and differences in football across the Nordic countries

Similarities
Nordic welfare state
Equality as a cornerstone in political activities and education
Strong public administration for sport and physical activities
Strong civil society for sport and physical activities
Phases of change in the history of football
The status of football within the global football system

Differences
Status of football compared to other sports within the sporting culture
Popularity of football as a spectator sport
Number of participants
Pace of development in women's football
Level of professionalisation and commercialisation
Amount of academic research on football

for it. Finnish baseball, moreover, was developed to serve the interests of national defence and remained the dominant team sport for a long time until ice hockey later emerged as the most popular team sport. Football's turn did not arrive until the 2000s. On the other hand, Sweden did not participate in World War II, and quickly industrialised and urbanised both before and after the war. This, together with the construction of the welfare state, laid a strong foundation for success in football. Iceland, a nation with a small population, on the other hand, is an example of a different kind of growth into a football country. Success in football on the international stage required focusing resources for the benefit of a handful of sports, including football (McGinn, 2020). Table 2 brings together the main similarities and differences we have discussed so far in this conclusion.

Nordic countries in the global football context

The Nordic countries are seen as similar welfare societies with distinctive characteristics (de la Porte et al., 2022; Tin et al., 2020). The welfare objectives are expected to be advanced also in sport as well. That is, sport organisations need to take into account equality and equal opportunities, ecological and social sustainability as well as financial transparency. As national associations and clubs receive funds from the public sector, they are required to operate in a morally and ethically sustainable manner. Shortcomings and misconduct are handled and sorted out together with all stakeholders. When looking at Nordic sport, especially football, in the global context, there is a growing transnational consciousness and connectedness. While neoliberal pressures of marketisation and commercialisation will probably continue, these forces will be adapted and *glocalised* by Nordic countries via their deeply institutionalised Nordic model. Moreover, certain elements of the Nordic model may be extended to and perhaps embraced by other societies, as global audiences are interested in and susceptible to this model (Giulianotti, 2020).

The Nordic countries, it can be argued, share a common value system. This is evident in, for example, the ambition of the schooling systems to provide all-round education for each generation (Giulianotti et al., 2019). In sport clubs, educational goals that reach beyond sporting achievements, which have been an integral part in the sporting and physical activities context, facilitate the development of participants. When contemplating the increasing global connectivity of Nordic countries, they offer values, ideas and practices with the prospect of a positive impact beyond the Nordic region. As this collection has demonstrated, football has been a driver in breaking barriers for women and, despite the challenges that remain (see Skogvang, 2023, in this volume), has provided a vehicle for ethnic minorities to live and express their identities (see Duarte Dias, 2023, this volume). As Bennike et al. (2023, this volume) show, as a sporting form football has been moulded to be more accessible to a broader range of participants so as to yield health benefits. As football leadership and organisations become more evidence based, the Nordic countries can benefit from their high level of education and academic skills in creating innovations and insights. This opportunity has already been recognised by football associations and some clubs over the past decade, who have set up research and development departments that draw on data to create knowledge, provide insights and assist decision-making.

Political practices today are marked by continuously securing alliances and partnerships. Within Europe and the European Union, countries have joined together in different coalitions to collaborate, for example, on environmental issues, energy supply and financial questions. Despite the differences, the Nordic countries seem to form an entity within the global football system, just as they do within other international communities. Their voice may be better heard this way as opposed to speaking up alone, because the international media, as de la Porte et al. (2022, p. 1) puts it, at times even "iconises" the Nordic countries for how they have successfully combined international competitiveness, equality and a high level of trust in social institutions. It is also possible for the Nordic countries to take advantage of their reputation as the "world's happiest nations" in the global football community. Indeed, they have cooperated in various forms for decades. The formerly organised Nordic Football Championships, which were staged in both men's and women's football, serves as an example. A more recent example is a letter addressed together to FIFA, criticising the labour regulations and situation in Qatar, the host country for the men's World Cup 2022. In addition, four of the Nordic countries have submitted a joint bid for the 2025 European Championship (UEFA, 2022).

When viewed from the standpoint of elite football, Nordic countries will continue to fulfil a feeder role and their national leagues will serve as a stepping stone towards stronger leagues – another relevant illustration of global connectivity. In the constantly growing women's football, the Nordic countries (especially the Scandinavian ones) have played a crucial role in attracting a significant number of players from abroad (Agergaard & Botelho, 2014). An indicator of football's strength is that all five countries have qualified for major men's and women's tournaments, a demonstration of the growing level of individual players. Similarly, the gradual professionalisation of national leagues has attracted players from abroad to join the Nordic leagues. Both push and pull factors are thus at play in the migration pattern of Nordic football. Besides through players, Nordic supporters also encounter other football cultures through global media. There emerges a sense of belonging to those sport organisations that receive extensive television airtime, resulting in many becoming followers of clubs in countries such as England, Spain and Italy (Hognestad, 2009).

The Nordic countries – where in international comparison, research funding provided by the public sector is relevant – have been cooperating in science and research for a long time. Today, they are increasingly looking for cooperation and synergies in new research activities as well. One example is the 1st Nordic Football Conference, organised in Finland in 2022, which attracted a range of participants from the academic community – including many of the authors of this book – as well as football associations from the Nordic countries and beyond. The conference addressed researchers, practitioners as well as students and stimulated discussions that went beneath the surface. Due to the interest shown, the second edition is being planned with the involvement of various Nordic countries. The aim is to continue the present format, with a university and a football association co-hosting the event. As for this edited collection of chapters – the first with this sort of scope – it has attempted to increase the understanding of the football domain of Nordic countries as well as contribute to its development – while also applying crucial critical perspectives. Our intention has been to look at football as a broad social phenomenon, in which considering moral and ethical considerations is inevitable.

Plentiful potential avenues remain for future scholarship that did not fit within the limited scope of this book. We recognise that our selection of chapters has covered rather traditional approaches to football within the social sciences. It is also absolutely necessary to explore topics such as good governance and responsibility in football organisations; regional equality in football participation within and across countries; disability football; and the social impact of the game. In order to further develop our understanding about the changing societal and economic context in which football actors operate, research on the hybridisation of sport organisations as well as the migration of players, coaches and other football practitioners would also be fruitful paths of study.

References

Agergaard, S., & Botelho, V. (2014). The way out? African players' migration to Scandinavian women's football. *Sport in Society*, 17(4), 523–536.

Andersen, S. S., & Ronglan, L. T. (Eds.) (2012). *Nordic elite sports: Same ambitions – different tracks*. Copenhagen Business School Press.

Backman, J. (2018). *Ishockeyns amerikanisering: En studie av svensk of finsk elitishockey* [The Americanisation of ice hockey. A study of Swedish and Finnish top level ice hockey]. Malmö University.

Bennike, S., Randers, M. B., Krustrup, P., & Ottesen, L. (2023). Football fitness – more of the same, or a path-breaking concept? *This volume*.

de la Porte, C., Eydal, G. B., Kauko, J., Nohrstedt, D., Hart, P. T., & Tranøy, B. S. (Eds.). (2022). *Successful public policy in the Nordic countries: Cases, lessons, challenges*. Oxford University Press.

Duarte Dias, T. (2023). Playing like a Swede, fighting like a Kurd: Ethnicity and aesthetics in Swedish football. *This volume*.

Giulianotti, R. (2020). Afterword: The Nordic model and physical cultures in the global context. In M. Tin, F. Telseth, J. O. Tangen, & R. Giulianotti (Eds.), *The Nordic model and physical culture* (pp. 235–244). Routledge.

Giulianotti, R., Itkonen, H., Nevala H., & Salmikangas, A. K. (2019). Sport and civil society in the Nordic region. *Sport in Society*, 22(4), 540–554.

Goksøyr, M., & Olstad, F. (2002). *Fotball! Norges Fotballforbund 100 år* [Football! The Norwegian Football Federation 100 years]. Norges Fotballforbund.

Green, K., Sigurjónsson, T., & Skille, E. Å. (2020). *Sport in Scandinavia and the Nordic countries*. Routledge.

Halldorsson, V., & Johannsson, O. (2023). Iceland: Preserving the balance between amateurism and professionalism. *This volume*.

Hjelseth, A., Skogvang, B. O., Telseth, F., & Augestad, P. (2023). Norway: Inclusion, exclusion and modernisation. *This volume*.

Hognestad, H. (2009). Transglobal Scandinavian? Globalization and the contestation of identities in football. *Soccer & Society*, 10(3–4), 358–373.

Horgby, B., & Ericsson, C. (2020). *Fotbollsföretagen och demokratin* [Football companies and democracy]. https://idrottsforum.org/wp-content/uploads/2020/06/horgby-ericsson200615.pdf

Huhtanen, K., & Itkonen, H. (2022). Palvelutuotantotehtävät suomalaisten liikuntaseurojen muodonmuutosten lähteenä [Public service provision as a source of transformations in Finnish sports clubs]. *Liikunta & Tiede*, 59(4), 91–102.

Isotalo, K., Itkonen, H., & Nevala A. (2020). Miksi Suomesta tuli vuosikymmeniksi jääkiekko- mutta ei jalkapallomaa? [Why did Finland become a hockey country but not a football country for decades?] *Ennen ja Nyt: Historian Tietosanomat*, 20(3), 2–23.

Itkonen, H., & Salmikangas, A.-K. (2015). The changing roles of public, civic and private sectors in Finnish sports culture. *Public Policy and Administration*, 14(4), 546–556.

Laine, A., & Vehmas H. (Eds.). (2017). *The private sport sector in Europe: A cross-national comparative perspective*. Springer.

Ljunggren, J. (2020). *Den svenska idrottens historia* [The history of Swedish sport]. Natur & Kultur.

McGinn, M. (2020). *Against the elements: The eruption of Icelandic football*. Pitch Publishing.

Rafnsson, D., & Kristjánsdóttir, H. (2023). Don't wait for change. Just do it: Women's football in Iceland. *This volume*.

Skogvang, B. O. (2019). Scandinavian women's football: The importance of male and female pioneers in the development of the sport. *Sport in History*, 39(2), 207–228.

Skogvang, B. O. (2023). Breaking barriers in the past and for the future: Women's football in Norway. *This volume*.

Storm, R. (2012). Danish elite sport and Team Denmark: New trends? In S. S. Andersen & L. T. Ronglan (Eds.), *Nordic elite sports: Same ambitions – different tracks* (pp. 224–236). Copenhagen Business School Press.

Szerovay, M. (2022). Shifting dominant logics? The organisational field of Finnish sport clubs in the 2010s. *Sport in Society*, 25(1), 70–85.

Taylor, M. (2006). Global players? Football, migration and globalisation 1930–2000. *Historical Social Review*, 31(1), 7–30.

Thorlindsson, T., & Halldorsson, V. (2019). The cultural production of a successful sport tradition: A case study of Icelandic handball. *Studies in Symbolic Interaction*, 50(1), 237–266.

Tin, M., Telseth, F., Tangen, J. O., & Giulianotti, R. (Eds.). (2020). *The Nordic model and physical culture*. Routledge.

UEFA. (2021). *The European club footballing landscape*. Retrieved November 15, 2022, from https://editorial.uefa.com/resources/0272-145b03c04a9e-26dc16d0c545-1000/master_bm_high_res_20220203104923.pdf

UEFA. (2022, October 13). *Four bids to host UEFA Women's EURO 2025*. Retrieved October 14, 2022, from https://www.uefa.com/insideuefa/news/027a-165683db82e8-d33d29ee48fc-1000--four-bids-to-host-uefa-women-s-euro-2025/

Index

Note: **Bold** page numbers refer to tables and *italic* page numbers refer to figures.

Academy Classification scheme 107
Act on Receipts from the State Football Pools 13
Act on the Promotion of Sports and Physical Activity 144
aesthetic appreciation 221–222, 226
AIK 65
AIK-Hatets Vänner 182
Allsvenskan 68, 87, 183, 205–206, 213–214, 219
amateurism 27, 60, 106, 179, 195, 198
amateurs 95, 96–99
"Anglophile losers" ("*Anglofile ta-pere*") 198
association capital 83
associative democracy 14
audiences 33, 83, 89–90, 192, 222

Betrideildin 207
Black Army 84, 185
Brann Bataljonen Bergen ("the Brann Batallion Bergen") 199

Christiania Fotballclub 52
City of Gothenburg 90
Cold War 1, 70
commercial football 59–60
commercialisation 18–19, 59, 61, 81, 83–84, 86, 88, 108, 151, 156, 194, 237; impact on Swedish football clubs 83–84
commercial logic 82
commercial sector 11, 15
commitment trap 122
communicative action 109
company-governance model 85
competition logic 82, 86

Constitution of 1849 11–12
consumer preferences 209
corporate capital 83
corporate model: democracy and 86–87; new 90–91; reactions to 87–88
corpothetics 222
critical juncture 121, 124, 126
cultural positioning 195–198
culture 165, 179–180, 184–186

Dalkurd FF 219–229
Damallsvenskan 73, 88
Dam projektilen project 142
Danish Ball Games Association (DBU) 12–13
Danish football: consolidation 13–15; distribution of club size *17*; early years 11–13; elite-level (commercial) football clubs 18–20; football clubs 12, 18–20; grassroots football 16–18; organisational system of *15*; participation numbers and clubs *14*
Danish Football Association (DBU) 127
Danish League Association (LA) 15
Danish Leisure Act 13
Danish Women's Football Union 13
DBU *see* Danish Ball Games Association (DBU); Danish Football Association (DBU)
democratic logic 82–83, 86–88, 91
democratic voluntary organisations 81
Denmark: consolidation 13–15; current landscape of football 15–16; early years of football 11–13; elite-level (commercial) football clubs 18–20; football clubs 12; foundation of DBU

12–13; grassroots football 16–18; organisational system of football 15
despair factor 214–215
DIF *see* National Olympic Committee and Sports Confederation of Denmark (DIF)
differences 233–238
differentiation period 143–144
dispersion model 113
diversification 19
Djurgårdens IF 65
double democratic principle 14

economic variables 209–211
elite-level (commercial) football clubs 18–20
Eliteserien 207, 211–212
Elite Women's Football Association 88
Enemmän kuin peliä: Naisten jalkapallo tasa-arvon tiellä maailmalla ja Suomessa (More than a game: Women's football on the way to equality worldwide and in Finland) (Vares) 135
engaging sponsors 19
ethnicity 221–222, 224–226; and aesthetics 221–222; defeat and 224–226; Kurdishness and Swedishness 219–221; lower leagues to national arena 223–224
European Union (EU) 1, 70, 239

facilities and stadium development 19
FAF *see* Football Association of Finland (FAF)
farmers football 221
FF *see* Football Fitness (FF)
FIFA World Cup 3, 69, 158
Figures of former Finnish marks (FIM) 96
FIM *see* Figures of former Finnish marks (FIM)
Finland: building national identity 27–28; consolidation 28–31; early years of football 25–26; football dwarf 31, 34; fragmented football 31–34; gender equality 137, 146, 147; globalisation 31–34; industrialisation 25; international football community 26; internationalisation 30; modernisation 25–26, 28, 31; number of players abroad 30; Olympic success 27; popularity of football 27, 31–34; professionalism 33; public sector 28; sporting life 29; spread of football 26–28; urbanisation in 26, 28, 31; *Veikkausliiga* 32; women's football 29

Finnish Championship 26
Finnish elite football in 1970s and 1980s 96–99
Finnish football: consolidation 28–31; crisis of 1990s 32; early years 25–26; economic recession 31–32; establishment 31; female players 32; formation of new top league 32; fragmented football 31–34; global football 31–34; globalisation 32; ice hockey, success of 31; internationalisation 30; modernisation 25; number of players 29–30, 32; popular football 27, 31–34; professionalisation 33; spread of football 26–28; *Veikkausliiga* (Pools League) 32; women's football 29
Finnish football, professionalisation of: amateur rules 94; amateurs 96–99; full-time players 100–102; Futisliiga 99–100; players' income 99; semi-professionals 96–99; shamateurism 96–99; sources and methods 95–96; transition towards professional league 99–103
Finnish women's football: 1999 Women's World Cup 141; challenges of 139, 147–148; consolidation period (1982–1992) 139–140; *Dam projektilen* project 142; differentiation period 143–144; early stages 136–137; gender equality 147; globalisation 145–146; goal-oriented activities 147; initial enthusiasm and organisation (1971–1982) 137–139; international success 146–147; number of registered women and girl players 136; organisation of 147; popularity (2001–2009) 142–143; professionalisation 147; research on 135; rise of girls' football (1992–2001) 140–142; sponsor 140
first FIFA championship for Women's football 157
floating shares 19
Football, fair play & business – the history of Danish club football (Grønkjær & Olsen) 11
football as health-enhancing activity 119–120
Football Association of Finland (FAF) 26, 135, 138, 147
Football Association of Iceland (KSÍ) 166

Index

football capital 83
football clubs 12
Football County Unions (FCUs) 13
football dwarf 31, 34
Football Fitness (FF) 119–120, 124–126; creation of new path 123–126; path-breaking concepts 121–122; as prevention and treatment 120
"Football Fitness as Prevention and Treatment" 120
football in Denmark 12
Football Yearbooks 135
freedom of assembly 12
freedom of association 12
Frenchwoman Stephanie Frappart 146–147
Futisliiga (Football League) 99–100
Futisliiga, formation of 99–100, 103

GAIS 65, 188
gender equality 147, 154, 164
The Gender Equality Council 154
globalisation 3, 31, 34, 145
glory factor 214–215
golden age of football 183–184
Gothenburg 180–181
Gothenburg Alliance 188
Gothenburg rivalries 180–181
governance models and logics 81–83
governance, problems of 83
grassroots football 15, 16–18
gubblag 69

Habermas' colonisation thesis Habermas' colonisation thesis 109
Homo Ludens (Huizinga) 112
hooliganism 184–186
Hovedserien 207

ice hockey 31–35
Iceland: gender equality 164–165, 167–169, 172
Icelandic championship 40
Icelandic clubs 42, 45
Icelandic football: amateurism 42–43; attendance at football matches 46; children and adolescents 45; consolidation: 1948–1973 41–43; early years: 1899–1911 38–40; English Premier League 46; facilities and weather 41; foreign influence on 40; independent republic 41; interest in English football 46; in media 41; national teams 46–47; "non-elite" system 44; number of players abroad 43, 47; popular football: 1974–2000 43–44; present and future: 2001–2022 44–47; professionalism 43; sports-for-all policy 44–45; spread of football: 1912–1947 40–41; summer sport 43; women's football 42, 44; World Cup 42
Icelandic Football Association 41
Icelandic Sagas 38
Icelandic Sports Model 44
Icelandic sport clubs, organisation of 45
Icelandic women's football 42; changes in visibility and attitude 166; equality 168–169; future challenges 171; media 169–170; method 166–167; role models 170–171; societal transformation 172; structure 167–168; UEFA and 163
Icelandic women's football: 1900s and 2000s 1–2; in global football context 238–240; international football community 233; locating 2–5; modernisation 2, 25; popularity, participation and international ranking 236; shared history and emergence of 1–2; similarities and differences in football 238; social equality 1; urbanisation 2
IFK Göteborg 188
IFK Norrköping 65
informal sector 11
institutional pluralism 113
international inspirations of football support 195–198
International Women's Football Tournament (IWFT) 157
Íslensk Knattspyrna (Football in Iceland) 166
IWFT *see* International Women's Football Tournament (IWFT)

Kanarifansen 199
Klanen (The Clan) 195, 199
Klaveness 160
Kopparberg/Göteborg 90
KR Reykjavík 39
Kurdish DNA and fighting spirit 226–227
Kurdishness 219–221

Landsfodboldturneringen 206
Landslagsskolen initiative 111
lifeworld 109

Malmö FF 189
market logic 116
Meistaradeildin 207
Mestaruussarja/Mästerskapsserien 207
Ministry of Education and Culture 144, 147
modern supporter culture 184–186

Naisten laji: Kirja jalkapallosta (Women's sport: A book about football) (Ruohonen) 135
National Olympic Committee and Sports Confederation of Denmark (DIF) 13, 120
neoliberalism 1, 3, 31, 70
networking 180–181, 183
new corporate model 90–91
NIF *see* Norwegian Sports Federation (NIF)
non-amateur football 56
Nordic Council 1
Nordic countries: women's football 135, 138
Nordic football associations 2, 94, 233
Nordic leagues: average match-day attendance in 206; development of 206–207
Nordic model 1–2, 233, 239
Nordic societies, development of 2, 106
Nordic spectator studies: attendance and satisfaction 207–208; consumer preferences 209; economic variables 209–211; future research perspectives 214–215; quality of viewing 211–212; sporting contest, characteristics of 212–214
Nordic sports model 2, 38, 94
Nordic welfare state model 1, 28
normative trap 122
Norsk Tipping 55
Norsk Toppfotball 107, 159, 193
North Atlantic Treaty Organisation (NATO) 1
Norway: climate 54; gender equality 58; industrialisation 51, 53; modernisation in 51, 60; urbanisation 51
Norwegian Confederation of Sports (NIF) 106
Norwegian Elite Football (NTF) 107
Norwegian football: attendances at top football matches 60; children 60; commercialisation 59–60; consolidation 53–55; early years 51–53; exclusion 61; future of 60–61; gender equality 58; inclusion 57–58, 61; in international football community 58–59; league system 54–55; modernisation 51; narratives 51; NFA cup 54; Olympic Games 54, 58; popular football 55–60; professionalisation 55–57; scientific approach 56–57; spread of 53–55, 57–58; women's football 57–58; World Cup 54, 58
Norwegian Football Federation (NFF) 106, 106, 150, 193, 193
Norwegian School of Sport Science (NIH) 56
Norwegian Sports Federation (NIF) 54, 195
Norwegian sports model: centralisation–regionalisation 108; commercialisation–democratisation 108; elite–grassroots 108
Norwegian University of Science and Technology (NTNU) 207
Norwegian women's football development 151–159; FIFA and UEFA 158; future 160–161; phases 152; pioneers and development 156–158; playing for charity, entertainment and fun 152–154; strong league organisation, the equal-pay-deal, collaboration 158–159; women's movement and struggle 154–156
Norwegian youth football: Academy Classification scheme 107–108, 110–111; centralisation/dispersion 112–113; colonisation 113–115; empirical and methodological context 107–108; Habermas' colonisation thesis 109; national talent development curriculum 111–112; professionalisation and market logic 108, 110–111; systematisation 108
NTF *see* Norwegian Elite Football (NTF)
NTF-Sport 108
NTNU *see* Norwegian University of Science and Technology (NTNU)

organised football, types of **123**
organised supporter cultures 193–195
Örgryte IS 65, 188
Osoitteena futis project 144
Östersunds FK (ÖFK) 90
outvasion Vikings 46

path-breaking concepts 121–122
path dependence 121
People's Home 70
popularity, participation and international ranking of football 236
preformation phase 121
professional football 123–124
professionalisation, defined 95, 108
professionalism 33
public sector 28

quality clubs 113

rational amateurism 69
recreational football 122–123
reflection trap 122
representative democracy 14, 82, 92
research on Norwegian football supporters 193
Rosenborg BK (Trondheim) 209
Rosenska Pokalen (football cup tournament) 65

Scandinavia 1, 3, 205
Scandinavian sports model 71
Scania rivalries 182–183
shamateurism 95
shamateurs 96–99
shock globalisation 86
similarities 231–233
social semantics 224
social transformation theories 163–164
societal transformation 172
spectator project (*publikumsprosjektet*) 200
sport and physical activity 2, 4, 120
sport for all 2, 45, 106–107
sporting contest, characteristics of 212–214
Stelpurnar okkar 163
Stockholm Olympics 26
Stockholm rivalries 181–182
Stockholm Sports Association 65
Stockholms Stolthet 86
STS Cup 140
Subway National League (*Kansallinen Liiga*) 145
sunk cost trap 122
Superligaen 206–207, 212
supporter activism 200–201
supporter cultures, Norwegian: challenges 202; commercialisation and 194; cultural positioning 195–198; defined 194; international inspirations 195–198; new football ritual 198–199; professionalisation and 194; research on 193; rise of organised 193–195; supporter activism 200–201
Sweden, football companies and democratic framework: corporate model 86–88; democratically governed club to company-governed model 85; governance models and logics 81–83; impact of commercialisation 83–84
Swedish Ballgame Association 65
Swedish Central Association for the Promotion of Athletics 65
Swedish Club Football: urbanisation 187
Swedish club football, rivalries in: 2000s football boom 186–187; background 179–180; golden age of football 183–184; Gothenburg 180–181; history of rivalries 187–190; hooliganism 184–186; modern supporter culture 184–186; Scania 182–183; Stockholm 181–182
Swedish clubs 71–72
Swedish football: *Allsvenskan* 68; clubs 71–72; conflicts 74; consolidation, 1924–1958 67–70; early years, ca. 1860–1903 64–65; English influence 72; FIFA 67; first national league 67; gender equality 70–71; Olympic Games 66; popularity, 1959–2000s 70–73; present and future 73–74; sport clubs 64–65, 65, 68; sports organisation 65; spread 1904–1923 66–67; *Vasaloppet* 68; women's football 69, 71; youth football 71
Swedish football, ethnicity and aesthetics in 219–229
Swedish Football Association (SvFF) 90, 142
Swedishness 219–221
Swedish Series 67
Swedish Sports Confederation 65–67, 69, 74, 82, 126, 186
Swedish sports model 74, 81–82
systematisation 108
system world 109

talent development in sports 19, 111–112, 165
TFK *see* Toppfotball Kvinner (TFK)
The People's Game 200

Tifo 202
Toppfotball Kvinner (TFK) 152, 159
Toppserien 152
Twin Clubs 181
Tyrsö FF 91
2000s football boom 186–187

UEFA *see* Union of European Football Nations (UEFA)
UEFA Champions League 101
UEFA Playmakers programme 144
Umeå IK 89
uncertainty of outcome 208, 213, 215
Union of European Football Nations (UEFA) 137, 155, 158, 163, 206

Vålerenga Kjerke (Vålerenga Church) 201
Veikkausliiga (Pools League) 32, 99–100, 102–104, 205, 207
Veikkausliiga/Tipsligan 207
Viking clap 46
voluntary sector 11, 13, 21

WCL *see* Women's Champions League (WCL)
welfare alliances 21
Whose-Game-Is-It-Anyway-Tradition 200
WLA *see* Women's League Association (WLA)
Women's Champions League (WCL) 152
women's football: commercial football 88–90; development of 151–152
Women's League *(Naisten liiga)* 145
Women's League Association (WLA) 15
Women who win – Football history 1887–2013 (Weber) 11
World War I (WWI) 1, 26, 52
World War II (WWII) 41, 54, 69, 233, 237–238
World Women's Invitational Football Tournament (WWFT) 157
WWFT *see* World Women's Invitational Football Tournament (WWFT)

youth football 71